ACCEPTED FABLES

Jordan Massee

COMPILED AND EDITED BY
RICHARD JAY HUTTO

Henchard Press Ltd.

Publisher	Henry S. Beers
Editor-in-Chief	Joni Woolf
Cover Design	Julianne Gleaton
Layout and Design	Daniel Emerson
Operations Manager	Gary Pulliam
Associate Publisher	Richard J. Hutto
Executive Vice President	Robert G. Aldrich
Photo Restorations	J. L. Sibley Jennings, Jr.

Printed in the USA.
2nd printing.

Library of Congress Control Number: 2004118300

ISBN: (10 digit) 0-9762875-5-2
(13 digit) 978-0-9762875-5-1

Henchard Press Ltd. books are available at quantity discounts with bulk purchase for educational, business, or sales promotional use. For information, please write to:
Henchard Press Ltd., 3920 Ridge Avenue, Macon, GA 31210, or call 866-311-9578.

DEDICATION

This volume of memoirs is dedicated to my parents
WILLIAM JORDAN MASSEE & ETHEL BROWN MASSEE;
to my sisters
EMILY MASSEE BROWN & MARTHA MASSEE DEVAUGHN,
and to my governess
FRÄULEIN ALWINA EICHLER.

"HISTORY IS ACCEPTED FABLES."
NAPOLEON BONAPARTE

Preface

Although Jordan Massee is often mentioned only in terms of refracted glory – his relationships with the great and near-great – it would be a disservice to dismiss his own gifts of keen observation and astute recollection. His early world of calling cards, chauffeurs and governesses, annual "cures" at European spas, and biannual shopping and theater trips to New York with his parents were all the more unusual in the still-ravaged South of the early 20th century. His re-creation of them offers us a rare first-hand glimpse into a vanished world. When his family's wealth and the privileges it afforded were lost, Jordan refused to surrender to self-pity and remorse but continued to live his life with the same appetite and intensity, even if on a less-grand scale.

To those who knew his larger-than-life father, it came as no surprise that he served as the model for Big Daddy in *Cat On a Hot Tin Roof.* Jordan's friend Tennessee Williams was not the only writer who drew inspiration from the senior Massee, however. Truman Capote and Jordan's cousin, Carson McCullers, did as well, and Jordan writes here of his father's pique that McCullers would have "borrowed" one of his own stories without his knowledge.

Had Jordan completed the book he envisioned, it would have been a multi-volume set. I have included here his entire outline of chapters so that the reader may appreciate the missive he intended. Some will be sorely disappointed that he did not write a particular chapter to which they looked forward while others will be, with good reason, relieved. Rather like the wealthy relation who periodically threatens to cut someone out of his will when displeased, Jordan sometimes dropped titillating hints of tales to be included in his book. What emerges instead is, to be sure, sometimes juicy gossip but more often than not a cogent and valuable preservation of stories in danger of being lost forever.

Perhaps it is fitting that the book is unfinished as Jordan was as well. He brought a child-like glee to each day (this was, after all, a man who was photographed coming down a child's sliding board in his late seventies) and his appetite for learning was enormous. He was just as well-versed in the latest New York Review of Books as he was in the cast listing of the Metropolitan Opera's Atlanta productions from the 1930s. As much polyglot as polymath, Jordan never stopped learning. We would do well to follow his example.

I am particularly indebted to Jordan's great-nephew, Bob Bonner, who serves with me as the co-executor of the estate. He was with Jordan to the end to assure him of his family's love and acceptance, and he has been no less supportive in our efforts to publish Jordan's book. If I have misread Jordan's handwriting in transcribing the chapters of his book, no one is at fault except me. If the reader fails to appreciate Jordan's wit and candor, then the fault lies with the reader. Admittedly, few will be interested in the full genealogical recollections of the early chapters but they are presented here as Jordan's legacy to his sister's descendants. His legacy to each of us can only be determined individually. As I said at his funeral, "Each of us thought that Jordan loved us best, and each of us was correct."

Richard Jay Hutto

TABLE OF CONTENTS

(only those chapters in boldface were written)

Introduction

For a long time I have wanted to set down those recollections of my family and a society that has almost completely vanished. I am seventy-seven and my sister Emily is ninety. Soon there will be no one left who remembers these people or their way of life. Most of the events recorded are seen through the eyes of my father. Both Carson McCullers and Tennessee Williams considered him the finest raconteur they had ever encountered. Even before his death in 1961, I wanted to preserve in his own words all the wonderful stories that delighted so many people throughout his long and colorful career. I took numerous notes during the period of 1946-1950, when I had returned to Macon to work for him, and during his subsequent visits with me in New York. I also wanted to obtain factual information regarding his life and accomplishments. That proved more difficult, since he maintained that nothing he had to say was of interest to others unless it was funny. This was no false modesty, since he was not unaware of the magnitude of his achievements, which were not appreciated in Macon, the city he had done so much to develop.

It was always easy to get him to tell us, again and again, the story of "Cousin Hugh and the Hat," or the story of "Pappy Bates and the Ice": all he needed was a good audience, and his own family was the best. Whenever Emily, Little Emily and I get together, Bob Bonner, Little Emily's husband, says we tell each other the same stories over and over, as indeed we do. We never tire of these stories, and they keep our childhood alive. I've noticed that Bob never leaves the room when we recount the tale of "Uncle Jack and Miss Johnson."

Like every born storyteller, Daddy liked to entertain, but getting the serious side of his life story from him was like pulling eyeteeth. He would answer specific questions readily enough, but usually without the colorful details that characterized the humorous anecdote. By the time he made his last visit to New York, in the summer of 1961, I was convinced that the best way to preserve the stories would be to record them on tape, whenever the mood struck. Unfortunately, I found the tape recorder as incomprehensible as I now find the computer; but Alan Kelly, who shared the apartment on West End Avenue with me, agreed to act as technician. However, we were able to record his voice on only one occasion. He was in good form, but one member of his small audience created so much disturbance with her laughter and repeated interruptions that the result hardly represented his best effort, precious though it is to the family. Furthermore, none of us reckoned on the noise of the traffic coming through the open windows, which was picked up by the sensitive microphone. I referred to the tape in setting down the account of "Cousin Hugh and the Hat," but it was of little use. Fortunately, my memory is good and Emily's even better when it comes to names and dates; and her memories go back thirteen years earlier than mine. Whenever possible, I have checked dates and other references with friends and relatives, on tombstones, and in old newspapers. In particular, I have tried to make the account of Daddy's construction of the dam at Jackson as historically accurate as possible, without forfeiting the humor.

Over a period of many years, Daddy told his best stories many times, until they had acquired, through trial and error, a perfection of form worthy of the great storytellers of world literature, without losing their captivating spontaneity or inexhaustible fund of colloquial expressions. The process was unconscious. His only criterion was audience response. Once the stories had reached their final form, they varied in repetition only in detail, depending on his mood and audience. Much of the richness of detail is now unfortunately lost. He regarded the stories as factual accounts of events in his life, what we now call oral history, except that with him the darker side of life was best forgotten, or at least not recalled. He never used vulgar or obscene language, or told a story in questionable taste.

He was by temperament as well as philosophy an eternal optimist. There were events in his life that would have broken a lesser man, but he survived, and without bitterness. Only rarely did he reveal the depths of his own feelings or the nature of his disappointments. His zest for life colored every perception and transformed the most mundane incident into an absorbing and entertaining story through his unique vision.

My Grandfather Brown's stories were filtered through my father's sensibilities, but he never failed to capture the older man's character and personality. My mother testified to that. Grandpa was as conservative as Daddy was flamboyant, and far more eccentric. He had a dry sense of humor, all his own, and certainly was not lacking in appreciation of his favorite son-in-law's broader humor and outrageous extravagance. They came to adore each other. Whenever Daddy was out of town, Grandpa would save the letters to Mother and read them over and over.

Initially, I planned to record only what Emily and I most fondly remembered of Mother and Daddy, Grandpa Brown, and our sister Martha, who died nearly thirty years ago, but I gradually realized that these memories would be more meaningful within a broader context, and decided to include friends, relatives, and those servants who became members of our family. More and more I realized the importance of giving some idea of the place and the ever more distant time in which the events occurred. Also, for me personally, it was especially important to include, however inadequately, a tribute to the memory of Fräulein Alwina Eichler, my beloved German governess, friend, and constant companion. For the most part, Daddy and Grandpa Brown speak for themselves; Mother, Emily, and Martha through their relation to them; but Fräulein has only me to speak for her. She came to us when I was seven, a crucial age in a child's life, and her influence on me was incalculable. I am everlastingly indebted to Fräulein for her guiding intelligence, goodness of heart, and single-minded devotion to me. She accompanies me through all the days of my life.

In the sections devoted to the Massee and Brown backgrounds, I have tried to keep genealogical data at a minimum. Particular dates are included only to clarify relationships and to specify which of several individuals bearing the same name is referred to. Roots are important, but to me ancestors are interesting only when I know something about them individually that reveals a unique personality or that sheds light on the attitudes and customs of a bygone era. More factual information is available elsewhere.

As to origins, both Daddy's and Mother's ancestors were more or less evenly divided between the English and the Irish, with a single exception, seven generations back. All of them came to the New World in colonial times, prior to the American Revolution.

There was no need to set down these recollections for my sister Emily or myself; we live with them always and continue to share them daily; and little need for Emily Brown Bonner, our parents' only grandchild, who was already grown when they died. My real purpose is to preserve the record for Lawson Bonner Anderson and Robert Bonner, Jr., the two great-grandchildren, both quite young when my parents died. They have their own memories but these are necessarily limited. Now there are three great-great-grandchildren: Lawson Anderson, Lane Anderson, and Lauren Massee Bonner, who never knew these forebears at all; and there will be generations to come, all descended from my sister Emily and her husband Jim Brown, who will surely have some curiosity about their ancestors back in the nineteenth and twentieth centuries.

Let's not forget the words of Jean Paul, "Memory is the only paradise from which we cannot be driven."

January 1992

My sister, Emily Massee Brown, died April 1, 1994, six weeks before her ninety-third birthday. She had been in excellent health until a week before her death, which resulted from a fall in front of her home. Her memory was phenomenal, and I am deeply indebted to her for names and dates, as well as numerous anecdotes I had forgotten or never knew. Without her help and encouragement I would never have undertaken this book of memoirs, aside from the history of the Jackson dam and my father's story of "Cousin Hugh and the Hat." Without her it was not easy to go on writing.

My niece, Emily Brown Bonner, died June 23, 1997, at the age of seventy-two. Her unexpected death leaves a void that can never be filled.

October 1997

MASSEE-JORDAN BACKGROUND

THE OLD HOME PLACE

From 1818 to 1826, the United States government made one treaty after another, pushing the Indians westward, until 1838, when they were forcibly deported to the Indian Territory (later in Oklahoma), in one of the most disgraceful episodes in American history. The territory between the Ocmulgee and the Flint Rivers was secured by a treaty with the Indians in 1818, and the counties of Early, Appling, and Irwin were created in that year. From the upper part of Early, Dooly County was formed in 1821, and the same year Houston was formed.

Houston County was surveyed in 1821 and lots were distributed by the Lottery System in 1825. Some of the fortunate drawers of lots settled on their land, and others sold the rights.

Among the first pioneers to settle in what is now Macon County was Needham Massee. He purchased lots of land numbers 20 and 21, each containing 202 1/2 acres, more or less, aggregating 405 acres; also that portion of lot number 13 lying on the west side of where the Southwestern railroad would run, containing about 30 acres. All lands were in the eighth district of Houston County (now Macon County).

Lot number 20 was originally drawn by, and granted to Benjamin Moore, in 1825; then, almost immediately transferred to James Bell, who, in turn sold it to William Davis for $212.00. In November of the same year, Davis sold Lot 20 to Needham Massee for $500.00.

Lot 21 was granted to Pacetty's Orphans of Clark's district in Camden County in 1827. Dennis Pacetty sold the lot in 1829 to William W. Seals for $210.00; and Seals, in turn sold the lot to Needham Massee in July 1830.

Needham Massee (1779-1859) and his wife, Sara Little (1781-1850), built the Massee Plantation House in 1827. They had three sons and eight daughters, all born prior to 1827.

After the death of Sara Little Massee, Needham married Permelia Ann Braswell of Fort Valley, in 1852. Under the terms of his will, he left his property in trust "for and during the natural life only" of his second wife, Permelia, then to be sold to an heir who could get a good endorser.

Drewry Washington Massee, "the Old Doctor," (1819-1903) was the youngest son of Needham and Sara Little Massee. Drewry's oldest son, Oliver Jerome Massee (1849-1915), married when he was nineteen, and bought the place from his grandfather's estate, in 1868. Jerome's endorser was his uncle, Marion Bryan. Cotton was 4 cents a pound. Jerome planted the whole place in cotton, gathered and sold it at 49 cents, and paid off the entire debt in one year.

Portions of the land were subsequently sold. The American Camellia Society Headquarters and Gardens, directly across Highway

49 from the Massee house, occupies land sold by Oliver Jerome Massee to Dave C. Strother and Dr. MacArthur shortly after Mr. Strother moved to Fort Valley from South Carolina in 1903. Dave Strother eventually planted camellias on the land. In 1965, he donated the property to the American Camellia Society, which he helped found.

Oliver Jerome Massee married Laura Isabella Jordan. They had four sons and one daughter, all born at Massee's Lane. On his death, Oliver Jerome Massee left the property to his five children. Laura Massee (Mrs. John Crocker Walker) sold her share to her four brothers: Marion Howard Massee, William Jordan Massee, Oliver Jerome Massee, Jr., and Thomas Drew Massee. Finally, Laura Massee Walker purchased the entire property from her four brothers, becoming sole owner of the Massee's Lane plantation and home. She lived there until her death in 1960. Her oldest son, Felton Jordan Walker, continued to live there with his wife, Mary Vinson.

The place is now owned by John Crocker Walker III ("Johnny"), Laura's grandson. The Old Home Place, as Daddy called it, has remained in the family for six generations, covering a period of one hundred sixty-six years.

Throughout the years, the principal crops grown on the plantation were cotton, peaches, and peach seeds. The Massee house is not large, but is constructed on 12 x 12 beams, suggesting upper stories were planned but never realized. Johnny Walker now owns 465 acres of land, comprised of the original lots 20 and 21, minus 35 acres on one side of the drive from the highway to the house.

After the death of Oliver Jerome Massee, the Slappeys, who had for years owned the adjoining plantation, arbitrarily changed the name of Massee's Lane to Slappeyville. At the request of Aunt Laura, Daddy took the matter to the Georgia State Legislature and the original name was officially restored. Massee Lane is now the accepted form.

NEEDHAM MASSEE

Needham Massee was born in North Carolina in 1779 and moved to Wilkes County, Georgia, in 1802. He married Sara Little in 1805. She too was born in North Carolina, in 1781. They moved to Jones County, Georgia, then lived for a time at Fort Hawkins, now Macon, Georgia. From there they came to Houston County, settling on the land at Massee's Lane in 1826.

Needham was a captain in the War of 1812. He was a member of the Society of the Cincinnati, which was organized by George Washington in 1783, and made up of American and French officers, to perpetuate remembrance of their turning, like Cincinnatus, from war to peace when their task was done. He became a member through his father, Drewry Massee I, and his grandfather, John Massee, who fought through the entire length of the Revolutionary War.

Needham and his wife Sara had three sons and eight daughters. The youngest son, Drewry Washington Massee, was born in 1819.

In Needham Massee's will, dated February 11, 1858, he directed that: "my old negro Piety be exempt from sale by the Executors or any one else that she remain as part of my Estate unsold with the permission of living with any of my children that she chooses and I further direct that before the division made among my grandchildren in Item Fourth, the Executors reserve from the proceeds of the aforesaid property five hundred dollars, the interest of which they pay or cause to be paid annually to that one of my children with whom the said Piety is living, and at the death of Piety or so soon thereafter as convenient I direct that the five hundred dollars so reserved be divided equally among my grandchildren."

Needham Massee and his wife Sara Little are both buried in the family cemetery, a short distance behind the house. His tombstone reads:

> *"In memory of Needham Massee, who departed this life, July 22, 1859, in the 80th year of his life. His trust being in God, his hope well-founded."*

TWO COUNTRY COUSINS

Needham Massee refused to sell the right of way for the railroad through his property, but gave the right free of charge with several reservations, one being that the train would stop at Massee's Lane whenever he flagged it down. The railroad company was more than delighted with the arrangement, thinking the old man wouldn't be traveling much. The first train ran July 4, 1851, from Macon to Oglethorpe.

Needham took to traveling to Macon and to Oglethorpe with greater and greater frequency. Stopping and starting a train was an expensive proposition in relation to one passenger's fare, which was reckoned in cents. Finally, the railroad company re-negotiated, this time on terms more favorable financially to Needham than those originally offered.

Not long after the railroad was built through his property, Needham Massee was visited by two elderly cousins who came from the country down around Reynolds, Georgia. Neither of the cousins had ever seen a train. Hearing a frightening noise in the middle of the night, they jumped out of bed and ran onto the front porch, still in their nightshirts, to see what was happening. A train was passing about a quarter of a mile from the porch, sending up sparks into the dark sky. When it had passed, one of the old men said to the other, "Thank God it missed the house!"

On their trip home, they rode the train to Oglethorpe. When they got thirsty they fetched a dipper of water from a bucket at the end of the railroad car; but before they drank, they offered water to each of the other passengers on the train.

Nathan Bryan

(January 29, 1793 - January 26, 1868)

Aunt Aileen (Mrs. Dave Massee) wrote disparagingly of the Bryans: The Bryan family was and still is great for honesty, great for kindness, ability to make fortunes, etc. The very poor relics of a fine family are that way because the men, living on sandy soil, hardly making a living, married second-class women, uneducated, no family background. They raised cattle and hogs, fished baskets in the river, and brought beef, pork, and channel cats to market on Saturdays.

She maintained that Grandmother Massee looked down her nose on the Bryans who lived on the edge of the Flint River swamp. Since her husband's mother was Susan Elizabeth Washington Bryan, she was probably disdainful only of those Bryans who did not live up to their family reputation. Aileen's description is interesting because it specifies those attributes separating the successful from the unsuccessful members of the same family. Obviously, blood was not the criterion.

Littleton ("Little") Bryan, my father's great-great-grandfather, was the richest man in Houston County at the time of his sudden death, in 1836, from eating too much barbeque. His estate was valued at seventy-five thousand dollars, a heap of money. He was the first banker in the county and kept the funds in an old brass-bound trunk under his bed, along with a shotgun. After his death, Nathan II adopted the practice when he moved from Pike County to the Bryan home on the Flint River in order to take charge of his father's estate and minor children.

Nathan Bryan II married Mary Lofley (1802-1879). Aunt Aileen admitted that Mary was "a true aristocrat and far better educated than her husband." She was a great-granddaughter of Daniel Marshall, the first Baptist preacher in Georgia, a matter of great pride to some members of the family. Mary Lofley Bryan lived until 1879, and my father remembered going to her funeral when he was a boy.

Susan Bryan Massee died in 1901. Shortly after Daddy married, he took my mother to meet her. The old lady showed Mother a gold locket containing a picture of Daddy as a child. Mother thought she was giving her the locket, until she said, "Certainly not. Jordan has been my grandson a lot longer than he's been your husband." After that, Mother didn't like her, unaccustomed to being refused anything; but Daddy adored his Massee grandparents.

Both my parents had numerous Bryan progenitors, but any connection between the two lines is purely conjectural.

MARTHA GOODWIN RAINES CARSON
(November 29, 1808 - June 21, 1862)

My favorite house in Macon is the Raines house on the corner of Georgia Avenue and College Street. It was built around 1848 for Cadwallader Raines by Elam Alexander, the master architect responsible for many of the finest Greek Revival buildings in Macon, including the imposing Cowles mansion on Coleman Hill, overlooking the city.

Raines came to Macon from Baldwin County, where he always signed his name Cadwallader; but he used the shorter Cadwell after moving to Bibb County. His sister, Martha Godwin Raines (1808-1862), married Joseph Jefferson Carson (1802-1875). They were my father's great-grandparents and were married in the Raines house.

When Daddy and Mother bought the McCaw house in 1910, they had already considered both the Cowles house and the Raines house, but neither had central heating or adequate bathrooms. Emily was bitterly disappointed when she learned that the house on College Street her father had purchased was not the Raines house. I first became aware of the house and its fantastic interior when Miller Lyndon and I played there as children. At that time it was the home of his grandparents, Dr. and Mrs. George Twiggs Miller. Mrs. Miller, "Katy," was the favorite grown-up of every child in the neighborhood. We especially enjoyed running up and down the free-standing stair in the center hall rotunda, spiraling from the main level to the cupola on the third floor. The house is now the home of Lee and Kitty Oliver.

Cadwell Raines died in 1856. The extraordinary story of his widow, Parthenia Thurmond Raines, is included in Rose Hill Rambles, published by The Middle Georgia Historical Society. This delightful little volume gathers together six tours of Rose Hill Cemetery, plus additional rambles to the less accessible spots, conducted by Calder Willingham Payne, Macon's most knowledgeable social historian. If, wandering through an old cemetery, you have ever wished the dead could speak, rest assured they can—through Calder Payne and his equally wondrous wife, Eugenia Coleman.

My father was inordinately proud of all his Carson cousins, going back to Alfonso Carson and his daughter Mabel. He insisted the Carsons were smarter than other people. Which reminds me of a silly woman who asked me, when I was three or four years old, "Who do you love the most: your mother or your father?" I replied, after some thought, "I love my mother the best, but my daddy's the prettiest." The Carsons may have been the smartest but they certainly were not the prettiest. However, photographs of Cousin Mabel, my father's first flame, are lovely; and I think Marguerite Waters Smith, the mother of Carson McCullers and Rita Smith, must have been good-looking when she was young. Rita was very pretty, but she took after the Smiths or the Waters. There were no other beauties among the Carsons I knew—but they were all smart.

HENRY TERRELL JORDAN
(December 25, 1825 – March 5, 1896)

I know very little about Henry Terrell Jordan, my father's maternal grandfather. He was born on Christmas Day 1825 and died March 5, 1896, and served valiantly in the Confederate Army. Henry Jordan married two Carson sisters. The first, Martha Goodwin Raines Carson (1834-1854), died when her daughter Laura Isabella Jordan was born. Subsequently he married Martha Carson's sister and moved to Texas, where he became very rich, or so the legend goes. Laura Isabella Jordan married Oliver Jerome Massee.

The Jordans came to this country from Ireland, prior to the American Revolution. Of Norse origin, Jordan is the Anglicized version of MacSiurtain, a surname of the Gaelic type adopted by one of the hibernicised Norman families which acquired extensive terrioty in Connacht after the invasion of 1172. It signifies descendants of Jordan, i.e. Jordan d'Exeter. Though Jordan is a common English name, very few of the Irish Jordans are of English descent.[1] In England the name is pronounced jor'dn (circumflex o as in orb); in Ireland, jur'dn (circumflex u as in urn).

DREWRY WASHINGTON MASSEE
(May 27, 1819 - June 27, 1903)

Drewry Washington Massee, Daddy's grandfather, has long been referred to as "The Old Doctor." He was too old to fight in the Civil War but offered his services as either a doctor or a civil engineer. He had degrees in both fields, a rare combination; and, according to my father, he had a thorough knowledge of both Greek and Latin. The need for doctors was far greater, and he eventually served at the notorious Andersonville Prison as Assistant Chief Surgeon. During his service there, he kept detailed records of his activities and expenditures. Out of his own pocket he paid for quinine from Mexico, smuggled through the Gulf blockade. Like many veterans of the Civil War, he was extremely reluctant to talk about his experiences, so Daddy heard little directly from him.

He married Susan Elizabeth Washington Bryan (August 8, 1828-March 20, 1901) and had thirteen children.

Many years later, friends and relations persuaded him to claim restitution from the federal government for the money he had spent at

[1] Irish Families, Their Names, Arms and Origins, by Edward MacLysaght; Hodges Figgis & Co. Ltd., Dublin, 1957.

Andersonville on behalf of those poor Yankee prisoners. His records, along with all receipts, were taken to Washington by an old friend, Charlie Crisp, who was speaker of the House. Crisp had volunteered to handle the claim. Shortly afterwards, Crisp dropped dead on the floor of the House. He was succeeded as Speaker by his son, another Charlie Crisp. Young Crisp never found the papers. There can be no question of the honesty of the two Crisps, and the papers were of no value to anyone except Drewry Washington Massee. It seems unlikely that any papers found in the office of the deceased Speaker of the House would have been thrown out. Perhaps someday they will be located in the National Archives, where there are still warehouses full of uncatalogued material. The Old Doctor was apparently not too upset over the loss; he hadn't wanted to make the claim in the first place. After so many years the money due him, with interest, would have been considerable.

A Letter From the Old Doctor

I have in my possession a letter from my great-grandfather, Drewry Washington Massee, to his brother. He had two brothers: James and Needham; I think the letter was to Needham Warren Massee (1815-1854), who was married in September 1847. Drewry Washington was twenty-eight years old when the letter was written, and he gives an interesting picture of his life at that time. The entire contents of the letter are as follows:

June 9th 1847
Georgia Houston Cty

Dear brother, I was surprised to see, in a late letter of yours received by Father, that you had written to me twice for I have not received the scratch of a pen from you since you left for the promised land not even so much as for my name to be mentioned in the letters to the rest of the family and well might I think you had forgotten me; it now being nearly months and only seen you twice and heard nothing from you only through others and that too often promising to write to me after you arrived in the fair Canan. I have a few half dimes to get to pay for letters, and I am willing to pay for some from you if you feel disposed to correspond with me; there appears to be but little news of importance through our action, the most of the volunteers I understand have returned home. R. Grigg poor fellow was unable to get nearer home than three miles this side of Columbus his Father is gone after him, he is in a low state of health as our country is gone. My family and myself are in good health and hope this may find you enjoying the same blessing, about the first of April Susan had a spell of sickness and as she recovered from it she got a fall from a horse which I was fearful would prove fatal, but she soon convalesced and is enjoying pretty fair health at present, Father's nervous irritation seems to grow worse he had well nigh lost the use of his little finger on the right hand, he has subjected himself to a magnetic treatment, and I am trying the Electra Magnetic machine on his nervous system which seems to be beneficial, for at one setting it has nearly restored the flexibility of his finger.

Crops are generally tolerably good through this section, though my corn crop is sorry my cotton is as good or better than usual at this season. I think there could be a full cotton bloom found in my field tomorrow, I have sixty acres in cotton this year the most of which is tolerable good. My wheat was sorry, our crops are suffering for rain at this time.

From the statements of yours of 11 of May to Father we shall be looking for you and your ___?___ soon, unless it is as the Negro said all talk and no drink the cider, as to my part brother I think if you would unite with some amiable and worthy lady you would be better satisfied in mind, and have a chance to prepare for future life for I consider there is but little solid pleasure to be found in this life much less while man is in an isolated state and his fond anticipations are based upon ___?___ boisterous tide of time by the uncontrolled bark of chance, he having no resting place but is here today and tomorrow somewhere else, and throwing away with one hand that which the other accumulates, therefore I hope I shall be able soon to congratulate you upon your happy exit from a single to a married life.

Your affectionate Brother in haste
D. W. Massee

Young Jordan with his father, who was the model for Big Daddy in Tennessee Williams's Cat On a Hot Tin Roof.

DADDY'S EARLY YEARS

The Fourth Generation

Jordan Massee was the son of Oliver Jerome Massee (May 3, 1849-June 7, 1915) and Laura Isabella Jordan (April 17, 1852-November 22, 1913), the second of five children:

Marion Howard Massee
(December 31, 1869-November 18, 1927)
William Jordan Massee
(August 1, 1873-October 19, 1961)
Laura Carson Massee (Mrs. John Crocker Walker)
(September 28, 1876-April 8, 1960)
Oliver Jerome Massee, Jr. ("Jack")
(September 6, 1879-April 6, 1932)
Thomas Drew Massee ("Dave")
(November 30, 1882-March 18, 1970)

Daddy's Boyhood

I doubt there has ever been born a completely happy child, but my father came close. He was born happy, or as they say today his genes predisposed him towards a state of well-being and satisfaction. Coupled with that, he had the good fortune to be born on a farm, one of five children, of loving parents. His father was severe but just, and he was his mother's favorite son. From the start he was a mischief maker, accepting with equanimity the inevitable consequences. Only once, when his parents were away, did an aunt punish him by making him stand in a corner facing the wall for an hour.

In a profile many years later Harry Stillwell Edwards wrote:

The story properly opens with Jordan as a little boy sitting on the margin of a private fish pond somewhere below Fort Valley, thirty odd years ago. He was there by special invitation cordially extended. There can be no doubt as to this, for he extended the invitation himself and promptly accepted it. The shadow that fell across his cork, presently, drew his attention to a man behind him, and an upward glance revealed a rather severe countenance dominating the situation.

"Mornin," said the boy, pleasantly. "Hope you don't mind my catching these little fish. You know they are mighty bad on trout beds!"

"No," said the newcomer, slowly the countenance relaxing a trifle, "but I don't want you to disturb the big ones. It's the breeding season, as you seem to have observed. What luck?" The boy drew up a string of "goggle-eyes."

"Pretty good, sir; but it's hard work." He drew a finger across a sweatless brow and shook it. The stranger saw a little wave in the grassy margin to the right and a slight movement of the rushes there. Bending over he drew up another string with three four-pound trout on it. "Ha!" he said comprehensively.

"Yes," said Jordan, "I tied them out over there to keep them from bothering my bait. Goin' to turn 'em loose when I leave."

Even as a boy Jordan Massee exhibited those qualities of humor and imagination that were characteristic of the man; but what set him apart from most boys were his dreams and the determination to make those dreams come true. Although his formative years were spent at Massee's Lane, he always dreamed of a better life. He was born less than ten years after the Civil War, one of that generation of men who set out to create a new South. Unlike most Southerners he never looked back. With his faith in himself and his willingness to work he was ready.

In my father's own words, "I was born on the first day of August, 1873, the day Baring Brothers, the great London banking house, failed. Born in a panic and been in one ever since." It was just eight years after General Robert E. Lee surrendered at Appomattox. He grew up in the wake of the Civil War, during those terrible years of reconstruction, when life on a farm in Georgia cannot have been easy. His father was too young to fight in the war, but when not yet sixteen was sent with a slave by wagon to Florida to fetch a load of salt. When he returned, the war was over.

As a boy, Daddy must have heard accounts of the Civil War, but he had singularly little interest in that tragic period in American history. His thoughts were always on the future.

For many years after the war, no man could successfully run for public office against a Confederate veteran. Daddy was no more than five or six when General John B. Gordon, a great war hero, came to Houston County to speak. He was running for the state senate, or some other important office. Prior to the speech there was a picnic honoring the great man. Daddy had a toy boat which he was playing with on the edge of a pond. The General crept up from behind and with his boot pushed Daddy into the water. Everyone was amused except Daddy. The General was not known for his honesty, having cheated half the men in the county, but when he spoke, all that was forgotten. Addressing the crowd he said, "Some people say I'm a crook, but I want you to know I never stole anything but once in my life and that was on the retreat from Gettysburg. I was leading my troops south when I spied some mules in a field. Now we needed mules desperately, so I went over to look at them. Branded on each mule were the letters 'U. S.' Now I always thought 'U. S.' spelled 'us,' so I took those mules." The audience went wild. Needless to add, General Gordon was elected to office by an overwhelming majority, and eventually became Governor of Georgia.

A Grand Old Noble Duke
Joseph Drewry Massee
(August 31, 1857 - November 24, 1939)

The greatest influence on my father in his formative years, apart from his parents, was his uncle, Joseph Drewry Massee. His fondest memories of childhood and adolescence involved Uncle Joe. All four of the Massee boys—Marion, Jordan, Jack, and Dave—adored him. Their father thought that boys should work hard and get a good, practical education; Uncle Joe thought they should learn to enjoy life. He taught them to hunt, to fish, to swim, and to play poker—all the things their father considered frivolous. Grandfather Massee, although a strict disciplinarian, was not opposed to pleasure, so long as it didn't interfere with the serious business of earning a living. The war and the terrible years of reconstruction had taught him that life was a long hard struggle, but Uncle Joe appears to have learned a different lesson from the late unpleasantness.

Joseph Drewry Massee was born in 1857, the seventh of thirteen children born to Drewry Washington Massee and Susan Bryan, eight years younger than his brother Jerome, my grandfather. He had three daughters but no sons, which may account for his extraordinary devotion to his nephews.

From as far back as Daddy could remember, Uncle Joe was noted for his humorous tales, in which fact was never allowed to interfere with fancy. My mother thought that after Uncle Joe had told a story several times he came to believe it himself, but I don't think that was the case. His imagination was so great, truth was simply irrelevant. He was a born fabulist.

Years ago, farmers drove into Macon with a load of watermelons, peaches or whatever was in season, and sold their produce directly from the wagons. Broadway, south of Cherry Street, was a veritable farmer's market. One day Daddy bought the two largest watermelons he had ever seen, from a wagon in front of his office. The melons were sitting on the floor, beside his desk, when Uncle Joe blew in, unexpectedly, from the country. When his uncle saw the watermelons, Daddy said to him, "Uncle Joe, I'll bet you never saw a watermelon as big as those."

Uncle Joe eyed the watermelons contemptuously and replied, "Nubbins, just nubbins. Your father came over to my place some years ago and said to me, 'Joseph, my four boys are coming down to see me tomorrow and I want the two biggest watermelons you've got.' I told him to go out in the patch and pick as many melons as he wanted. Now you remember, Jordan, your father was a tall man, well over six feet. He walked out in the field thumping those melons without leaning over, just walking along thumping. Now those were real melons."

After the death of his first wife, the mother of his three daughters, Uncle Joe married again. A few years later, his oldest daughters married and left home. On the death of his second wife, he was left with only Mabel, his youngest child, to look after him. When Graham Bell came to ask for her hand in marriage, Uncle Joe said, "Well, I think I ought to tell you, she's mean as the devil." He needn't have worried: Mabel continued to take care of him until he died, more than twenty years later, and she did marry Graham Bell.

Around 1910 or 1911, while Daddy owned the Macon Railway and Light Company, the streetcar motormen went on strike and threatened to burn down his house on College Street. News didn't travel fast in those days, but when Daddy got home late that afternoon, Uncle Joe was sitting on the front steps with a loaded double-barrel shotgun on each side. He said to Daddy, "They may burn it down, but I'll get four of the sons-of-bitches before they do!" How he found out about the threat and got to Macon no one ever knew.

When I was about five years old, Daddy said to Mother, as we were finishing dinner, "Has that boy ever met Uncle Joe?" Within minutes of learning that his only son had never met his favorite uncle, we were on our way. When we drove up to his house, between Massee's Lane and Marshallville, Uncle Joe came running out. Ignoring Mother and me, he said to Daddy, "Jordan, you should have been here this morning when I needed you. I drove my buggy over to the Cummins' field and tied the horse to a fence post. I walked down the hill and there was a coachwhip, eighteen feet long. That snake chased me up the hill, where I grabbed a big stick. Then I chased the snake back down the hill. Just before we got to the bottom, I struck at the snake but missed him and broke the stick in two. Seeing that, the coachwhip chased me back up the hill again. This time I was able to jump in the buggy and grab my shotgun. When I took aim, that snake stood on the tip of his tail, eighteen feet tall, and said to me, 'That's not fair, Joseph, that's not fair!'"

At this point in the story, I turned to Mother and asked, "Can a snake talk?" They all laughed at me, and I was embarrassed without knowing why. Daddy always said that I never liked the old man after that, which wasn't true. I was as fascinated by him as everyone else was, but saw him only once again.

Shortly before his death, in 1939, Mother took Martha and me to see him. She had always been his favorite among the wives of the four Massee brothers. He was dying of cancer and I still remember how ravaged he looked. Years later when Martha was dying, I hoped that she had forgotten.

Long after he taught the Massee boys to enjoy living, he undertook the same course of instruction with the four Walker boys—Felton, Jerome, John, and Charles—the sons of Daddy's only sister, Laura Massee Walker.

Daddy always spoke of Uncle Joe as "a grand old noble duke."

Richard Drew Massee, son of my father's Uncle Jasper, set down the following story:

Uncle Joe told me this story. He said one day he and his father (Dr. Drewry Massee) went out to clean the well. First, they took down the railing around the well, then they put the ladder into the well and the Old Doctor descended. While Uncle Joe was pulling up the ladder, his father called to him to go after something he had forgotten. Instead, Uncle Joe went to the barn where he took off the bell that hung around the neck of the old blind mare. He went back and walked around and around the rim of the well, slowly ringing the bell.

His father called in vain for help, expecting every minute the old blind mare to fall in on top of him. Uncle Joe let him stew mercilessly in his agony for quite a while, then deliberately took the bell back to the barn and performed his errand.

The next day, when the Old Doctor was relating his harrowing experience, he saw a cunning smile on Joe's face. The truth of the situation dawned on him and, as Uncle Joe told it, "He beat me most to death."

Pappy Bates and the Ice

Marshallville was divided between Baptists and Methodists. Once a year each denomination held a week of revival meetings to remind the faithful of their reward in Heaven and to reclaim any backsliders. First the Baptists had their week of meetings, and then the Methodists had theirs.

Marie Bates attended every meeting at the Methodist Church; her husband attended none. After meeting, the faithful would walk home. When they passed Pappy Bates' house, he would be sitting on the front steps darning socks and sewing buttons on his shirts. The message was clear. At the last scheduled meeting, the preacher announced, "We have had a most successful week. Everyone is back on the side of the Lord except for Mr. Bates. I have decided to extend our meetings a few more days, in the hope that we may bring him around."

The pressure was so great that Pappy Bates finally agreed to attend one meeting, if for no reason other than to keep his wife quiet. One revival meeting was enough. He saw the error of his ways and was born again. From then on, Pappy attended church every time they opened the doors, sang louder, and prayed more fervently than anyone else in the congregation.

A few weeks after all that happened, my grandfather told Daddy, who was seven or eight years old, to ride into town and get some ice from Pappy Bates' store. In those days ice was quite a luxury. Great blocks were cut from the frozen lakes in New England during the winter months. The ice was tightly packed in sawdust and bound in burlap bales, which could be stored for months. Eventually the bales were shipped by railroad to the South.

When Daddy arrived at the store, Pappy told him, "I'm sorry, Buddy, the train failed to stop here this morning and went on to Oglethorpe, but don't worry, that same train will stop here on its way back to Macon in about an hour and you'll get your ice then."

Daddy whiled away the time—he was in no hurry—and when the train arrived, he and Pappy Bates were waiting on the platform. They put the huge bale on the wagon and took it back to the store. As soon as Pappy cut open the bale, he started scooping out sawdust with both hands. He scooped and scooped, until finally he found a small ball of ice, about the size of a man's fist.

Just at that moment, the Methodist preacher walked in and slapped Pappy on the back. "Good day, Brother Bates, How are you?" In a voice trembling with anger, Pappy shouted, "God damn it! Don't call me brother. I never had but one brother and he was killed at Gettysburg."

DADDY RECALLS HIS FIRST THEATER

This is the way my father recalled his first theater: "My father had an uncle, Marion Bryan, who was a rich old devil. He loved a dollar more than I do my right eye, and I haven't got but one. When I was about eight years old—maybe nine—he took me to the theater. I'd been to Macon plenty of times, but I'd never been inside the Opera House, or any other theater.

On our way to Macon, he took a twenty-dollar gold piece out of his pocket and held it in his hand. 'Buddy,' he said, 'this is a minstrel show and it's the funniest show on earth. There are four acts. If you don't crack a smile from the time the curtain goes up on the first act until the time the curtain comes down on the last act, this twenty-dollar gold piece is yours.'

After the first act, neither of us smiled."

THE SILVER DOLLARS

Daddy and his older brother, Marion, worked one summer at the packing plant in Marshallville. Packing peaches in those days was hard work. At the end of the season each received seventy-five silver dollars, the most money they had ever seen all at one time. They discussed what they would spend the money for and decided they would each buy a good shotgun. Their father didn't approve. He said, firmly, "No. That's a lot of money and you must put it in the bank to help pay for your education."

Uncle Marion thought that was final—they would have to do what their father said—but Daddy would have none of it. He said to Marion, "What's the use in having money if you can't spend it the way you want?" It took many hours to persuade Marion to disobey his father, but finally he agreed. The money was theirs to do with as they chose, so they threw it all in the well.

When their mother heard what they had done she started crying at the thought of what their father would do when he found out.

That night he said nothing. The boys felt sure he had been told, but still he said nothing. Finally, Daddy could stand the suspense no longer, and said, "Let's get it over, Father; aren't you going to punish us?"

"No," their father said, quite calmly, "The money was yours. You worked hard for it, but it was a very foolish thing to throw it away." And that's all he said.

A few days later, the well digger came to clean the well, which he did once a year. When he came up with one hundred and fifty silver dollars, Grandfather pocketed the money, and the subject was never mentioned again.

The Correspondence

When Daddy was a young man, a girl from Atlanta came to visit relatives in Marshallville. Joe Barnes, his best friend, was very much taken with the girl's charms and beauty. In fact, he fell head over heels in love with her.

A couple of months after the young lady had returned home, my father said to his friend, "Joe, what do you hear from that good-looking gal from Atlanta?" Poor Joe replied, "Well, Jordan, I wrote seven or eight letters to that girl and never once got an answer, so I broke off the correspondence."

John Crocker Walker

(March 1, 1868 - October 21, 1936)

Although five years older, John Walker was a friend of my father long before he married Laura Carson Massee. His father, Charles Addison Walker, came from Sumter County; his mother, Luisa Crocker, was from Macon County. John was born at the old Walker-Trick house on East Main Street, Marshallville, in 1868. Charles Walker died when John was only seven years old, and life was very hard for Luisa, left with three boys and two girls. John attended elementary school in Marshallville, where he and Daddy became friends. Both were poor students. All classes were conducted in one room, regardless of grade. Mr. Walter Fredericks was their teacher for the first eight years. The teacher for the final year was Mr.

Hollingsworth, John Walker's brother-in-law.

While still boys, John and my father were sitting on a fence when a caravan of Gypsies passed. Attached by a rope to one of the wagons was a beautiful black stallion, which the Gypsies had no doubt stolen along their way south. John called to one of the men, "How much you want for the black horse?" The man replied, "Five hundred dollars." "I'll give you ten," John shouted. "Sold," said the Gypsy; and the deal was closed. Until Uncle John's death in 1936, Daddy always called him "Gypsy."

After leaving elementary school, John went to work in a store in Winchester owned by his uncle, William Hamilton Felton. One day, Daddy dropped by to see John, who immediately asked him to mind the store while he went down the street for lunch. While he was gone, Daddy noticed a pile of watermelons of various size and shape. One by one he weighed the melons on the produce scale and indicated the amount with chalk on the bottom of each melon. When John returned, Daddy remarked casually, "I'll bet you a dollar that melon weighs thirty pounds." John was sure it weighed no more than twenty. Having fallen in the trap, John picked a melon and said, "What about this one?" Daddy lifted the melon, apparently to better estimate its weight, and said, "Forty pounds." And so they spent the better part of the afternoon betting on the weight of melon after melon. Not wishing to push his luck too far, Daddy finally said, "Pay me, John; I've got to go now." Later, John discovered the deception, but I doubt that he got back one penny of his money.

Eventually, John Walker and Mr. Tom Taylor founded The Georgia Banking Company in Marshallville. There was another bank in the town, but the new venture flourished. They also owned jointly two large farms. When they finally parted company it was agreed that one would divide the property and the other would have first choice. Mr. Taylor drew up the division, and John chose the bank. He was still president when he died at the age of sixty-eight. John Walker was an unusually kind and gentle man, according to all who knew him. During the depression, he took many risks rather than see friends and neighbors lose their property.

Uncle John and Aunt Laura had four sons: Felton Jordan Walker (1899-1960); Jerome Massee Walker (1901-1990); John Crocker Walker, Jr. (1909-1986); and Charles Carson Walker (1911- 1994).

Eastman College

Daddy bought 2,000 bushels of cowpeas at 50 cents a bushel. He borrowed the thousand dollars from Ware's Bank. Mr. Burk Baldwin and Daddy's father endorsed the note. A few months afterwards he sold the cowpeas in New Orleans for $1.00 a bushel. He was sixteen or seventeen years old at the time. With the thousand dollar profit, Daddy went to business school in Poughkeepsie, New York.

It was Eastman College. Old Man Eastman died and Mrs. Eastman married one of the teachers, Professor Gaines. Gaines was head of the school when Daddy was there. Mrs. Gaines' daughter married Timothy Woodruff, the Lieutenant Governor of the State of New York. Eastman College was the finest business school in the country.

Daddy attended school in Poughkeepsie for a year, then went home.

COLUMBUS, GEORGIA

After his return from Eastman College, Daddy went to Columbus, Georgia, for two years. While there he boarded with his mother's cousin, A. A. Carson, the prosecuting attorney for that district and "a helluva good speaker." Carson' daughter, Mabel Carson, was in the class with Laura Massee at Cox's College, in LaGrange.

Apparently, Daddy and his Cousin Mabel were very much in love. He went to LaGrange as often as possible under the pretext of visiting his sister, Laura. The head of the school remarked, "I've never seen a fellow so devoted to his sister." There is a charming photograph of Mabel, Aunt Laura, and Daddy taken at the time. It is said that Daddy and Mabel Carson wanted to get married but both families opposed the union because of the kinship. They were second cousins, which doesn't seem too close, by the standards of that time, or now, but the legend of a thwarted romance persists. More than fifty years later, Carson McCullers became intrigued with the story and insisted that had they been allowed to marry she and I would have been double first cousins, which is not true at all, but she liked it that way.

Mabel Carson married someone else and died in childbirth. According to Marguerite Waters Smith, mother of Carson McCullers, my father was grief stricken. Marguerite, known to everyone as "Bebe," grew up hearing stories from her mother, A. A. Carson's sister, of the dashing young man who almost married Mabel. Her mother would often remark to her children, "As Jordan Massee would say, 'A rolling stone gathers no moss.'" Bebe said she was grown before she discovered that Jordan Massee hadn't originated the platitude she grew up with.

In Columbus, Daddy worked for the A. G. Rhodes Furniture Company, as bookkeeper. When he left, Mr. Rhodes begged him to stay. Later in life, when Daddy was in the brick business, Rhodes wanted him to come to North Georgia where he owned a whole mountain of shale. He offered to put up all the money and allow Daddy to pay him back for his half out of the profits. Daddy told me that he declined the proposition because he didn't know anything about making brick out of shale, but I think the real reason must have been that nothing on earth could have persuaded him to abandon his own brickyard in Macon. Even when he was building the hydroelectric plant at Jackson, he continued to operate the Bibb Brick Company.

Until the end of his life, Daddy insisted that the three hottest places were Fort Valley, Columbus, and Fiddler's Green. When Martha and I, as children, asked him where Fiddler's Green was, he told us, "It's ten miles the other side of Hell."

Brown-Lawson Background

Hugh Lawson
My Great-Grandfather
(August 26, 1799-May 20, 1856)

Hugh Lawson, my mothers' grandfather, married (1) Sarah Bryan (January 5, 1808-July 27, 1847). They had thirteen children, nine daughters in a row, then four sons. Emily Bryan Lawson (Mrs. Robert Hardy Brown, March 3, 1841-May 14, 1889), my grandmother, was the youngest daughter.

Some of us, in my generation, got tired of hearing about the distinguished Lawson line, especially from Mary Carolyn Richardson Davis. She had me spend many a lunch hour in the genealogical department of the New York Public Library, which was on the top floor, with no air conditioning, and infernally hot. I was to find the name of the ship on which the Lawsons came to America. She knew the year, but that was all. I'm afraid I failed poor Mary. A few years later, on a visit to Macon, I called on Mrs. Tom Stewart, a long-time favorite. While we were talking, Cousin Mary blew in, unexpectedly. Without further ado, she announced in triumph, "Jordan! I have discovered the name of the ship that brought the first Lawsons to America." She couldn't have been more pleased with herself if she had found the Holy Grail.

I said, "Mary, I've lost all interest in the Lawson line. I'm busy working on the Jordan line. They are descended from the kings of Ireland." Mary was not descended from the Jordans, who are on my father's side. The effect of my remark was like puncturing a balloon. Mary soon made a hasty retreat, and after she had gone Mrs. Stewart said to me, "Jordan, have I ever told you how much I love you?"

Hugh Lawson was greatly admired for his fine upstanding character, but the portrait of him, which now belongs to Emily Brown Bonner, my niece, shows a man stern and unbending, and very homely. My mother used to say, half apologetically, "He was always frail, but so aristocratic looking."

I have a copy of a letter from Hugh Lawson to his oldest child, Sarah Penelope Lawson (1828-1907), who later married Thaddeus Oliver, and was the mother of Hugh Oliver and James Oliver, of whom I shall be writing more later. The letter is dated 1838, so Penelope was ten years old. The letter is folded and addressed on the reverse side. The grandmother referred to would be Penelope Frank (1785-1866), the second wife of James Campbell Bryan (1766-1832). I don't find this letter to Penelope very endearing. However, Emily has letters from Hugh Lawson to his youngest daughter, Emily Bryan Lawson (my grandmother), which are quite charming. These letters were written in 1854, when she was thirteen years old. They were written from "Pine Retreat," the Lawson plantation in Houston County. His daughter was in Buena Vista, Georgia.

The "Margaret" referred to by Hugh Lawson in the letter dated September 28, 1854, must have been his half-sister, who was born in 1790. Apparently, she never did get a husband. The "Hudy" mentioned in the letters of Feb. 25 and Sept. 28 is probably Hugh Oliver. I am unable to identify "Anna" or "Ben," mentioned in the Sept. 28 letter.

After the death of her husband, Thaddeus Oliver, in the Civil War, Mrs. Oliver (Sarah Penelope Lawson) and her two sons, Hugh and James, went to live with her brother, Hugh Lawson—son of the man who wrote the letters—at Pine Retreat. She taught school at Andrew College in Cuthbert and also at Montpelier College in Monroe County. Eventually, she came to Macon to look after Emily Bryan Lawson (Mrs. Robert Hardy Lawson) during her youngest sister's final illness. After my grandmother's death in 1889, Mrs. Oliver, along with Hugh and James, remained to keep house for Grandpa Brown, and to assist in rearing his three children: Mattibrian, Lawson, and Ethel. When Mattiebrian was old enough, she took over running the house, under Mrs. Oliver's supervision. The Brown residence on Poplar Street remained the home of Mrs. Oliver and her two sons until my mother married in 1899.

Mrs. Oliver's presence was a mixed blessing in the Brown household, since she was a rather difficult woman. Whenever Grandpa Brown would ask, "Mrs. Oliver, will you have a cup of coffee?," she would reply, "Yes, Capt. Brown, if it's hot." Or, if asked if she would like a piece of steak, "Yes, Capt. Brown, if it's tender." Nevertheless, my mother must have been fond of her, since she said she planned to name me Penelope had I been a girl. My father responded, "Over my dead body."

Finally, after leaving Macon, Mrs. Oliver went to live with her sister "Tomie," Mrs. George Archer Ferrell in Seale, Alabama, where she died in 1907.

Letter From Hugh Lawson
To His Daughter Sarah Penelope Lawson
When She Was in Twiggs County
With Her Bryan Grandmother in Tarversville
Houston County May 12, 1838

My dear Daughter;

I think the time long and I think it a little strange you do not write to me. Have you forgotten that you have a father? I received a letter a few days past from brother Nathan, which informed me that you had gotten well, and were enjoying good health. I hope you are good and dutiful to Grandma, to aunt Martha, and to Mr. Cooper. Do you my daughter read your bible, and do you say your prayers night & morning? I shall be very sorry to learn that you neglect either. Remember thy Creator in the days of thy youth. You are young, but not too young to die. After death you can make no preparation for eternity. Life is the time, to seek and serve the Lord and to secure an interest in Heaven. Remember my daughter, that every day we live, leaves one less, and that when we quit this world, there are but two places, Heaven, and Hell. Make your choice and choose the good part which shall not be taken from you.

If you will let me know when the examination comes on, I will try to be at it. Give my love to brother Nathan and tell him I am much obliged to him for his friendly letter. Say to sister Martha that I made inquiry for a bonnet the same day I received your letter; but could not get such a bonnet in all Hawkinsville. We are mostly in health, some complaints of bad colds. Your Mother and all the family send their love to you. Give your Mother's love and mine to Grandma, aunt Martha, uncle Calvin, Nathan, George and Susan.

Your father
H. Lawson

A Letter From Hugh Lawson (1799-1856)
To His Youngest Daughter Emily Bryan Lawson (1841-1889)
In Bunavista
Houston Cty. Feb. 25, 1854

Well now, I do want to see my own sweet, sweet Pink, that black eyed Pink. The way I would buss her, is nothing to nobody. But I hope you are doing well, and behaving well, and getting good lessons. And you are studying Latin, wonderful. I can't talk latin when you come home. One old fellow, who lived a good while ago, and 'tis said, he was right smart too (I believe they called him Dr Johnson), said he had seen many ladies, who knew all about latin, but never met with one who knew english. And them was english folks too. They used the same language we do. Now you know your old father lives in the back woods and don't know every thing. But I suppose its genteel to talk latin. You are my youngest daughter, my pet, you must be made genteel, a perfect Pink. Well, you are young, but I am too old, to dig up dead folks to talk latin with them, if I could. Since I live with english folks, and associate with that kind of people only, I would be very glad to understand the english language, so as to be able to speak it and write it correctly. I want to talk with my own sweet pink when she comes home. Don't forget how to talk english, for I cant talk latin.

Be a good girl, be kind and dutiful to bro. Thad & your sisters. I shall be very sorry, if you are not a good girl both in, & out of school.

Read your bible, say your prayers night and morning, ask for protection and direction, for wisdom and for a new heart. Remember your Creator. Give my love to bro Thad, your sisters, and help Hudy. Ma & all send love to you.

Your own father
H. Lawson

P. S. When I leave this country, if I should happen to fall among them folks that talk latin, then I'll study latin.

H. L.

Letter from Hugh Lawson
To His Daughter Emily Bryan Lawson
In Bunavista, Georgia
Houston Cty March 22, 1954

Last Monday's mail brought a welcome letter from my own dear pink. Bless that sweet pink, I wish I could give her a kiss right now. I do love my sweet blackeyed pink. I hope my own little daughter is behaving well and making good use of her time. Pink wants a hat, and a pair of shoes. I wonder if little girls wear Kossouth hats in Bunavista. Well here's a five dollar bill, buy a hat and a pair of shoes. Bryan Brown is complaining, the rest of our relatives are all well so far as I know. Some little sickness in our black family; white family all up. My health is feeble, but better than it has been. We have planted our corn, except our new land. We have not commenced planting cotton, we are very dry and in much need of rain. Ma has a new garden and has just got it sown, some seeds are up, and some coming up.

All join me in love to Thad, Nep, Mollie, Pink and that sweet little boy Hudy.

Your own father
H. Lawson

A Letter From Hugh Lawson (1799-1856)
In Houston County
To His Youngest Daughter, Emily Bryan Lawson (1841-1889)
Who Was in Beuna Vista, Georgia Sept. 28, '54

Well I want to see my own sweet Pink. I thought, I must talk to her a little while Mrs. Leverette, my overseer's wife, died last sunday morning. She has been looking for death a long time. She was a member of the baptist church, & I think a good woman. She seemed to be in her senses to almost the last breath, and was entirely resigned. I trust she is now in heaven. Mr. Leverette has six small children. What he is to do with them I cannot tell. I heard yesterday from Anna, she & babe are doing well. Your Ma went to Tomie's yesterday, alls well there. All were well at Bryan's a few days past. My white family are up. Margaret has been sick, but is up. Rose physicked her some, but not enough I reckon to get all the evil out of her. Rose is playing with Anna, Shine with Martha, Your Ma & Hugh have rode out this evening to look up a weaver & Robert has gone with Ben to carry Wheat to Mr. George Walker's Mill. We want some nice flour for my pretty Pink when she comes home. Bless my Pink, I wish I had her in my arms now.

I got a letter from Amanda Howell a few days since. I think they are pleased with their country. She had just return from Florida. While in Florida she saw William Howell. Reuben Howell & his wife have parted. I do not know what is the cause of difficulty. I reckon they dont love one another, well as I do my Pink. There is no white person here this evening, but Margaret and I. But we keep at a very respectful distance from each other. She stays in your Ma's room & I in mine. I wish you would send along some smart fellow, who would carry her to California. They say women are scarce there. May be so, she would get into market. I dont think she ever will in Georgia.

Give my love to all and a good share to Pink.

Your own father.
H. Lawson

Stephen Williams Brown

My great-grandfather, Stephen Williams Brown (1804-1866) had a sister named Nancy Brown Small. Nancy's daughter, Maria Small, married Curtis Leary, who was the brother of Hannah Leary (1804-1845), Stephen Williams Brown's wife.

There was some talk about Maria, that her husband, Curtis Leary, forced her to leave his house. She took her little daughter and went to live with her uncle, Stephen Williams Brown. One day Curtis Leary rode over to the house on his horse and picked up his daughter, who was playing in the yard, unattended. He placed the child in front of him on his horse and rode off. They went to Texas, and Maria Leary never saw either of them again.

Maria's parents sided against her, but Stephen Williams Brown sympathized with her and told his children that they were always to treat Maria with the greatest kindness and respect.

I do not know what my great-grandmother, Hannah Leary Brown, thought of her brother's conduct, but it is assumed she agreed with her husband. In any case, Hannah died long before Maria. Stephen's second wife was Mary Saxon, known to her adoring step-children as "Aunt Mary."

When Maria was dying, Stephen told her he thought her Hawkinsville relatives should be notified. Maria begged him not to call them in, but he did let them know her condition. The relatives would not come to see her but said that when she died he could send her possessions on to them.

This story was told to me by Cousin Emmie Baxter, who got it from Mattiebrian Brown Benton, Mother's sister. Somewhere, perhaps in Texas, there may be descendants of Maria Leary. I wish they could know her tragic fate.

From what I know of Stephen Williams Brown, I like him best of all my ancestors, with the exception of Grandpa Brown. He was a loving husband and father, with the patience of Job and the face of a Roman god.

A BIOGRAPHICAL SKETCH OF ROBERT HARDY BROWN

(September 8, 1836 - November 24, 1914)

WRITTEN BY HIS DAUGHTER MATTIEBRIAN BROWN BENTON

(July 21, 1868 - December 8, 1932)

I do not know when my aunt wrote this biographical sketch of her father. The manuscript, in her handwriting, was given by her son, Robert Benton, to my sister. In preparing this copy, I have corrected a few dates known to be in error, and eliminated an ambiguous reference to "three children."

I have not included Mrs. Benton's outdated list of Robert Hardy Brown's descendants.

—JM

My father, Robert Hardy Brown, son of Stephen Williams Brown and Hannah Leary, was born in Houston County, Georgia, September 8, 1836. His father and mother had been married in Lenoir County, North Carolina, and had moved almost at once to Twiggs County, Georgia. There, their first child, Bryan Williams Brown, had been born in 1827. Just before the birth of my father, who was the fifth child, Stephen Williams Brown had built a home on the edge of Houston, almost to the Pulaski County line. This was a two-story house, built after a style very common in middle Georgia.

I know little of my father's childhood. His father was a successful man, a hard worker and one who talked little. It was said he managed his plantation and his sons, scarcely speaking a word. Hannah Leary Brown became almost stone deaf, consequently her children were brought up largely by their Negro nurse. She died in 1845 when Robert was only nine years old. He was said to resemble her closely. I have been told by my aunt, Martha Lawson Brown, that she was noted for her neatness, her love of flowers, her hospitality, and that she made the best doughnuts in the county. My grandfather, Hugh Lawson; my grandfather, Stephen Williams Brown; and his brother, Dempsey Brown were all near neighbors and all had large families.

They built a school house equidistant between the three homes and guaranteed the salary of the teacher. He was usually from New England and boarded with the three families, turn and turn about, in orthodox fashion. Of my father's brothers, Bryan, Marshall, William, John, and Calvin, he was particularly devoted to the eldest, Bryan. They married sisters, Martha Jane and Emily Bryan Lawson, and these two, "Aunt Martie" and "Uncle Bryan," were the only grandparents I ever knew. The Brown Boys were all tall men, six feet in their stockings, broad shouldered, with fine carriages, thick hair, wonderful teeth, and well-shaped limbs.

Bryan and Marshall were very handsome. William was fine-looking—when I knew him—with abundant iron-gray hair and a long beard. John died early of typhoid fever, and I heard little of him. All the brothers were noted for their extreme neatness, teeth, nails, etc., for well-brushed clothes and a generally trim appearance. They cared little for books, but were omnivorous readers of newspapers, keeping in close touch with local and national politics. Only Marshall was said to have a taste for literature.

When Robert was a few months old, my grandfather fitted up a spring wagon, drawn by a pair of fine horses. He took his wife and baby and went back to North Carolina to see the kinfolks. They were gone for about a year. I do not know where the other boys were during this time, probably with Dempsey Brown's family. This was in 1837, long before any railroads were in Georgia, or along that route. I have often wondered what that little cavalcade must have looked like; it has always seemed to me a tender and loving thing to do and I am glad Hannah had that pleasure before she died. She died early in her 42nd year, in child bed—the baby died also—it was her only girl. A niece of Stephen, "Cousin Betty," kept the house until Stephen married again.

It is said this silent man spoiled his children outrageously—never punishing them himself or allowing anyone else to do so.

When Bryan married Martha Lawson, she greatly endeared herself to the little boys. Calvin, the baby, who was a delicate, nervous child, and a very naughty one, was greatly devoted to her. When the boys waked up at night and cried for food, it is said Stephen thought nothing of having the cook come to the kitchen and make batter-cakes for the little wretches! I could never get my father to admit this, but "Aunt Martie" said it was true. Yet this same Stephen refused to buy a pound of wheat when his crop was a failure. He said he had never bought a pound of flour in his life and that he never intended to do so. It seems there was enough wheat to make about a barrel of flour. This was kept for high days and holidays—on other days, the family lived on meal. William told me once that he got so tired of meal in various forms that he had never willingly eaten any since that memorable year!

Robert was the delicate one, always excepting Calvin, and was never made to do any farm work—all he ever did was to feed the pigs and go to mill on Saturday, when he said it often interfered with his plans for fishing. The older boys, Bryan, Marshall, William, and John worked in the field and also making cabins—real pioneers—but not Robert. I have thought perhaps Stephen's circumstances must have been better, for he seems to have been a fine farmer and a good manager. He married the second time Mary Saxon. He proposed on Sunday; she asked him to return the following day for his answer, when she shyly handed him "Yes" in a little verse. Aunt Martie knew it, I wish I could remember it, Stephen thought it was very fine. "Aunt Mary," the boys called the step-mother. She called my father "Robbie," much to my amusement, for all his brothers called him "Bob." She told me once he was always nice to her; indeed I think all the boys were, except Calvin, who was a great tease, and always a privileged person on account of his health.

I am sorry my father would never talk of old times—I know so little of his early life. Once he bought a grape-fruit, thinking it was a big orange and that he was getting a great deal for his money! Stephen had a mahogany desk where he kept his money—always some gold, and once my father said he thought it best to show children money and not to hide it as if it were tainted. Just a hint here.

Robert went to the school I have spoken of before. I saw the little house once. It was not the "little red school house," but it had a red door! Here he played with the Lawson girls and his cousins, Dempsey Brown's girls and boys. Once he and one of the older boys (John, I suspect), told Emmie Lawson (Robert's future wife) and Eugenia (Dean) Brown, one of Dempsey's girls, to paint their faces with blackberry juice, that is would make them "so pretty"—and when the little maids did so, laughed at the sight. Whereupon the little girls in great distress went to the brook and with soap and sand almost rubbed their faces and hands raw.

He was sent to school in Twiggs and afterward to Perry, Georgia, to a Mr. Crussland, said to have been an excellent teacher. I saw Mr. Crussland once and gazed at him with awe, too much frightened to ask him about my father's school days. He did say, however, "Robert was always a good pupil." My father regarded him highly. Robert studied bookkeeping and accounting, but I do not know where. Before the war he was clerking in Hawkinsville for Ard Rawls. He taught school a few months also. I have a vague recollection that my mother went to him a short time. Perhaps this was just as he left school himself. He taught in Hawkinsville, for Eugenia Pate Stetson told me once that she was a pupil and how wonderfully he taught arithmetic! When the war broke out he volunteered from a strong sense of duty. He told me once that he never felt the South had the shadow of a chance to win, that he could not go with hope or enthusiasm, but only that wiser and older heads thought it was the only way—how much easier and happier if he could only have agreed with them. The family were aghast when he volunteered—they all thought Camp Life would kill him. I was told that William's wife (Martha Pope Brown) was particularly kind in fixing his outfit and that he was very generous after he was established when the war was over, making her a present of some silver forks (a handsome present for those times).

He never talked much to me about his war experiences—once he told me how bad the biscuits were they tried to make—this was when I complained at supper. He said he never cooked much—that he used to write letters home for the men in his company, they taking his turn for him in the cooking.

Mr. Huest(?), father of the famous Lula Huest(?), was in his company, and I think Mr. Frank Heath of Leesville, Georgia, long deceased.

He was several times offered promotion, but always declined it—because he loved the company and also because Calvin was for a time at least, a member. My Aunt, Mrs. Oliver, always called him "Lieutenant"—that was his rank when he came a-wooing my mother. Cousin Jim (Admiral Oliver), then a small boy of five or six, was very jealous and used to beg my mother not to marry him. The daguerreotype taken in his uniform shows a very thin and delicate young man. His service he told in his own words.

At the surrender in Goldsboro, North Carolina, he had his horse, and so rode home. I asked him once what he did with his uniform. He replied that he had no money to buy clothes, so his step-mother cut off the buttons, replaced them with plain ones, and he wore it as long as there was a piece. His father had a stroke of paralysis and was helpless for many months. One story shows the poverty of those days; a severe storm had blown down the chimneys of the house—how to buy brick and mortar was a problem. Finally, "Aunt Mary" suggested that there were bags and bags of goose-feathers she had saved for years in the attic. So they were sold for enough for the material and Robert and the free servants replaced them. Robert sold his horse and bought corn from the farmers—this he carted into Hawkinsville, where the Yankee regiment bought it for their horses, paying in gold and U. S. money. Then he bought more corn and made a little money. He has told me of his first trip to Hawkinsville, nine miles distant, driving a cart to which two oxen were hitched—all the horses had long since been given to the Confederacy. It was a very hot July day and the oxen persisted in making for every shady spot. I have forgotten how many weary hours it took to cover those nine miles.

When he married my mother, she brought him ten thousand dollars in money. With this he had a fine start. It is significant, I think, of their relation, that I never in my life heard her speak of their money. In fact, I never knew anything of it until a few weeks before her death.

He had a notary come to the house and had her to deed the home (for which he had paid $10,000) to her three children. He told me that he had the house in her name, so that in case of his death she would have that much more than her share of his property. My father was always devoted to my mother, loving her and caring for her in a really remarkable way. She was always frail and delicate, and he never forgot it. He was what is known as "a good provider," and did much of the marketing, hiring of servants, etc. He was truly "the head of the house," and bore all its financial burdens. On the other hand, she gave him all honor, and to the household and to the world they were one. He cared for her in many little ways, waiting on her like a woman. After her illness of two years, when I think now he must have early realized it was fatal, he re-doubled his devotion, doing everything possible for her comfort and pleasure.

It has been a life-long habit to keep a household expense book—every cent spent was entered—he footed up the pages and entered the monthly bills. When the expenses grew heavy as her illness advanced, she worried, so he at once discontinued the life-long practice, saying he would keep track through his checkbook.

He was a very indulgent father, wanting us to have the best in food, clothes, and education, yet I was afraid of him for many years, and perhaps never loved him as he deserved until after my mother's death. He never struck me but once, but I always thought the whipping unjust, and it was years before I forgave him. Because it was so unusual I have never forgotten it.

Is this an ideal picture of a devoted husband? He was devoted, but not ideal—delicate, in poor health always, nervous and high-strung, he was often irritable and wounded those he loved best. Yet his love and devotion far outweighed his faults. He used to "preach" as we called it, walking back and forth, pouring out in vigorous English his opinions of everything and everyone. This criticism belied his kind heart. He had great native ability, a marvelous memory, keen judgment, great financial acuteness. His honesty and fairness in business were proverbial—truly "his word was his bond."

After my mother's death, he became a very tender father, especially to his daughters. He always had a tender heart toward women, and a sympathy for them. He often said life was unfair to women. He welcomed aluminum in the kitchen, and all household helps, because they lightened women's burdens.

He wrote to my mother every day when they were separated and, after my marriage brought me to Augusta, he wrote to me about every day. He gained flesh as he passed middle life, and grew to be a fine looking man, with deep, intensely blue eyes set beneath a square over-hanging brow, a fine erect carriage, intelligence and alertness in every movement. Never can I forget his love and kindness when I kept house after my mother's death, or his pride in my housekeeping, etc.—and his generosity after my marriage.

To go back a little, Robert Hardy Brown and Emily Bryan Lawson were married January 10, 1866 at Pine Retreat, by Reverend B. F. Tharpe. He had baptized my mother and she had boarded in his home when she went to school in Perry. She was much attached to him and to his family. It was a bitter cold day. The quaint cards bear the name of her sister, Mrs. Oliver, a war-widow and her second brother, Hugh Lawson. Her dress was dark green and she had a pretty shawl. Aunt Rosa came from Twiggs and brought Cousin Sarah who was too delicate to leave behind. The wedding was at twelve o'clock. After a luncheon, the pair drove to Aunt Mattie's, twelve long miles away. They boarded in Hawkinsville, where Robert worked in a cotton warehouse.

In 1868 they came to Macon, boarding at "The Brown House," "The Lanier House," and with a Mrs. Freeman—where she lived I do not know, though I have a hazy idea that it was on Second Street. I was born July 2, 1869—in Houston County at Aunt Mattie's—named in honor of her and her husband—my father's dearly loved elder brother, my mother's former guardian and my Aunt Mattie—the sister who had been mother to Emily. My parents boarded until my brother's birth, January 6, 1872. He was born at Pine Retreat and named for the dear brother killed at nineteen in the War, Robert Lawson. With two small children, it was best to have a home.

So a home on Plum Street, not far from Cotton Avenue on the right-hand side was purchased. This was a comfortable house with a large lot. I remember we had a large vegetable garden in the rear, and it was a real adventure to go to the very end, climb the fence and gaze into the alley! My first clear memory begins with this home. I remember the confusion with furniture coming in when the three bedrooms were the only comfortable places in the house. Aunt Nannie (Mrs. Halliburton she was then), came to help Mamma. We all had grippe, and I remember her as she sat in a low rocker, patting Brother with one hand who was by this time extremely delicate and a "bad" baby, while she wiped her nose with the other! My father's health was very bad and it was feared he would have tuberculosis. I remember it was told that Dr. Fitzgerald, his physician, came one day with two five gallon jugs, one full of corn whiskey, and one of cod liver oil, and said "take every drop of both these jugs, then come to see me." Papa said he did not know which was worse, the corn whiskey or the oil!

He was a clerk in a cotton warehouse, Campbell and Jones, I think, then afterward a cotton buyer. He soon dealt in stocks and bonds. I remember how strange I thought it was he did not have a store and sell something, shoes or groceries. Once someone asked me what his business was and I replied, "Oh, he lives by his wits," in all innocence, for I always believed he had more wits, or sense, than most people. The lady to whom I made the remark came to Mamma to apologize, for she believed I had been taught this remark by curiosity seekers.

Papa and Mr. W. G. Solomon formed a partnership for selling stocks and bonds, in 1885, I think. He was for many years a director of the Exchange Bank and when elected President of the Central Georgia Bank, he did not own a dollar's worth of stock, but had to purchase some shares to qualify.

He was for nearly thirty years President of the Bond Commission of the City of Macon, and it is said managed the affairs with the utmost fidelity and success.

He was an Alderman for a few terms, and one of the directors of the Southwestern Railroad for many years.

His many friends were very loyal and he loved them very much and was much grieved when so many preceded him to the grave. Dr. John Baxter, Judge J. J. Gresham, Major Fletcher Hanson, Mr. Charles E. Campbell, Mr. Lee Jordan, Dr. James Etheredge, his kinsman by marriage, Mr. Exham Philips, and many others. To his brother, Bryan Brown, he was greatly devoted. They wrote to each other almost every day—sometimes Uncle Bryan would write twice, to even three times a day—short letters, but telling the most intimate details of business or home affairs.

Uncle Bryan's penmanship was almost illegible, so all he wrote was safe, no one but Papa could read it! Papa, on the other hand, wrote a beautiful hand but was very careful not to write anything he did not wish the world to see. He might talk extravagantly when he "preached," but he never went too far when he sat down to write.

Although so delicate, so nervous and high-strung, he was rarely ill enough to go to bed. I nursed him through the three illnesses when he had to be in bed—once with "La Grippe" on Poplar Street, once on Orange Street, and at the last. He had little faith in drugs, or doctors, often saying that quinine and calomel were the only ones that ever amounted to anything. He was always a good patient for me, however, and took both medicine and nourishment beautifully.

In closing this very inadequate sketch, I must speak of his love for his nephew, Pope Brown, eldest son of William Brown. He was like an elder son and he took the keenest interest in his success and in his career. All of his people were dear to him, indeed the Browns had the reputation of being very "clannish." John, eldest son of Marshall, was a great favorite also, and the daughters of Bryan: Sallie and Rosa. Of Mamma's people he was very fond—Aunt Martie was like his own sister, Aunt Neppie, Aunt Nancy, Aunt Tommie, Aunts Rosa and Mag, he loved them all. Cousin Laura Bunn was like a daughter to him for many years and Cousin Jim Oliver and Cousin Hugh were very dear to him. He loved little children, especially little girls, and to him a pretty woman was always one of Mamma's type, slender, delicate, and refined. An erect carriage and neatness were always admirable in his eyes.

Addenda

"All of his goodness to us I shall never forget. As my mother looked to him for advice and counsel, so too did we, and we shall miss him sorely. He was always particularly sweet to me, and I loved him for it."

—Mary C. R. Davis
(extract from a letter)

"I am always recalling with tender, grateful memory, the countless, beautiful kindnesses with which my dear Uncle blessed my youth. I have loved and admired him ever since I can remember. He was so wise and good in so many ways. I never knew anyone who did kind deeds more beautifully than he did."

—Laura L. Bunn
(extract from a letter)

An Autobiographical Outline by Robert Hardy Brown

In 1904, Grandpa Brown, who was then sixty-eight years old, prepared an outline of his life, presumably at the request of his oldest daughter, Mattiebrian Brown Benton. The original, in his handwriting, was given by her son, Robert Benton, to my sister Emily. It is included here exactly as Grandpa wrote it, with only a few changes in punctuation: I was born September 8, 1836, in Houston County, Georgia.

Reared on a farm, and did some farm work. Stephen Brown was my father; Hannah Leary Brown my mother. They came from North Carolina in 1820, 1825. I received an Old Field education (that is, mostly country school). Went to school 1855. Jeffersonville Twiggs. 1856, Perry, Houston County.

Each year to the noted educator, James E. Crosland.

Later, in the fifties, I was employed in general merchandise store, as salesman and book keeper, office man, in Hawkinsville, Pulaski County, Georgia,

And up (to) the beginning of the Civil War.

Enlisted and went to the war, in the third Dawson's Battery of Artillery.

Soon the Battery took the name of Anderson Battery.

Dawson, too old, resigned. Anderson made Captain.

After the camp of instruction, he, the Battery, was sent to the Western army.

That is, sent to Tennessee and Kentucky.

From Nashville, we receded gradually, slowly but surely: Murfreesboro, Tullahoma, Chattanooga, Missionary Ridge; Chickamauga, Dalton, Resaca, New Hope, Marietta, Atlanta, Lovejoy—by Griffin, and on to Macon—this place.

We were engaged in the little but fierce battle of Griswoldville, and back to Macon, Ga.

Thence to Hawkinsville, to Doctortown by River Boat, and thence by R. R. to Savannah.

From Savannah, we escaped the enemy by the skin of our teeth, over the 3 Rivers at Savannah by cover of night, on Pontoon Bridge made of rice boats tied together, into South Carolina.

This was marvelous as well as close and dangerous escape.

No one knew better than I did, for I was detailed and required to go over in the evening, and return, for a report as to the readiness of the bridges; which I did.

I probably was the first to cross, and return, and one of the last that crossed that night.

Sherman was on our heels, and in Savannah next morning in full possession.

On to, through South Carolina, to Branchville—had spat at this place, thence to Saulsbury, and thence to Greensboro, where we laid down arms, about 9th or 10th, April. General Lee surrendered April 9th, 1865.

We returned, as a company, to Hawkinsville about 1st May, 1865, and there disbanded and took our paroles of our captain—ragged, hungry, destitute.

I think each of us received $1.60 silver.

I was Lieut. in the Battery, hence I had a horse, which I bartered for 150 bushels (of) corn. Sold the corn, and began (a) little store on less than $100, about 1st July, 1865.

By the close of the year, had made (a) little money, and closed out to get married.

I married Miss Emily Lawson, daughter (of) Hon. Hugh Lawson, of Houston County, January 10th, 1866.

We were neighbors, went to the same schools, except she took college course during the war.

Began business again in Hawkinsville in 1866 and 1867: Rawls and Brown Dry Goods and Groceries. J. W. Lathrop, Savannah, was silent partner.

Made no money. I sold out and came to Macon, 1867, in (the) Fall.

Went in cotton warehouse as a clerk.

Health failed me. I quit in the 70's.

Was elected an alderman City Macon, because no one was against me.

Served my term. Two years. Was glad to get out.

We had just three children born to us. All three living: two in Macon, one in Augusta.

My wife died 1889. Noble Christian woman, too good for this earth. Now must be in the upper heaven.

1888 I was made President of the Central Georgia Bank, Macon, having served long time Director Exchange Bank.

Am still President Central Georgia Bank.

About 1892 was put on the Board Bond Commissioners City Macon, and made President of the Board, which office I have held since, and hold now.

This put(s) me up to date, and more than sixty-five years old—I don't say how much.

June 18, 1904

It must have been very difficult for my aunt to get her father to set down these bare facts. He always refused to discuss his war experiences, except with his old body servant, Lucius. Although a lieutenant in the war, Grandpa was known to most people in later years as "Captain Brown."

A PUBLIC HANGING

Grandpa Brown told my father about a poor Negro sharecropper who was sentenced to be hanged for killing another man over a game of cards. He was taken by wagon from the county jail in Hawkinsville to a great oak tree, a few miles from town, where public hangings were held. Just before reaching his final destination, the poor man passed his own piece of land. His wife, completely distraught, ran after the wagon shouting, "Joe, what's to become of me and the children? It's time for the new crop. What am I to plant?"

Joe looked down at her mournfully as the wagon slowly moved on and said, "I don't give a damn what you plant; this here sheriff's got me plum discouraged."

Mother's Generation

My mother, Ethel Oliver Brown, was the daughter of Robert Hardy Brown (September 8, 1836-November 24, 1914) and Emily Bryan Lawson (March 3, 1841-May 14, 1889). She was the youngest of three children:

Mattiebrian Brown
(Mrs. William Nelson Benton)
(July 2, 1868 - December 8, 1932)
Robert Lawson Brown
(January 6, 1872 - March 2, 1912)
Ethel Oliver Brown
(Mrs. William Jordan Massee)
(September 30, 1879 - August 25, 1958)

Laura, Sarah, and Nancy Bunn

Rosannah Stuart Lawson, the seventh of Hugh Lawson's nine daughters, married Hugh Lawson Bunn. They had three children: Laura, Sarah, and Nancy. Only Nancy, the youngest, married. She and her husband, Adiel Adams, lived in Macon. Laura and Sarah taught school, as did their father.

Laura Bunn had a crippling form of arthritis, which was very painful, but until the end she was able to care for her needs. She was studying in Germany when her arthritis became pronounced. The doctors there were able to detail the progress of the disease but were unable to give her anything that would ameliorate the condition.

Lula Johnson (later Mrs. Comer) grew up in Marshallville, Ga. When she inherited $5,000, my father thought she must be the richest girl in Georgia. She took the money and went with Laura Bunn to Paris to study French. Later she taught French at Wesleyan College.

Laura and Sarah lived with sister, Nan in Macon, where Laura died. After the death of Nan, Sarah went to live with her cousin, Mattiebrian Benton. Although Sarah was considered the frail one, she outlived both her sisters. Cousin Laura and Cousin Nan were greatly beloved by everyone in the Lawson and Brown families; Cousin Sarah, less so.

When Sarah was left alone, Mattiebrian Brown, without consulting her husband (Nelson Benton) or her son (Robert Benton) invited her to come and live with them in Augusta. She had many barrels and crates of books, which she stored in my mother's garage, at the house on College Street. I still remember her periodic visits of inspection, although I was a very small child. A tiny little old lady, always dressed in black. Mother's chauffeur would open the containers to make sure the books were all right.

While living with Auntie, she decided to visit her Bunn relations in Cove Spring. She missed the train two days in succession. On the third day, Uncle Nelson took the day off from work, to be sure she got on the train. In Atlanta, where she had to change trains, she missed the connection. Auntie had more patience with Cousin Sarah than did Uncle Nelson—or my mother.

The letter from Cousin Laura to her cousin, Mattiebrian Benton, is the most endearing of all the Lawson letters I have seen. I am unable to identify the baby "Sol," referred to by Cousin Laura.

A Letter from Laura Bunn (Daughter of Hugh L. Bunn and Rosannah Stuart Lawson) to Her First Cousin, Mattiebrian Brown Benton

Pension Schmidt
2 Köthener Strasse
Berlin, Prussia
Dec. 15th 1895

My dear Cousin:

Your delightful letter came yesterday—and for fear I may soon become too "percluse des mains" to write to you at all—and also because I always want to write to you I am going to send you a brief reply. The letter that came from you yesterday is the fourth I have had from you since I left Macon. I could cry to think you have sent others that have lost their way. I am distressed, too, about cousin Marion's and cousin Jim's letter. I hope they made no mistake in the address. I receive frequent letters from Madame Hugon—but no letters have been forwarded to me from Paris. What a long, long way the "Minneapolis" has gone—and the poor little wife at home! You must send me her address, and some day I will send her a little letter.

I am really very much troubled about you. Those severe colds just at the commencement of winter are no trifles. You must take your tonic faithfully and have cod liver oil, too. I remember you grow tired very soon of your medicines and I fear you will need one to remind you of them and to insist on your taking them. I have been wishing for you so much of late. A German Xmas is something to be seen—and I am watching all I can of the busy preparations for it. It has not been very cold, although we have had snow several times—but oh, how dark and damp the days are! And how wet and dirty the streets are! I suffer so much all the time that I am disposed to view the world with a jaundiced eye—and I exclaim "Quel sale temps! Quelle sale ville! Quel sale monde!" I am in danger of losing practically all the enthusiastic admiration I cherished theoretically for this great German nation. I have such a few pleasant people, but I find the Germans of this house, those among whom I live, and move and have my being, tout à fait antipathiques—especially my landlady. And then we have such vile things to eat! I try to go out for a walk every day, even when it rains, but I do not walk in the Thiergarten now. The streets, with the display of Xmas goods are so gay and attractive. I go along with the crowd and gaze into shop windows. Booths have been erected in every open square, and this Sunday evening these impromptu shops are doing a thriving trade. They call to-day the Silver Sabbath—but next Sunday, the last before Xmas, will be the Golden Sabbath—and all these itinerant shop-keepers expect to become only a little less wealthy than Croesus or an American. I wish to go out after dark next Sunday afternoon and inspect all these queer little shops. There are forests of little fir trees on every open place and in the streets, waiting to be bought up. The two ladies from America of whom I wrote you always have a little tree for themselves. They have spent so much time in Germany they have adopted many of the German customs. They have been working furiously for two weeks writing their Xmas letters and making and sending off presents to distant friends. Miss Scammon told me this evening she had mailed letters and packages to fifty-six friends in America and England! I think it is a beautiful and delightful thing to do—but it requires time, health, and money. The German ladies find Sunday a good time to do their fancy needlework—and all that I have seen, sew and knit and crochet all day Sunday with the greatest sang froid imaginable. I am sure you pronounce well—and if you do not speak fluently or easily, it is merely because you lack practice. I am not advancing just now in either German or French. I learn the lesson in French literature and recite it—and that is really all, except the little reading I do. I have been almost too unwell to do anything, and it has been hard to find a German teacher that suited one. I think now I have found one that will prove satisfactory. I shall settle with my physician and seek another who may give more energic medicines. This doctor tells me to be patient and cheerful—and meantime I am almost bed-ridden. I have just finished reading "Mosaïques"—a collection of short sketches and letters by Prosper Mérimée. This author is a little passé de mode now. Have you read anything by Daudet? Do you know this little French conundrum: Faites une sentence en nommante les noms de quatre auteurs Francais classiques. Racine, Boileau, de Lafontaine, Molière. (Racine boit l'eau de la fontaine Molière.) This fountain Molière is a very handsome one, at the side of the house in the Rue St. Honoré where Molière was born. I have often walked by it. You have my deepest sympathy in all that troubles and distresses you. I often wish for you—and now I should be so glad to spend the coming holidays with you. I shall continue to hope that some day we are to have some good times together. But any times together will be good for me. I am so glad to know the others are well. Does Ethel read as much as ever? Write me more about the little lady. What is she reciting now? I am looking forward to hearing her mandolin music. Please remember me with very much love to her—to uncle Robert and Lawson. If Aunt Nep is still with you give her an especial message of love from me.—I should love to have a chance to pat Sol's head and to feed him. My poor hand can write no more. Sweet, do take good care of yourself for me. I shall feel anxious about you all the time until I know you are well. I trust the Xmas time will be full of pleasure for you—and all the other dearly loved ones of the household. With warmest love for you always

Your cousin,
Laura

Daddy's Early Years in Macon

Courtship and Marriage

FROM COLUMBUS TO MACON IN 1893

Daddy left Columbus in 1893 and moved to Macon, which boasted a population of around 25,000. His brother Marion ("M. H.") and his sister Laura had gone to the World's Fair, in Chicago, and Daddy came to take M. H.'s place while he was away, hoping to land a permanent job later. M. H. worked for Willingham and Hendricks, "The Dixie Works," at the foot of Cherry Street. While M. H. was in Chicago, Daddy did his work and in the time left over did the work of M. H.'s assistant, Pringle Willingham, which greatly impressed Mr. Hendricks.

Mr. Hendricks pulled out and started Central Sash. Daddy went to him to get a job, but Hendricks was afraid that M. H., then at Willingham Sash & Door, would get trade secrets out of Daddy.

"Did it occur to you, Mr. Hendricks, that I could get a damn sight more secrets out of M. H. than he could get out of me," Daddy answered him, but didn't get the job.

Broadus Willingham pulled out and started Macon Plough Works. They made Terrill scrapers, just the one item. Daddy went to work for him.

Despite the great difference in their ages, Daddy and Mr. Broadus Willingham became good friends. He was always known as "Old Man Broadus," to distinguish him from his son. Later, when Daddy had become a very prosperous businessman, he and Mr. Broadus would fish together at Homossassa, Florida. Once, when they were out on the river, with a guide to row and locate the best spots for fishing, Mr. Broadus gave Daddy a cigar. Daddy tried to light the cigar but with no success. So he turned it around and tried to light the other end but still couldn't get it going. Thinking that Mr. Broadus wasn't looking, he quietly slipped the cigar into the water and took one of his own expensive Romeo and Juliets out of his pocket and lit it. Quick as a flash the old man said, "I saw you, Jordan, throwing away my cigar for one of your own Ro-me-o and Ju-li-ets," pronouncing each syllable, sarcastically. "When you worked for me you were glad to get a two-for-a-nickel cigar."

"Mr. Willingham," Daddy replied, "I'd still be glad to get a two-for-a-nickel cigar if I were still working for you."

The plough company burned down and Mr. Broadus Willingham didn't rebuild it. From there, Daddy went to work for Mr. A. D. Schofield, at the Schofield Iron Works, as bookkeeper.

DADDY RECALLS MR. SCHOFIELD

The Schofields were very big and rich and prominent in those days. And very arrogant. When I worked for Mr. Schofield, I wrote a very perfect Spencerian hand, and I was extremely proud of the neatness as well as the accuracy of my bookkeeping. Had a good memory, too. Customers would come in on the first of the month and ask, "How much do I owe?" I would quote the exact amount from memory and they would say, "Let me see that on the books." I was always right, to the penny, and Mr. Schofield was impressed.

One day I looked at my pen and there was a fine hair on the point. I tried to blow it off, but instead scattered several little ink spots on the ledger. Spots no bigger than pin points. I knew that when the ink was completely dry I could scrape the spots off with a sharp knife and leave no trace on the paper. Just then the whistle blew and I went out to lunch, leaving the page exposed, to dry. When I came back, there was a large hand drawn on the page in red crayon, with the index finger pointing to those little spots.

I said, "Mr. Schofield, did you do that?" And he said, "I did."

"Then you can take your job and go plumb to Hell."

In those days Mr. Schofield was the meanest man in the world. Later when he lost his money he got some of the milk of human kindness in him. It made a real man out of him, and he became as fine a man as there was in Macon. When he came into the bank to borrow a hundred dollars, he'd take off his hat and talk like a human being.

It's funny how some people change. You know, young Logan Lewis used to be a first class horse's behind. It took a world war to change him. Now he's as good a friend as I've got in Macon. Crosses the street just to speak, whenever he sees me coming. Damn good-looking boy, too.

LUMBER

After leaving the Schofield Iron Works, Daddy started the Massee Lumber Company. At first it was a brokerage firm and did no manufacturing. A couple of years later it was doing so well, M. H. Massee sold out at Willingham Sash and Door Co. and joined Daddy.

They needed so much capital to begin manufacturing, they took in M. H.'s brother-in-law, Gus Felton, and reorganized as the Massee-Felton Lumber Co.

In 1900 Daddy sold his third to Gus Felton for $35,000. Together with John Moore and Joseph Neel, he built and operated the Bibb Brick Company. Mr. Neel was in it for less than a year; John Moore, twelve or thirteen years. In 1914, when Daddy owned it all, he sold his brother, Jack Massee, 40 percent on credit, letting him work it out.

But I'm getting ahead of the story.

Uncle Dave and the Supreme Court

The Massee-Felton Lumber Company started a big sawmill in South Georgia, which Daddy operated. He gave his youngest brother a job there. Dave was sixteen or seventeen years old, and it was his first job. The mill was desperately in need of more land, or at least the right to cut timber. Most of the wooded land in the vicinity belonged to an old codger who had stubbornly refused to sell either his property or his timber. Daddy spent weeks trying to wear down the owner's resistance. He frequently rode over for dinner with the man and his wife. The meal invariably consisted of cornbread and greasy turnip greens cooked with fatty meat. He told the old man one funny story after another until finally he thought he was ready to sign over the rights to his timber. They were sitting on the countryman's front porch after a very heavy meal when Dave dashed by on his horse. The old man's little dog ran after the horse, yapping furiously. Dave drew his pistol and shot him. He intended only to frighten the dog and couldn't have hit him again if he tried, but the dog was dead. The old countryman was so angry he ordered Daddy off his place and told him never to come back.

Dave's job was to keep a record of the laborers' hours and prepare their pay envelopes. One Saturday the whistle blew at noon and, as usual, the envelopes were not ready. The workmen were all outside the office making a lot of noise while waiting for their week's pay. The racket made Daddy nervous and he said to Dave angrily, "God damn it, Dave, you've had all week to finish the books; why aren't the envelopes ready? Those men have worked hard and they want their money."

Dave replied, "You don't like the way I keep the books?'

"I don't like it worth a damn."

Dave slammed the book shut. "Then keep them yourself," and walked out.

Two days later Daddy received a telegram: "Come at once. Father." And he went. When he arrived at Massee's Lane, his father was standing at the top of the front steps waiting for him. He said, "Son, your mother and I are very upset. You have badly mistreated your little brother."

Daddy protested, "But Papa, let me tell you my side of the story."

"That won't be necessary," said his father sternly. "We want you to do three things: first, apologize to Dave; second, give him his job back; and, third, raise his salary."

Without further ado, Daddy did all three. The Supreme Court had rendered a decision and there could be no appeal.

COURTSHIP

Mother knew Jack Massee, Daddy's younger brother, before she met Daddy. Jack was an outstanding athlete and remarkably good-looking. Mother had lots of beaux, especially among the Mercer boys. Presumably, it was Uncle Jack who introduced Mother and Daddy. Not long afterwards, Daddy approached Grandpa Brown for permission to marry his daughter. He was rejected in no uncertain terms. About a year later he went back to Grandpa's bank to try again. This time he took with him his oldest brother, Marion Massee, hoping that Uncle Marion's reputation as a solid citizen in the community would help his cause.

After hearing Daddy's heartfelt plea, Grandpa, in a voice loud enough to be heard throughout the bank, replied, "Massee, I think Ethel is too young to get married, and I don't like everything about you. I do know you'll always take good care of my daughter, so I'll give my permission on one condition: that you and Ethel live with me."

Daddy, overjoyed, said, "Mr. Brown, I can assure you that we had no other intention!" Then Grandpa added, "I hope you realize, Massee, that Ethel is an expensive fad." In telling the story, Daddy always commented, "That was a truthful old man." That is how it came to pass that Mother and Daddy on returning from their honeymoon took up residence with Mr. Brown in his house on Poplar Street, where the Catholic Church rectory now stands.

Continuing with the story, Daddy recalled, "Mr. Brown was too smart for me. Ethel and I lived with him for about a year, as star boarders. Never missed a meal and never paid a cent. Mr. Brown came home from the bank one day and without a word handed your mother an official looking document. 'What's this, Papa,?' she asked. He told her, 'It's a deed to the house. I'm damned tired of you and Massee living with me. From now on I'm going to live with you.' And that's what he did, for the next ten years, until he died in 1914."

It turned out to be a happy arrangement for all concerned. Although opposites in every respect, Daddy and his father-in-law became utterly devoted to each other. Despite his eccentricities, Grandpa Brown was an extremely conservative man, but he was fascinated by my father's daring and flamboyance.

At times, Grandpa Brown could be highly critical of Daddy, but he brooked no criticism from others. When Daddy was touring with his prize racehorse, Felton Hatcher, his business partner, went by the Exchange Bank to have a little fun teasing the old man. He said, "Mr. Brown, Jordan should stay home and look after business instead of gallivanting around the country with a bunch of racehorses." Although those were Grandpa's own sentiments, he shouted, "Let me tell you something, Hatcher, when Massee gets back, he'll know more about the business in one day that you will in the rest of your life!" He came from behind the desk to make the point.

Once Mr. Brown observed, "When Ethel got married she didn't know one playing card from another. Now there are enough old decks of cards around the house to paper the walls in every room."

There was one thing Grandpa Brown and Daddy couldn't agree on, and that was who would get to read the morning newspaper first. Each insisted the other made a mess of the paper. They solved the problem by ordering separate subscriptions. Poor Mother was no better off with two messed-up papers than with one.

Towards the end of his life, Daddy said to me, "You know, Boots, if your mother and I had ever split up, I'm sure that old man would have gone with me, even though Ethel was his favorite child. But there was never any danger: there wasn't enough money for two piles."

A Wedding Amid Palms

"I started the Massee-Felton Lumber Company and operated it very successfully for several years. M. H. was working for Willingham Sash and Door Company. Had a good job; owned some small amount of stock. Well, he caught Pringle Willingham stealing the petty cash and wanted to prosecute him in the courts. O. P. Willingham and Mr. Broadus wouldn't allow this so they bought out M. H. to save the family name. Ethel and I were just about to get married at that time and Pringle was to be my best man. So we had to get a substitute right away."

Hillyer Rudisil was the new best man, or, as that generation expressed it, he stood up with my father. Mother and Daddy spent their wedding night at the old Kimball House in Atlanta. The Ocmulgee River is said to originate in a spring underneath that hotel.

Mr. Rudisil and his fiancee were married the following day. They joined Mother and Daddy in Atlanta and the two couples proceeded to New York, where they spent their honeymoon.

No account of Mother and Daddy's wedding could possibly equal the colorful account in the Macon Telegraph the next day, which was preserved by Laura Massee Walker, Daddy's sister. I particularly like the description of "a handsome man of magnificent physical proportions, whose face clearly portrays that firm manliness which characterizes him both socially and in the business world." No one knows why Mother was accompanied down the aisle by her maid of honor, Odille Taylor (Mrs. Charles Preston), instead of Mr. Brown.

My mother's dearest friend, Martha Hunt Cornell, was not in the wedding because her uncle had just died and Mrs. Hunt thought it would be unseemly.

Macon Telegraph, Macon, Georgia, November 9, 1899
WEDDED AMID PALMS
MR. WILLIAM JORDAN MASSEE and
MISS ETHEL OLIVER BROWN
BEAUTIFUL WEDDING
FIRST BAPTIST CHURCH FILLED
TO OVERFLOWING.

Reception Tendered the Wedding
Party at the Home of Capt. Robt.
Hardy Brown, Father of the
Bride, Immediately after
Ceremony—Bridal Tour.

An hour before the appointed time yesterday afternoon the First Baptist Church was filled to its utmost capacity by friends and acquaintances assembled to witness the marriage ceremony uniting Mr. William Jordan Massee and Miss Ethel Oliver Brown.

Waiting was made enjoyable by Mrs. Everett, who presided at the organ and beguiled the time with most beautiful selections, ranging from the musical classics to those simple and tender airs familiar from childhood, which speak to the soul and awaken sweet memories.

Promptly at 5 o'clock the father of the bride, Mr. Robert Hardy Brown, with Mrs. S. P. Oliver on his arm and followed by immediate members of the families of the contracting parties, proceeded up the main aisle of the church and took their places in the pews reserved for them.

After a few moments of breathless expectation there were heard the familiar tones of Mendelssohn's Wedding March, and the ushers slowly marched to their places in the following order: Mr. Bryan Brown Taylor with Mr. Joe Warren Turner and Mr. Charles F. Cater with Mr. William E. McAndrew.

Following these came the bride's attendants as follows:
Miss Mary Cooper of Perry on the arm of Mr. E. H. Coleman.
Miss Edith Stetson with Mr. Winship Cabaniss.
Miss Julia Huguenin with Mr. William Pitt Glover.
Miss Ann Sanford with Mr. G. E. Williams.
Miss Daisy Jeter with Mr. John Curd.

When these had taken their places the organ breathed a softer, sweeter tone, and the bride, on the arm of her maid of honor, Miss Odille Taylor, moved slowly toward the altar, while the groom, with his best man, Mr. Hillyer Rudisil, came from the pastor's study to await them. The pastor, Rev. J. L. White, preceded the conventional marriage ceremony by a few well chosen, eloquent and heart-stirring remarks, and the scene was made doubly solemn by the sweet, low organ tones barely breathing "Oh, Promise Me." Then a short, heartfelt prayer and the bride and groom, as handsome a couple as ever bowed their heads to these solemn vows, turned from the altar to walk down the aisle of life together.

It was the unanimous comment of the crowds who waited their turn to make their exit from the church that a more beautiful wedding had never been seen in the First Baptist Church.

The decorations of palms and white chrysanthemums were elaborate and arranged with perfect taste.

The bridesmaids wore charmingly becoming toilettes of pink organdy over pink taffeta silk and carried white carnations.

The maid of honor wore an exquisite gown of white organdy over white silk and carried an armful of pink carnations.

The bride's gown was of white liberty silk and gauze over white taffeta and she carried an armful of lilies of the valley. Since her debut she has been conceded to be one of Macon's loveliest girls, and as a bride, her sweet, gentle beauty was enhanced tenfold.

The groom, Mr. William Jordan Massee, is a handsome man of magnificent physical proportions, whose face clearly portrays that firm manliness which characterizes him both socially and in the business world.

From the church the bridal party proceeded to the home of the bride's father, where a reception was tendered them and invited friends.

Mr. and Mrs. Massee left at 7:10 via the Central of Georgia for an extended trip to points of interest in the North and East, carrying with them the best wishes of a host of friends.

POPLAR STREET

GRANDPA BROWN AND LUCIUS BROWN

My grandfather, Robert Hardy Brown, was born in Houston County, Georgia, a few miles from Hawkinsville. He was a delicate child and was never made to do much farm work. While his older brothers worked in the field and built cabins, Robert frequently went fishing. Their mother, Hannah Leary Brown, early became almost totally deaf, so the boys were largely brought up by their black nurse. Hannah died when Robert was nine years old.

He must have spent much time, even as a boy, with Lucius, one of his father's slaves, who was the same age.

Stephen Williams Brown, Robert's father; Dempsey Brown, his uncle; and Hugh Lawson, his future father-in-law; were all neighbors and had large families. Together, they built a school house equidistant from the three homes, and imported a teacher from New England. The children of the three families all went to school together.

In 1855, Robert Brown went off to boarding school, first in Jeffersonville, and the following year in Perry, to the noted educator, James E. Crussland. Lucius was sent along to look after him. Grandpa took his own furniture, as was the custom, and Lucius slept on a cot at the foot of his bed.

When the Civil War broke out in 1861, Robert volunteered from a sense of duty, although, as he told his daughter, Mattiebrian, years later, he "never felt the South had the shadow of a chance to win." The family was aghast. They felt camp life would kill him. Again, Lucius went along to look after him. This was not uncommon among planters' sons during the Civil War. He was twenty-four when the war began.

By the time they reached Virginia, both Grandpa and Lucius sorely needed new boots. Lucius walked from somewhere in Virginia all the way to Houston County in central Georgia, and back to Virginia with the boots. He could have kept on walking until he was in Union territory, but he didn't.

After the war, as soon as Grandpa and Emily Lawson, whom he married in 1866, set up housekeeping in Macon, Lucius came to work for them, as a servant, no longer a slave. Henceforth, he was Lucius Brown.

Over a period of many years, Lucius took care of Grandpa and his office at the bank. Every workday, Grandpa donned his frock coat and high silk hat and set off on foot for the bank, with Lucius, also dressed in frock coat and high silk hat, a few paces behind him. When the bank closed, the two of them came home together. The routine was followed six days a week, without variance, year in and year out.

He continued to work for Grandpa until around 1906. Emily doesn't recall his death. She was only five when the family moved to Orange Street, and Mother probably would not have told her when Lucius died.

Not long after Daddy got married and came to live with his father-in-law, he arrived home one evening just in time to see Grandpa Brown chasing Lucius down the street, shouting after him, "Don't ever put your foot inside my house again!" Lucius escaped into the night, and Grandpa returned to his room, still cursing.

Daddy was very upset by all this and told Mother what had occurred. He couldn't understand why she showed so little concern. Didn't she realize that her father couldn't get along without Lucius?

The next morning, Daddy got up before dawn to go hunting. He tiptoed down the stairs trying not to wake anyone. When he reached the door to Grandpa's bedroom, which was on the ground floor, he heard much laughter from within. The door was slightly ajar, so he peeped inside. Grandpa and Lucius were sitting on opposite sides of a table with a jug of whiskey between them. Both were in their shirtsleeves, with their high silk hats on, and both had their feet on the table. They were swapping stories of the Civil War. My grandfather never discussed his wartime experiences with anyone else, but he and Lucius had been through the war together.

Daddy understood then why Mother had shown so little concern.

Cousin Hugh and the Hat

Daddy Himself Tells the Story

Mr. Brown had two nephews, James Oliver and Hugh Oliver. Their father was killed at Gettysburg, and Mr. Brown practically raised those boys. Jim went to Annapolis and Hugh went to Mercer, where he studied for the ministry. Jim was not an outstanding student, but Hugh had a brilliant scholastic record. He could recite the Bible from cover to cover, from memory. The family all thought he was going to be a second Spurgeon, but it didn't turn out that way. The poor devil had hard luck. The biggest church he ever got was in Buena Vista at fifteen hundred dollars a year. But Jim Oliver, after graduating from Annapolis, had a distinguished career in the Navy. He became an admiral and was the first governor of the Virgin Islands after we bought them from Denmark. The whole family, my wife included, regarded him with great pride and respect. He married Miss Marion Carter of Virginia, who inherited Shirley Plantation, one of the great show places on the James River.

Every day I went by the bank to pick up Mr. Brown for lunch. One day when I walked in, he said to me, "Massee, I bought myself a new hat this morning," motioning to a large hat box on his desk. "Take a look at it."

I opened the box and found a brand new high silk hat. I admired the hat, as was expected, and put it back in the box.

About that time, Cousin Hugh, the preacher, blew in. I can see him now coming through the bank, back to where Mr. Brown had his office. He was a big man, with a big nose, and he had on the top of his head a little brown hat about the size of half a grapefruit. It was a derby, but turned up all the way round. It looked just like a nickel on a gate post.

When he got about ten feet from where we sat, he was grinning from ear to ear. Mr. Brown took one look at him and said, "Where in the Hell did you get that hat?" And that's all he said, from that day to this, verbatim et literatum et punctuatum.

The preacher stopped dead in his tracks and said, with awe and reverence, "Why, Uncle Robert, Jimmy sent me this hat from London!"

Without another word, mind you, Mr. Brown got up from his chair and walked out the back door. I knew just where he was going—he went through the alley behind the bank to Ed Lowe's bar—but the preacher didn't know. He must have been gone about an hour.

Cousin Hugh was utterly dismayed. While we were sitting there waiting for Mr. Brown to come back, the preacher, obviously very upset, said to me, "Jordan, what's the matter with Uncle Robert? I thought he'd be glad to see me, but he hardly spoke. I don't understand. He was downright rude."

Then the devil got into me and I said, "Parson, don't you know what was the matter?"

"Why, no, Jordan. Could I have offended Uncle Robert in some way?"

"No, it's not that. It's just that he begrudges you that hat Jimmy sent from London."

You could just see that sinking in. It seemed plausible enough to the preacher, and the devil only needs half a chance.

"Your Uncle Robert was mighty good to you boys. He couldn't have done more if you'd been his own sons. Now if you really want to show your appreciation, you'll give that hat to Mr. Brown."

But I could see that suggestion met with no favor. "You ought to swap hats with him."

I took the beautiful high silk hat out of the box and showed it to the preacher. "You take this new hat and leave the derby for your Uncle Robert."

Now I was the best brick salesman in the world—you don't have to prove that—but I had a hard time selling the preacher. He was obviously impressed with the hat—there probably weren't many high silk hats in Buena Vista—but on the other hand, the derby was sent to him by Jimmy, from London. He wasn't at all sure.

He tried on the high hat looking at himself in the mirror, turning this way and that, vain as a peacock. The hat fit him perfectly, but he still wasn't sure.

Finally, he put the hat on again and went up to the front of the bank, to the head cashier, and said, "Major Chesney, how does it look?"

Major Chesney said, "It looks just fine, Parson. You ought to have a hat like that."

Still not entirely convinced, he went up to Mr. Stone, the chief bookkeeper, and, shaking his finger in Stone's face, said, "Now do not deceive me, Stone, do not deceive me. How does it look?"

"I wouldn't deceive you, Parson, it looks fine. That hat just suits you."

By then the preacher was sold on the idea, and I figured I'd better get him out of there before Mr. Brown got back. That old man would have killed me if he'd known what I was up to, and I couldn't have done it if the devil hadn't gotten into me. So I put the preacher into my buggy, which was waiting out in front to take Mr. Brown home to lunch, and drove him to the station, just as fast as I could go. I bought him a ticket to Buena Vista and saw him get on the train.

When Mr. Brown returned, I was sitting there waiting for him. He'd had a few drinks and was ready to ride. He reached over and opened the box to get his new hat. When he saw the little brown derby, he shouted loud enough to be heard all over the bank, "Where'd that damned thing come from?"

"The preacher swapped hats with you, Mr. Brown. He thought you wanted the derby that Jimmy sent from London, so he took your hat and left you his."

Without another word, Mr. Brown took the hat and went to the front of the bank. He took out his pocket handkerchief and slowly dusted off a spot right in the middle of the floor. Then he carefully placed the derby on the spot he had dusted, and with both feet jumped up and down on the hat thirty-nine times. I counted.

He was a funny old man.

The Star Brand

Grandpa Brown was hipped on the subject of shirts. He owned fourteen identical white shirts, all the Star Brand, and fourteen detachable collars.

Seven shirts and seven collars were sent to be washed every Saturday, while the others were kept at home to be worn during the week. He had seven sets of cuff links, studs, and collar buttons. When the freshly laundered shirts and collars were returned, my mother put cuff links and studs in each shirt, carefully folded them, and placed them in his bureau, along with the stiff collars. Just before going to bed, Grandpa bathed and put on the shirt he would wear to work the next day. He slept in the clean shirt, so that when he got up the next morning, he was already half dressed. Before joining Mother and Daddy he had a demitasse of G. Washington instant coffee, which was brought to his room by the cook.

Although the bosom and cuffs of men's shirts were heavily starched in those days, there was never a wrinkle in Grandpa's shirt when he emerged for breakfast. He had another half cup of coffee, boiling hot, and read his own copy of the newspaper with the morning meal.

Sometime after Daddy became a member of the household on Poplar Street, he had a poker game for Mr. George Denman, from New York, who was in Macon on business. Just as the game was getting underway, Grandpa blew in. When Daddy introduced him to Mr. Denman, Grandpa said, with great formality, "I am most happy to meet you, Sir. What line of business are you in?"

Mr. Denman replied, "I manufacture shirts, Mr. Brown."

When Grandpa heard that, his ears pricked up like a mule when he sees a hole in the bridge, and of course he asked, "What brand of shirts, Sir?"

"The Star Brand," Mr. Denman replied, with obvious pride.

Grandpa turned abruptly and without another word left the room. Daddy was embarrassed and apologized to all the guests for his father-in-law's rude behavior. No sooner had the players settled down to their game than Mr. Brown reappeared. With a sweeping gesture, he brushed aside the cards and chips and spread a shirt across the poker table.

"There's one of your damned shirts," he shouted, "and the right sleeve is an inch longer than the left sleeve," producing a tape measure to prove it. My father could have gone through the floor, but Mr. Denman quite seriously measured both sleeves.

"You are quite right, Mr. Brown. I owe you an apology, and as soon as I get back to New York, I shall see to it personally that you receive satisfaction."

A few weeks later, Grandpa received a package containing seven white shirts, in his size, with a charming note from Mr. Denman assuring him that such a mistake would never occur again, at least not with the Star Brand.

UNCLE JACK AND MISS JOHNSON

When Daddy moved to Macon in 1893, he boarded with a Mrs. Singleton at her home on College Street. Mrs. Singleton took in young men who came to the city seeking their fortune, and helped these paying guests become gentlemen. Of them all, my father was her favorite, although there was an incident that tested her affection. At one meal, Daddy discovered a hole in the middle of his napkin so large he put it over his head. It was the thoughtless act of an irrepressible young man, and he was forgiven.

Marylu Tanner, who became our maid twenty-five years later, was working for Mrs. Singleton at the time Daddy was a boarder. He was courting my mother at the time. Marylu always remembered hearing him tell Mrs. Singleton, "If only Ethel will marry me, I'll give her anything she ever wants." In telling us, Marylu added, "That was one man who kept his promise."

Daddy and Uncle Jack were closer than any other brothers I ever knew. Jack was six years younger, so I doubt that they were very close in the early years. Daddy spent more time with Marion ("M. H."), who was three and a half years older. When Daddy left home to attend school in Poughkeepsie, Jack was only eleven years old.

After he left school, Daddy moved to Columbus, where he worked for two years. For part of that time, he lived in a hotel. Jack would occasionally visit him there. On one of his visits, Jack accompanied Daddy to a poker game, just to watch. When he grew bored, he said, "Buddy, I'm going down the path to the hotel and get some sleep." Daddy pointed out to him that in the city there were streets, not paths. Jack walked back to the hotel and went to bed, locking the door to their room from the inside. When Daddy got there, some hours later, he couldn't get in. He knocked but was unable to rouse Jack. Finally, he got a bell boy to crawl through the transom and unlock the door. By this time half the hotel was awake. Jack woke at last and said, "Why didn't you wake me, I would have let you in."

As an adult, Jack became so sophisticated and so elegant that Daddy nicknamed him "Baron." For years, he could get the Baron's goat by reminding him of going down the path in Columbus. Jack, in turn, throughout the years of their close association, always called Daddy "Brady," after Diamond Jim.

Uncle Jack went to Mercer University, in Macon, where he was an outstanding athlete. He was one of my mother's many beaux, and there are several pictures of him as a college student, in her scrapbook, which Emily and I treasure. Some say that he was very much in love with Mother; if so, it was a great mistake, from his point of view, when he introduced her to his older brother.

Jack's attendance at Mercer was cut short by a terrible accident. He slipped getting on a streetcar, and lost a leg. He spent a year or so back at Massee's Lane with his parents, recuperating. During that sad period, he and his sister Laura became very close.

Eventually he was fitted with an artificial limb and was able to resume an active life. Until his death in 1932, he could play thirty-six holes of golf in an afternoon, and in those days you walked around the golf course, you did not ride.

Following his recovery, Jack went to Poughkeepsie, to the Eastman Business College, which Daddy had attended some years before. While Jack was at school, Daddy made a business trip to New York. On his first evening in the city, he went to Rector's for dinner. When he walked into the restaurant he caught sight of Jack sitting in the waiting room with a good-looking girl with bright red hair. Jack saw Daddy entering and tried to hide behind the large menu he had been given to read, but Daddy walked right over and said, "Hello, Jack, I thought you were at school."

Jack explained, "I'm just in town for the weekend," and with considerable embarrassment, "I'd like for you to meet Miss Johnson."

"Delighted, Miss Johnson. I hope you and Jack will be my guests for dinner," Daddy responded.

The prospect appealed to Jack, who, like most young men in college, was living on a limited budget. "We accept with pleasure, but we'd better go to a less crowded restaurant. Miss Johnson and I have already been here for an hour and haven't gotten a table yet."

"I think I can arrange that," Daddy assured him, and called the headwaiter over, slipping him a bill, which Jack didn't see. "I'm Mr. Massee. Did my secretary call this afternoon and reserve my usual table?"

"Oh yes, Mr. Massee. She called around three o'clock. Please follow me." Daddy, and Jack and Miss Johnson followed the headwaiter across the crowded floor and were seated at a choice table. They were each given a menu, and Daddy immediately started studying the list of wonderful foods to choose from.

When he happened to look up, Miss Johnson was concentrating on her menu, but Jack sat staring into space, white as a sheet. "What's the matter, Jack? Aren't you going to order?"

Jack replied, "I haven't decided yet whether I'm going to eat or cut that son-of-a-bitch's throat."

It was not the only time Daddy ran into Jack in New York. Each time, he was with a different girl, but they all had red hair and they were all named Miss Johnson.

When Uncle Jack finished school, he moved to Macon and with Daddy's help got a job at Willingham Sash & Door Company. He boarded with Mrs. Singleton, as Daddy had done before him. One day, Mrs. Singleton phoned Daddy in great agitation, saying, "Jordan, I think you'd better come right away. There's a Miss Johnson here, from Poughkeepsie, and she says she's going to marry Jack."

On his way to College Street, Daddy stopped to speak to Jack, who was all for going at once to confront Miss Johnson; but Daddy told him that he couldn't risk losing his first job and that he himself would handle everything. He promised Jack he would return as soon as matters were under control.

When he arrived, he found Mrs. Singleton sitting on the sofa talking to a pretty young girl with red hair. He had never seen this one before. As soon as Mrs. Singleton had discretely withdrawn, Daddy calmly inquired, "Now tell me, Miss Johnson, what this is all about."

Greatly excited, Miss Johnson replied, "I've come all the way from Poughkeepsie to marry Jack and I will not be put off."

"Now Miss Johnson, let's be perfectly frank. Did my brother promise to marry you?"

"No," she admitted.

"Well, is there any reason why he has to marry you?"

"No," she further admitted.

"Then how do you propose getting him to marry you?"

"Well, I will, you'll see. He'll marry me or I'll make you all sorry he didn't."

Now, Daddy didn't like being threatened, so he said, "Miss Johnson, I own this town. And if you give me any trouble I'll have you arrested and put in the dungeon underneath the courthouse, and you'll never be heard of again."

Miss Johnson began to cry and Daddy began to cry. Feeling genuinely sorry for the girl, he started on a different track, "You have made a terrible mistake. Jack doesn't have a dime to his name. If there is any scandal, he'll be fired, and I don't intend to support the two of you. Now, let me buy you a ticket back to Poughkeepsie, and you take this hundred dollar bill to cover expenses."

Miss Johnson perked up immediately. She put the hundred dollar bill in her purse and let Daddy take her to the station, where he bought a ticket and put her on the train.

As she was leaving, Miss Johnson said, "What a nice brother you are!", just as cheerful as could be.

Jack was waiting for him in great apprehension, "Jordan, tell me, tell me, what happened?" Daddy told him in full detail. When he had finished, Jack sighed, "My God, if I had known it was that easy, I would have asked her to stay over for one more night before she went back to Poughkeepsie."

Jordan enjoying the sun deck en route to Germany.

The Bibb Brick Company

History

Centuries before the coming of the white man this area was recognized for the quality of its clay deposits. As my father used to say, "The richest soil this side of the Nile." Macon has long been the center of the manufacture of clay products, especially brick, hollow tile, and sewer pipe, as well as ornamental ceramics. At one time the Standard Brick and Tile Company produced more brick per year than any other organization in the country, which is the same as in the world. Only one company, in Chicago, came anywhere near.

The Bibb Brick Company was started in 1902 by W. J. Massee, Joseph N. Neel, and John T. Moore. When Neel and Moore withdrew, the company was reorganized with W. J. Massee as president, O. J. Massee, Jr. as vice president, and W. W. Mosley as superintendent. Jordan Massee sold his younger brother Jack 40 percent of the stock in the new company, to be paid for out of his profits, over a period of years. It was the beginning of an extraordinary partnership that lasted until Jack's death in 1932. In every business venture they complimented each other.

The Bibb Brick Company plant occupied an area of twenty acres, with spur tracks from the Central of Georgia and Southern Railroads running alongside the kilns, making loading of cars easy and expeditious. The company owned clay beds conveniently located about a mile and a half distant to which the company had its own railroad with engines and clay cars for hauling the raw material to the plant. In the clay pit an automatic shovel dug out the clay and loaded it into the cars, operated for many years by Mr. Schoonmaker. At the plant, the company used two large Chambers brick machines, with a capacity for making 200,000 bricks per day, or about 14 car loads a day, over sixty million bricks or more than 4,000 cars annually. In 1926, the employees on the yard numbered about 150 men.

In 1914 the Bibb turned out 60 million bricks, and in a three year period made between $200,000 and $300,000 net for the stockholders, besides salaries of $30,000 for Jordan Massee and $25,000 for Jack Massee.

The Bibb office was on the premises, located at Tenth and Oak Streets. In addition to Jordan and Jack Massee the office force consisted of Pappy Bates as bookkeeper, Emmet Fetner as treasurer, a secretary or two, and M. H. "Duke" Massee, Jr. as favorite salesman. The books were kept in a large, walk-in vault, which fascinated me when I was a child. From time to time the company bought additional land to ensure an adequate supply of clay for any foreseeable future.

In 1926, Jordan Massee, Jack Massee, and J. P. Stetson organized the Bibb Sewer Pipe Company, the largest, most up-to-date, and thoroughly equipped plant of its kind in the South. The company manufactured different kinds of terra cotta products, but made a specialty of sewer pipe while the sewer pipe company was a separate organization, the directors of the Bibb Brick Company were largely interested in it. The two companies used jointly the ample yards of the latter. One hundred and twenty-five men were employed. From this plant, Jordan Massee sold the City of Miami its first sewer pipe. Eventually, the Bibb Sewer Pipe Company was sold and became W. S. Dickey Clay Manufacturing Company.

In the early 1920s, the selling agent for the Bibb Brick Company was the Massee Brick and Tile Company, located at 10th Street and Pine. This organization brought together Marion Massee, Jordan Massee, Jack Massee, and Marion's two sons, M. H. Massee, Jr., and Cleve Massee. Later, the Standard Brick and Tile Company was established as the selling organization for the Bibb Brick Company and the Cherokee Brick and Tile Company. The Cherokee was owned by William Elliot Dunwody, Sr., and Sam Coleman. Their plant was operated by Kenneth Dunwody, the gifted son of W. E., Sr., Sam Coleman, Jr., and M. H. "Duke" Massee, Jr., my father's nephew. Both worked for the Standard. The office was located on Broadway between Cherry and Poplar.

In practice Mr. Dunwody and my father controlled the company, as they had controlled their individual companies, although Kenneth Dunwody and Jack Massee operated the two plants. Sam Coleman, Sr., was more or less a silent partner. His sympathies were invariably with my father but he voted as Mr. Dunwody told him to vote. He had several other business interests and sense enough to know that the brick business was in capable hands. Mr. Sam was a gentleman to the manor born, and there will be more of him in a later chapter.

Mr. Dunwody was a trial to my father and to Mr. Coleman. He had several nervous habits calculated to annoy those around him, ranging from having to have something in his hands to play with, to more serious matters. His desk was not more than fifteen feet from my father's but he would often dictate letters which were then typed and placed on Daddy's desk. He also wrote to various members of Congress with suggestions on how to run the country. He even corresponded with a brick manufacturer in Belgium whom he had never met. The Belgian didn't know that Mr. Dunwody knew no more about how to make brick than a dog knows theology. His son, Kenneth Dunwody, on the other hand, knew all there was to know and kept abreast of the latest mechanical developments. Mr. Dunwody, Sr., had a secretary, one of whose duties was to spy on my father and Mr. Coleman, along with running the Lutheran Church. He once bought a Dictaphone so that he could dictate letters even when his secretary was absent. On one such occasion he dictated a long letter to one of his competitors. When the secretary had typed the letter she was informed by the machine that

Mr. Dunwody had changed his mind and to destroy the letter. After she had destroyed the letter and typed several others, the families never spoke again, "I've changed my mind. Don't destroy that letter. Send it at once!" That was enough to try the patience even of a Lutheran.

Several times I went on business trips with Daddy and Mr. Dunwody, usually to Miami. We traveled in a Pullman compartment. Daddy slept in the lower berth, Mr. Dunwody in the upper berth, and I on the narrow couch on the opposite side.

I was intrigued by Mr. Dunwody's money belt, having never seen one before. He slept in his underwear which I thought most odd. Before retiring to the upper berth, Mr. Dunwody went through a series of calisthenics, despite his age and the limited space. These were repeated next morning. I will say he was quite agile for a man of his age. The sound of snoring in that compartment was deafening. Mr. Dunwody usually wore earplugs.

Daddy and I once took a trip to Cuba with Mr. Dunwody and his wife. We stayed at the Seville-Biltmore. I drank a daiquiri and Miss Bessie and I danced the Charleston, much to the amusement of Old Bill. She was older than my mother but dressed like a flapper. On our return to Macon, I reported all this to my mother. Her silence indicated disapproval. The Dunwodys lived in a large Tudor style house in Rivoli. After their sons married and built their own houses, Old Bill and Miss Bessie lived alone, and she did all the cooking. Mr. Dunwody would buy two ears of corn for dinner whenever a vegetable wagon stopped in front of his office. This was completely alien to my father's nature, as was everything Mr. Dunwody did.

In the fall of 1931, the Bibb Brick Company was re-financed and reorganized with W. J. Massee as chairman of the board and sales director, Henry K. Burns as president, and Jack Massee as vice president and operating general manager. Mr. Burns, who acquired a large stock interest in the corporation, came to Macon twenty-five years earlier. He and his brother, H. M. Burns, were the largest distributor of automobiles in Alabama. When they came to Macon, they continued their business and organized the Georgia Finance Company, out of which grew motor finance companies in Macon, Gainesville, Athens, and Knoxville. In 1930, Henry Burns took over the Schofield interests in J. S. Schofield Sons Company.

Government jobs, under the Roosevelt administration, were a boon to the reorganized Bibb. Labor and production costs were low resulting in mass production. Within a month the company was awarded contracts for the brick and hollow tile for a Cochran public school job, the Jacksonville Post building, the Miami post office, the Cave Springs School for the Deaf, the Fort Valley and West Point post offices, and the Fitzgerald Baptist Church. Mr. Burns' interest in the reorganized Bibb Brick Company marked his interest in the brick and tile business. Eventually, he built the Burns Brick Company, the most modern plant in the entire South, designed by his son, Henry Burns, Jr. According to my father, Henry, Jr. was a mechanical engineer of genius, with an appropriate educational background. After my father got out of the brick business he took great delight in watching the Burns Brick Company battling Dunwody and Coleman at the Cherokee. Daddy always liked Mr. Burns although he had a very low opinion of him. He did not like Henry Burns, Jr. but admired his extraordinary ability. Everyone's favorite member of the family was Derry Burns, the chief salesman for Burns Brick Company.

My father and his brother Jack had a very special relationship with the men who worked in the yard. The work was hard and particularly grueling in the hot summer months, which extended from the beginning of May through September. Jack Massee was a hard taskmaster but the men had great respect for him. If they got in serious trouble with the law they counted on his help to keep them from being evicted from their homes. Sunday mornings, a number of workers would gather at our side door to get Daddy to bail out their friends who had been arrested for drinking and gambling on Saturday night. Daddy always paid the fines in order to have a full crew Monday morning. Once, when I went with him, Daddy said to the jailer, "I want a discount today, there are so many." The jailer preferred cash to a jail sentence and determined the amount of the fine himself. Though unorthodox, justice was swift and effective. Every Christmas two or three dozen workers would gather first in the Jack Massee's backyard on Vineville Avenue then in our yard for a round of whiskey.

When Jack Massee died, the pallbearers were twelve black men who had worked at the Bibb Brick Company. In the mid-thirties, Mr. W. T. Anderson wrote the following piece for the Macon Telegraph:

George Was a Gentleman
By W. T. Anderson

We were leaving New York down 50th Street to reach the sky-way built along the North River water front, and entered at 51st Street. A red light stopped us, at Seventh Avenue. As we waited, a familiar-faced Negro approached, wearing a cap marked "theater." He was smiling and looking into the car inquisitively.

"These look like some of my folks from down in Georgia," he said.

"Where are you from?" I asked. "Macon, Georgia, Sir," he replied.

"Why, we are from Macon, too!" "Is that so," he replied. "Do you know Mr. Jordan Massee?" "Oh, yes," I replied. "We are newspaper people, from the Macon Telegraph and the Macon News."

"Well, I declare. How is Mr. Massee? I used to work for him. I have been up here about six years, and it sho does me good to see people from my old home." "What is your name?" "My name is Jones, sir – George Jones. Please tell Mr. Massee howdy for me, and give him my regards. It sho does me good to see my folks, and I am pleased to have met you."

The light changed, and we moved on, waving him farewell, as he backed away with a cordial "good-bye," and "yaw-yaw-yaw." We felt as George did, that we had been cheered with greetings from an old friend and acquaintance in a strange land.

And it is peculiar what a gratifying sensation one gets upon encountering a person from home. No matter how snooty and reserved we may be toward these same people when we meet on our home streets, we could embrace them as long lost brothers when they are in far-off country. George was a gentleman, and we appreciated his speaking to us.

Other large brickyards in Georgia were run by the Englishes in Atlanta, the Bones in Milledgeville, and the Bickerstaffs in Columbus. Largely due to the high cost of transporting brick, the manufacturers stayed out of each other's territory. They were all very friendly. I was a child when Daddy said to me, "Boots, don't ever get into a fight with the Bickerstaff boys." There were six or seven brothers, all of whom called him "Uncle Jordan." They had only one sister and felt that her husband mistreated her. At a big horse race the brother-in-law rode his own horse and won the race. When he rode triumphantly past the grandstand, all the Bickerstaff brothers shot him simultaneously. There wasn't even a trial. It was a matter of family honor; anyhow, who was to say which brother fired the fatal bullet?

My father enjoyed selling brick and tile more than anything he ever did, especially when his nephew, Duke Massee, accompanied him on business trips. In addition to specific job lettings, they regularly called on their best customers to persuade them to carry a larger stock. On one visit, when they came out of the contractor's office, Duke was laughing fit to be tied, so Daddy asked him, "Duke, what the hell are you laughing at?" When he could speak, Duke replied, "Uncle Jordan, I knew we weren't going to stay there long; that man wouldn't let you get in a word edgewise." Whenever Duke laughed his eyes almost shut and he got red in the face. He was one of the best audiences Daddy ever had, and those trips together were joyous occasions for both – and highly productive. Like my father, Duke worked hard but enjoyed life. Their interests were identical. I cannot speak too highly of Duke and his wife Eulalee and their family into the third generation.

Daddy was also devoted to Sam Coleman, Jr., who in later years was a good friend of my sister Martha and her husband, Bill Devaughn. I think that Sam loved my father more than his own.

After the crash, when almost all building had come to a standstill, Daddy got many a government contract because the Major or General in charge was thankful to get a plug of Humbug Chewing Tobacco. Daddy always carried extra for emergencies.

Despite the more spectacular achievement of building the dam and hydroelectric plant near Jackson, Daddy thought of himself as a brick manufacturer and took great pride in the buildings built of brick from his plant. When we were in Rome in the Summer of 1926, an Italian newspaper hailed him as "King of the Brick," and published our picture standing outside the Coliseum. Near the end of his life, Daddy boasted, "I've shot more birds, caught more fish, played more poker, and sold more brick than any other man in Georgia."

CONVICT LABOR

During an acute labor shortage, my father leased a number of convicts, black and white, from the State of Georgia, to work in his brickyard. He asked Judge Lawton Miller, his lawyer, to draw up the contract, but Miller refused since he didn't approve of convict labor. Daddy built a large brick dormitory, with showers and a swimming pool for the convicts, a radical procedure for Georgia in 1910. When Judge Miller saw the accommodations and sampled the food provided, he apologized to Daddy and said, "Jordan, you deserve a medal for public service."

One of the convicts assigned to the brickyard was Porter Stocks, an attractive young man from a wealthy Atlanta family. He had been sentenced to twenty years hard labor for killing a man alleged to have dishonored his sister. Porter never regretted the act, nor did the Stocks family.

One day young Porter walked into my father's office with a rod and reel and said, "Jordan, I've just figured out that you're paying the State of Georgia seventy-nine cents a day for my services. Well, this morning I fetched a big bottle of drinking water for your office, which ought to be worth about seventy-nine cents, so I'm taking the rest of the day off to fish down in the old clay pit."

Little wonder that Porter Stocks became a pet of my father's and was given special privileges, some of which were strictly illegal, including a key to the compound. He kept street clothes in Daddy's office and every Saturday night would ride into town to one of the public gambling houses, but he was always back in time for early morning inspection. It is also no wonder that he was hated by the state's superintendent, as mean a man as ever walked in shoe leather.

Finally, through his family's influence, Porter was pardoned by the governor of Georgia. Unfortunately, the day before he was to be released he was found dead from a bullet wound. Both the sheriff and the coroner pronounced his death suicide. His father came down for the inquest. Later, in private, Mr. Stocks said to Daddy, "Jordan, you were mighty good to my son and I know how much he admired you. I find it difficult to believe he killed himself, particularly on the very day before he was to be freed, but I'll take your word for it, and only your word. Did my son kill himself, or did someone else kill him?" Daddy assured Mr. Stocks that in his opinion it was suicide. Forty years later, when I pressed him for the truth, he told me, "Never in a thousand years would that boy have shot himself, but if I had told his father what I really thought there would have been another killing, as sure as your name is Boots."

Only one convict ever escaped alive from the compound. He had a sack of gold coins which he kept hidden. One day he and the gold and one of the guards all disappeared and were never seen again.

There was another convict laborer who attracted my father's attention, a black man imprisoned for life. He was a very silent man and had little to do with the other convicts. After work hours, when the others were making merry, singing or playing cards, he sat alone, deep in his own thoughts; but he was the best worker ever employed at the brickyard. After a year or so, Daddy approached him and said, "Jim, I want you to tell me how you came to kill a man." Somewhat reluctantly he related how he was serving a brief sentence in Augusta, and in the same prison was a big bully, in for life, who constantly brutalized all the other inmates. One day, while they were eating, the bully spit in Jim's tin plate. "I took my knife and struck at him. I wasn't aiming to kill him, but I was mad, and it killed him."

Daddy said, "Now, Jim, if you're telling me the truth, I'm going to get you out of here," and he sent his own lawyer to Augusta to look up the court records. The facts of the case were just as Jim had described them. Daddy obtained a new trial and had his lawyer defend the accused. This time Jim was acquitted.

A few days later Daddy was walking around the plant, which he did every morning and every afternoon, when he saw Jim working as usual. He said to him, "Jim, what the Hell are you doing here? You're a free man now." "Yes, sir, I know," he replied, "But I'se gonna work for you the rest of my life. You can pay me whatever you think I'm worth, but whether you pays me or not, I ain't leaving." He was still there thirty years later when my father lost the plant.

The other story concerning convict labor didn't have such a happy ending. The State appointed its own Head Guard, a man who hated the convicts as much as they hated him. That man loathed every living creature except for his two police-trained dogs, two truly ferocious creatures. Every day he groomed those dogs by the hour and saw to it that they got the choicest cuts of meat from the canteen. He treated his dogs just like children.

Now there was one convict who was regarded as extremely dangerous. He was serving a life sentence for armed robbery and murder. One day he stole a shotgun from the Head Guard's locker and escaped. The guard figured he was heading south, through the swamp beyond the clay pit. Before unleashing his bloodhounds, he announced, "I'll catch that son of a bitch! Who'll volunteer to go with me?" When there was no response, he turned to Daddy and said, "Massee, I know you're not yellow." Under the circumstances Daddy felt he couldn't tell him he was scared to death to accompany him; so the two men mounted their horses and took off in pursuit of the escaped convict, with the two greatly excited dogs at the horses' heels. When they entered the swamp, the guard caught sight of the convict in the distance, and shouted to him to drop his gun. Instead, the man fired the shotgun but hit a tree. Although the guard knew the convict still had one shell left, he charged on, the dogs well ahead of him now, Daddy well behind. A second shot killed one of the dogs instantly. The convict threw the gun to the ground and started running, which was difficult since he was up to his knees in swamp water. The guard took aim and shot him dead. Slowly, the body sank into the mire.

He turned and rode back to where Daddy was waiting, accompanied by the remaining dog. When he reached Daddy, he said, "Well, I guess he got away."

Jordan in Pomerania with Baroness Gerda von Blumenthal and her cousin, Baroness Marion von Blumenthal.

W.J. MASSEE AND THE JACKSON DAM

INTRODUCTION:

Someone who was writing a book on the development of electricity in Georgia wrote Calder Payne for information. I told Calder I would send him what I had on Daddy and the dam at Jackson. Whether the book was ever completed I do not know.

In addition to copies of newspaper articles, I sent Calder these notes I made in 1961, during my father's last visit to New York. Except for the use of the third person, and the elimination of a few passages pertaining to "friends" of the family, these notes on the Macon Railway and Light Company are exactly as told to me. Eventually, dates should be verified, although my father's memory was well-nigh infallible. Some of the anecdotal material was not included in the copy prepared for Calder Payne.

JM
(February 1982)

Originally, there were several separate streetcar lines in Macon: one in East Macon, one in South Macon, etc. Mr. Jacob S. Collins of Savannah consolidated the several lines, forming the Macon Railway and Light Company.

On October 7, 1907, Jordan Massee and several associates, including Felton Hatcher of Macon and Judge Allen of Milledgeville, bought the Macon Railway and Light Company from Collins. They purchased 6,000 of the total 9,000 shares of the company for $80 a share: $480,000 for the property. Massee was president with a yearly salary of $25,000. They paid 6 percent cash dividends to stockholders during all the time Massee held controlling interest.

Mr. Jacob S. Collins ("Uncle Jake") came to Savannah as a chicken peddler. He got to be a very rich man. Owned two banks. He had an insane desire to be mayor of Savannah. In those days, Billy Osborne was the czar of Savannah, but he was an honest city boss, unlike the Tammany crowd. Collins wasn't acceptable to Osborne and he knew he couldn't get to be mayor without Osborne's support. But, finally, after many years, he decided to run for the office in spite of Osborne.

Massee went to Savannah to help him. Collins had rented the Opera House and had on a frock coat and a high silk hat. Now Osborne hired about five hundred roughnecks as hecklers and had them planted all over the theatre. When "Uncle Jake" got up to speak, they all crowed like roosters: "Cock-a-doodle-do." Finally, when they quieted down, Collins said, "I resign," and sat down. Mr. Brown, Massee's father-in-law, said Collins would never have sold the Macon Railway and Light Company had he not thought Massee wouldn't be able to make the second payment and he'd get it back, plus the down payment.

Soon the idea of a hydroelectric plant on the Ocmulgee River began to take shape in Massee's mind, so much current was needed to run the streetcars and light all the homes in Macon.

In the latter part of 1908, Massee, then age thirty-five, built the dam on the Ocmulgee River, near Jackson, after borrowing $5,000,000 for the project in the midst of a national financial panic. This was one of the few developments in the South which came through successfully in that period. Never had to go through reorganization or anything, and made a great deal of money for everybody connected with it.

The dam at Jackson is 1,300 feet across, 120 feet thick at the base, and 120 feet high, and has 170,000 yards of concrete in the dam proper. "$5.70 a yard paid the contractor. Couldn't be duplicated now for $40 a yard" (in 1961). Financing the dam was done through A. B. Leach and Company, of New York, by a system of underwriting.

Before deciding to finance the construction of the dam, Mr. Leach sent the best available engineers to Macon to assess the feasibility of the project in terms of water supply, availability of land, and demand for power in central Georgia. He also wrote the president of Macon's largest bank for a character reference, not for a report on Massee's finances, which he determined through his own investigators. Later, Mr. Leach showed Massee the banker's answer, which made no reference to character but stated that the whole project was sheer madness since there wasn't enough water in the Ocmulgee River to warrant building a dam. Fortunately, Leach's engineers thought otherwise.

"When Leach showed me that letter he took it out of a walk-in safe in his office. After I had read it he put it back in the safe, just inside the door, which he left open. He left the room for a few minutes and I reached inside the safe for the letter, and put it in my pocket. It's the only thing I ever stole in my entire life. But just as sure as I know my name is Massee, I'm sure Leach intended me to take it. I kept that letter as a memento of a first rate son-of-a-bitch." His name is best forgotten.

When A. B. Leach first agreed to finance the project, Massee and his associate, Felton Hatcher, were so elated they got drunk and marched, military fashion, late that night, up the middle of Broadway from Battery Park to midtown, where a friendly Irish policeman took them in custody and delivered them to their hotel.

On their return trip to Macon, Massee and Hatcher were so pleased with themselves they searched the train from one end to the other looking for someone to whom they could brag. Finally, in a smoking car, they spotted an elderly man with a long beard who seemed a likely prospect. The old man not only listened patiently to their story, he kept asking for further details. Finally, the man said, "I married a beautiful girl from Macon, Miss Nannaline Holt." Massee thought, "Oh! My God! This must be Mr. James P. Duke, who has built more dams than any other man in the country." Mr. Duke was delighted with the two brash young men and invited them to attend the ceremonies attending the inauguration of his latest dam in North Carolina. Massee loved a good audience, but after that he was more careful in his choices.

When the dam was completed, A. B. Leach and Co. sold bonds and took up the underwriting. Mr. Leach, whose duty it was to sell the bonds, hired Massee himself to sell the bonds. Massee took a party of bankers South in an all-steel private railway car. (There were only two, the Advance and the Federal, which belonged to President Taft.) Leach said, "Take anybody down there that will go, and I'm giving you an expense account of $25,000."

When the prospective investors arrived in Macon, Massee took them on a tour around the town. When they passed the Massee home on College Street, one of them said, "That's an imposing mansion. Who lives there?" Massee replied, without explanation, "That's the largest Negro boarding house in Macon." Another investor wanted only to see "smokestacks."

They played a lot of poker but Leach was a damned sorry card player.

Among the bankers was "Uncle" James I. Buchanan, President of the Pittsburg Trust Co. Leach told Massee, "Sell Buchanan first. Whatever he does, the rest will follow like sheep." When Massee presented his proposition, privately, to Mr. Buchanan, the banker responded, "Massee, I'm most favorably impressed with your project, and with you. How much did you and Mr. Leach expect me to invest?" Well, that was the one thing that Massee, who had never sold a bond in his life, had forgotten to ask Mr. Leach, but without hesitation Massee replied, "$300,000 worth." Buchanan bought the $300,000 bonds, and, as Leach had predicted, eleven other men each invested the same amount! Before revealing how much Buchanan had invested, Massee asked Mr. Leach how much he had expected Buchanan to take. Leach replied, "Around $25,000, maybe $35,000."

Massee recalled that one banker was from Toronto, another from Philadelphia. And two of the prospective investors were from England: Kitkat, manager of the London branch of the Bank of Scotland; and the son of the Earl of Weymouth, whose name was Newsome.

They hated each other like the devil hates holy water, and spoke to each other only when playing poker. Instead of saying, "I raise you," they'd say, "I put you up."

The son of the Earl of Weymouth wore trousers so high-waisted Massee suggested he have them made with armholes, eliminating the need for a vest. One of the English bankers arrived at Massee's house wearing heavy boots with cleats, as though he were on an African safari. When he saw the parquet floor in the front hall, he removed his boots before entering.

The other bonds were sold later on when the dam needed improvements. The $5,000,000 bonds were actually to pay for the dam. Then a like amount of $5,000,000 was issued in common stock, with no immediate value. "As Tom Troy would say, 'The Hope of the Future.'" Massee and his few associates took half of the common stock.

A close friend got 1,000 shares of this stock. He sold it for $15 a share, although Massee begged him not to. Right afterwards, Massee sold part of his stock for $37.50 a share. Within a few years, the stock sold at par for $100 a share.

When Mr. Leach found that a two-thirds majority in the Macon Railway and Light Co. would be insufficient for the purpose of the dam, he commissioned Massee to buy the remaining stock from Mr. Collins. Massee offered to buy the stock as cheaply as possible for Mr. Leach, but he said, "No, you buy the stock as cheaply as you can and I'll pay you $120 a share for it. The difference between what you have to pay and $120 is yours."

Massee recalled, "In one day, between sun-up and sun-down, I made $120,000, with no risk involved. I paid Collins $80 a share for the stock and sold it to Leach for the agreed $120. Your mother spent the $20,000 in one day, in New York, for a fur coat and some other things; but I don't remember what we did with the $100,000."

"Jim Campbell was the 'Co.' in A. B. Leach & Co. He was not only the 'Co.' he was Leach's brother-in-law. They were all right. I never would have fallen out with them had not Leach brought in a man named Philip Gosler. Got him from A. G. White Company, the biggest engineers that ever lived. Gosler was a Philadelphia Dutchman who graduated from the University of Pennsylvania. He stirred up all the trouble. Jim Campbell hated him worse than I did. All fell out. I resigned. Campbell finally said he'd make Leach fire Gosler if I would come back. But I didn't. Gosler was a damned smart man."

"Boots, do you remember my saddle horse, General Lee? I paid $2,500 for that horse and never got on his back. I kept him in the stable behind the house on College Street. Your mother has a picture of Mrs. Hazlehurst on that horse, and she looked damned good, too."

"Dick Rose was hired to exercise the horse, and he kept him in good shape. That's the horse I gave Jim Campbell and he brought him back up to New York. Campbell gave me that large Oriental pearl your mother wore in a brooch. Later I wore it as a stick pin. I know what that pearl cost because I saw the bill for it."

During construction, Massee motored from Macon to the dam site and back, almost every day. He and his car became familiar sights on the highway, where there was little traffic. One morning he was stopped by a motorcycle cop for speeding. In those days you could plead guilty and pay the fine on the spot, thereby avoiding having to appear in court at a later date. "What's the fine?" Massee asked. "Ten dollars, Mr. Massee," the officer replied, somewhat apologetically. "Here's a twenty dollar bill," said Massee, "I'll be back around five o'clock this afternoon. Don't bother me." The incident was reported next day in the Atlanta newspapers. I don't think my mother was amused.

Macon was not big enough then to use half the power from the dam. "I had one helluva time getting a franchise to go into Atlanta. It was Fred Seely who finally got it for me. He then owned the Atlanta Georgian, later the Atlanta Journal. Fred started the Atlanta Georgian. Sold it later and moved to Asheville, North Carolina, where he built Grove Park Inn and developed the Biltmore Industries, which Mrs. Vanderbilt had started."

Later, Massee sold the Macon Railway and Light Co. Wishing to provide for his brother Jack and Mr. Jack Nyhan, he made an agreement with the purchasing company to keep Nyhan and Jack Massee, both of whom had done outstanding work, and to keep the power rate in Macon at the same level for a prescribed number of years. Massee described Mr. Nyhan as a "clever Irishman, a wheel horse who worked night and day." Massee gave Mr. Nyhan full credit for building up the company. Unfortunately, Nyhan sold his stock for $10 a share. A shame. Eventually, when Massee sold the company, he sold his own remaining stock for $120 a share.

No sooner was the ink dry than the new owners fired Mr. Nyhan and Jack Massee and raised the rate of electricity in Macon to 10 cents. When Massee, now an outsider, objected, he was practically told to go to Hell. So, "out of pure spite and unadulterated cussedness" Massee built a modern steam operated plant, located near Central City Park, with which he waged a man-sized war on his old company. His new company gave employment to deserving men who had been fired by the management of the old company. Rates went down from 10 cents a kilowatt to 2 cents a kilowatt. The old company lost a lot of money; Massee's new company lost a little. The public was kept well informed through ads in the local papers.

While building the steam plant, Massee ran into all sorts of difficulties. A flood washed some of it away, etc. Of course Judge Felton and his gang saw to it that he couldn't borrow enough money in Macon, so Massee went to George W. Parrot, in Atlanta. He was a rich old man, built and owned the Piedmont Hotel and a big bank. Massee had once worked for him, at the Parrot Lumber Company, which was worth a million dollars.

Massee: "I need $50,000."

Parrot: "What sort of collateral you got?"

Massee: "None. Just my face."

Mr. Parrott let him have $75,000. He told Massee, "You and I know this $75,000 is the limit, I can't let you have any more; but no one else needs to know that. You can tell everyone that whatever it takes to finish that thing, I'm going to let you have, even if it takes a million dollars." And that was the story Parrot spread around in banking circles in Atlanta, and when Judge Felton came in the next day to find out if Massee had gotten more money, that is what Parrot told him.

Finally, the Yankees came to Massee and said, "Let's get together. We'll buy your steam plant, and on your terms."

Massee said, "O.K., but before we sign you must agree on a fair rate. That brings up the question, 'What is a fair rate?' Ten cents was much too high and 2 cents is too low to keep running. So let's add the two and divide by two, and agree on 6 cents." The management of the old company agreed and Massee sold them the steam plant.

"I punished them all right. Judge Felton came and sobbed on my neck and I finally sold it to them—the Georgia Public Service Company—but on my own terms. I told those people, 'I could close you up eventually, but I'll accept your offer.' And I sold it to them for what it cost: $300,000-$500,000."

"I made a new deal with them. Judge Felton drew up the contract. He was their man, but he also represented me! I said, 'That's perfectly all right. I know what I want and I can read!'" Throughout these years, Massee and Judge Felton remained good friends.

In the new contract, it was stipulated that the power rate would not go higher than 6 cents, but a few months later the big company filed a petition in Atlanta to raise the price to 8 cents. At his own expense Massee took ads in the local newspapers telling the public the whole story and stating that he would have the best lawyers protest the raise. For that purpose, he obtained the service of Judge Lawton Miller ("I'll whip them sure.") and, at the request of Judge Miller, also hired Pope Brock. Massee invited leading businessmen of Macon to join him in the office of the Governor of Georgia, in Atlanta, on a specified date, when the governor had agreed to review the facts. There were many businesses in Macon to which the power rate should have been of vital interest, including the largest cotton mill in the world. Only one Macon man joined Massee and his lawyers in the governor's office on the appointed day: Mr. P. L. Hay!

Massee, in disgust, apologized to the governor for taking up his time, and tore the written contract in two. He gave Mr. Hay one half "as a souvenir."

Some years later, in 1919, Harry Stillwell Edwards wrote:

But it wasn't a glide waltz all the way through. I know of black nights, when this man's back was to the wall and the dream was a nightmare. The vital thing is, not that the financial aid always came at the critical moment, but that the soul of the man was never shaken and that he came through with the same old smile, and that the few gray hairs he developed have dropped out and the brown are back again in their places.

The visible spirit of eternal youth, the incarnation of optimism, he is with us for always. When you go down Cherry Street after dark, look up at the white lights that turn night into day and think of Jordan Massee. They are the stars in his service flag; they are the unwinking stars in his wonderful dream—come true.

Emily Brown Massee

FOUR SUMMERS IN FLAT ROCK
(1903-1906)

In 1903, Mother and Daddy took Emily and Nancy to Hendersonville, North Carolina, for the summer. They stayed at a large resort hotel in town. Among their first contacts was Dr. Justice, in case Emily needed medical attention. When Daddy complained of the food at the hotel, Dr Justice arranged a meeting with Mrs. Siegling, who had a commodious summer house in Flat Rock and took in a limited number of selected paying guests. Due to Mother's and Nancy's strictness, Emily was a perfectly behaved two year old, so Mrs. Siegling agreed to take them, although there were no other small children. Emily and Nancy had their meals in a small room adjoining the dining room. The arrangement was satisfactory to all concerned.

Effie Siegling was a prominent socialite from Charleston who was married to a Confederate general much older than herself. They lived in the Robert William Roper house on the Battery, the grandest of all the ante-bellum mansions in Charleston, and owned The News and Courier, a Charleston newspaper. The Sieglings had one child, Rudolph, who, in 1903, was at prep school. By the third summer, he was at Princeton, where he became captain of the football team. Emily was crazy about Rudolph, and he was very sweet to her. Eventually, Rudolph became the editor of The News and Courier. Emily saw him only once after she was grown. She and Daddy were in a taxi, going from the Biltmore Hotel to Pennsylvania Station, in New York, when Daddy spotted Rudolph on the sidewalk. They got out of the cab to speak to him.

The Siegling establishment in Flat Rock was meticulously run, with the help of numerous black servants. Money never passed directly from Daddy to Mrs. Siegling. Once a week, Daddy placed the rent, in cash, in a vase.

Day to day life at Mrs. Siegling's was peaceful, genteel, and for Daddy, rather dull, although he was there only for long weekends, commuting between Macon and Flat Rock by train. There was no golf in the community and little to do except sit on the porch and rock. Occasionally, the guests went riding in Mrs. Siegling's carriage. Before the fourth summer was over, Daddy had grown tired of the place.

Nearby were the Bonclarken Club House and its surrounding cottages, now owned by the Associate Reform Presbyterians; and numerous large estates, most of which belonged to wealthy families from Charleston or New Orleans. The finest place in Flat Rock, however, belonged to the Nortons from Louisville, Kentucky.

Mrs. Siegling was older than Mother and took a special interest in her and in little Emily. An exciting diversion for Emily was picking mushrooms with Mrs. Siegling, who carefully supervised the selection.

From time to time there were other guests at Mrs. Siegling's. Only a few came regularly, among them Lillias Brown, from Aiken, with whom my mother kept in touch for years. There was a small house on the property which was rented one summer by a Charleston family named Jervey. Another summer, the house was taken by Wright Hunter from Savannah, an uncle of Jim Brown, Emily's future husband.

In their first summer, Daddy had Emily's go-cart brought up by train. The porter who unloaded the cart accidentally let it roll off the platform. Although the cart was destroyed, Daddy did not report the accident for fear the porter might get fired. He simply bought another go-cart.

Years later, during World War II, Emily and Daddy often went to the races in Miami. Sometimes, they spent two nights on the train, with only one day in Miami; other times they stayed over, in a hotel. The fast train out of Chicago hooked up with the Southern, which passed through Macon on its way to Miami. On several trips, Mr. Sam Coleman and young Sam accompanied them.

On one of the Miami trips, when they got to the Macon Terminal Station, an elderly porter recognized Daddy, who was on the board of directors of the Southern Railway, and asked Emily, "Is this the young lady whose go-cart I lost?"

When Emily replied, "It is," he added, "Anyone else would have reported me and I would have lost my job, but not Mr. Massee."

Those of us who grew up in the days when most travel was by rail remember with warmth and gratitude those nameless Pullman car porters whose efficiency and courtesy made traveling a pleasure. They were better paid than most black workers, North or South, but the work was arduous and the hours unbelievably long until the railway porters' union was founded.

In 1903, the Sieglings had a tennis court where the young people gathered, including the beautiful Martina Burke, who was exactly ten years older than Emily. Mother and Daddy knew Mr. and Mrs. T. C. Burke in Macon, where they had moved from Augusta, Georgia. They were among the most prominent Catholic families in Macon. Mr. Burke was a highly successful businessman. Their two daughters, Mary Henrietta ("Mae") Burke (1888-1965) and Martina Liguori Burke (1891-1964) were both born in Macon. Every advantage that money could buy was provided in raising the two girls. Mrs. Burke entertained beautifully; and, subsequently, Mae and Martina provided Macon with the only reminder of what lavish and gracious entertaining had been in earlier decades. The scale was reduced but the quality was not.

The Burkes lived in a large Queen Anne Revival house on Georgia Avenue, directly across the street from the Alonzo Schofields. When Mae was growing up she was quite stout, which is hard to believe for those who knew her later when she had become as slender as Martina.

As a girl, her best friend was Adele Daly, later the wife of Benjamin Cleveland Smith. Adele was small and thin, while Mae was downright fat. On hot summer days, Mrs. Burke made the two girls rest in the afternoon. They would take off their good frocks and lie down on Mae's big four-poster bed. One day Mrs. Burke, on entering the room, didn't see Adele, who was on the far side of the bed. "Where is little Adele?" she asked. Adele loved telling the story years later when she had grown stout and Mae had grown thin.

Mother and Daddy took Mae to New York with them on a shopping trip, and Mother helped her select her first tailored suit. Mae was only sixteen or seventeen at the time, but in a photograph taken in her new suit she looks a matronly forty-five. We used to tease Mae by saying we could blackmail her with that photograph. She attended St. Elizabeth's, a college in New Jersey, where she roomed with Adele Daly.

The summer that Mrs. Burke and Martina spent in Flat Rock at Mrs. Siegling's, Mae was in Europe, having just graduated from St. Elizabeth's. That was the summer that Emily and Mrs. Burke became good friends. They remained close until Mrs. Burke died in 1938. Every year she gave Emily a Christmas present, the first of which was a large rag doll which Emily named Mary for Mrs. Burke. During the summer, Emily would go to Mrs. Burke's room, by invitation of course, to button up her older friend's dress. Ladies' dresses were fastened in the back with countless small buttons requiring small, delicate fingers.

When Emily was seven or eight years old, she was the only child invited to Martina Burke's debut, a very formal party at the Burke residence.

After an unsatisfactory visit to White Sulphur Springs in 1906, Mother and Daddy took Emily and Nancy back to Flat Rock for their last summer at Mrs. Siegling's. The four summers in Flat Rock for Emily and Nancy were not all that different from their time in Macon. They stayed very much to themselves in their small, self-contained world, much as Anna Lockhart and I did thirteen years later. For Mother, they were peaceful summers spent in the unobtrusive company of a most remarkable woman from Charleston, Effie Siegling.

EMILY'S FIRST TRIP TO NEW YORK, 1905

On their numerous visits to New York, Mother and Daddy always stayed at the Holland House, located on Fifth Avenue at Thirty-Third Street. The old Waldorf-Astoria was on the north corner at Thirty-Fourth Street, where the Empire State Building now stands. Daddy was attracted to the Holland House by the quality of the food; Mother, by the quiet dignity of the establishment and the impeccable service. The Men's Dining Room, which excluded women, was presided over by Old Joe, the famous maître d'hôtel. J. P. Morgan was a frequent guest.

In the Ladies' Dining Room, Mother and Daddy always had the same table, discreetely located against a wall, away from the more conspicuous areas. Old Joe would frequently come over to bring Daddy a glass of draft beer. Mother never welcomed the attention because of his loud, booming voice, which could be heard across the room. On one visit, he told Daddy that he had been in a big poker game the night before: "There were two policemen, two firemen, another headwaiter, and one gentleman."

Naturally, Daddy asked, "Why the gentleman?"

Old Joe replied, with irrefutable logic, "Somebody's got to lose."

Whenever Mother and Daddy were in New York, they continued to stay at the Holland House until it was torn down. Most of the staff, including Old Joe and the best of the chefs, moved to the newly constructed Biltmore Hotel, on Forty-Third Street between Madison and Vanderbilt, and Mother and Daddy moved with them, establishing a tradition that was to continue until the forties.

Emily was four years old when Mother and Daddy took her to New York for the first time, along with the ubiquitous Nancy Flewelyn. They traveled by boat from Savannah to New York. While still in the Savannah River, Mother and Nancy both became seasick. Neither ever saw the ocean. They stayed in their staterooms until the boat was safely moored in New York Harbor.

Emily had a fine time, totally unrestrained. Mother and Nancy were too ill to look after her, and Daddy gave her the run of the ship. She had never before had such freedom.

One night a young man fell overboard. He was not reported missing until the next morning. The captain turned the boat around and returned to the area where he was thought to have been lost, but no trace of him was found. He was the son of a prominent Atlanta couple.

The days in New York were a great success. Emily was thrilled by the big city and delighted to find the F. A. O. Schwartz toy shop, quite near the hotel. She and Nancy took most meals in their room, while Mother and Daddy spent days shopping, which was the real purpose of the trip, and evenings at the theatre.

Returning to the hotel one afternoon, Mother happened to look up and, to her horror, saw Emily sitting in the window with her feet dangling out. She was in a state of shock by the time they reached the room. Nancy tried to reassure her, "It's all right, Baby, I had a tight hold on her sash." Emily was even more unconcerned than Nancy.

They returned to Macon by train, which meant crossing the Hudson River by ferry to reach the railway terminal in Newark. There were no bridges between Manhattan and New Jersey, and the tube under the river had not yet been built. The ferry had barely left the dock when Mother and Daddy discovered that Emily and Nancy were not on board. In the rush, they were separated from Mother and

Daddy when the gate closed and were left on the wrong side.

Mother took charge. She ordered the captain to go back and get her little girl and nurse. He insisted he could not turn around in the middle of the Hudson River, and that they could come across on the next ferry, an hour later. That seemed reasonable enough to Daddy but Mother would have none of it. Finally, when they were more than halfway across the river, the captain acceded to the voice of authority and turned the ferry around. By the time they reached the Manhattan dock a large crowd had gathered waiting to cross the river, but the captain allowed no one on board except Emily and Nancy. Mother was twenty-five at the time.

White Sulphur Springs

In late spring of 1906, Daddy, Mother, Emily, and Nancy went to stay at the old Greenbriar Hotel in White Sulphur Springs, West Virginia. Greenbriar was the most stylish resort hotel in America. Everyone in Society went there, or to the somewhat less prestigious Homestead. Daddy planned to travel back and forth between White Sulphur and Macon.

Greenbriar was very exclusive and very dressy. Mother liked all the dressing up and had clothes for every occasion, but Emily and Nancy got tired of all that. When the novelty wore off, life at Greenbriar appealed less and less even to Mother.

Daddy joined a group of elderly men for poker every morning. One day he made some mild suggestion concerning the house rules, which he thought rather silly. One of the old men looked over his glasses at Daddy and said, "You're a little young to be making changes. We've been playing poker here under these same rules since Lee surrendered at Appomattox." At lunch that day, Emily didn't like the meat served, so Daddy asked the waiter to bring her some turkey that had been on the menu the night before. The waiter informed Daddy that turkey was not being served for lunch. Daddy informed Mother that he had enough of Greenbriar. After lunch he told her, "You can do as you please, but I'm leaving."

Mother decided she didn't want to be left at Greenbriar, so she and Nancy quickly packed. They got to the station early, as usual. The ticket seller was busy and Daddy grew increasingly impatient. Finally, Daddy shouted to the man, "I want four tickets to Washington, and you'd better hurry, I can hear the train coming 'round the bend." With total unconcern, the man replied, "Don't get excited, there's no rush. That train is going due west to Cincinnati. The eastbound train for Washington isn't due for another four hours."

Daddy had no intention of spending any more time in White Sulphur Springs, so he bought four tickets to Cincinnati. The travelers spent the night in Cincinnati and returned to Macon through the Bluegrass country, with numerous stops to see racehorses.

Grandpa Brown expressed surprise at their early return, although he should not have been surprised at anything his son-in-law did. The family spent the rest of the summer in Flat Rock; but the next year, Nancy said to my mother, "Baby, couldn't we just stay home and rock and fan?" It was not to be.

Hendersonville, 1907

In the summer of 1907, Mother and Daddy and Emily went to Hendersonville, North Carolina, to look for a house. Daddy located a very large house with four bedrooms downstairs and four bedrooms upstairs, and a vegetable garden in the backyard, the first summer home he ever rented. The rest of the household arrived by train: Nancy; her sister Nicy; the automobile with Isam Fann, the chauffeur; the carriage, with coachman and two matching horses, David and Rucker; the buggy, with Mack the butler as coach; Emily's cart and pony; another servant; and much luggage. Daddy and Emily met the train; Mother did not.

They all set off for the new house, driving up the main street, with the pony cart bringing up the rear. It fell to Daddy's lot to drive Emily and himself in the cart. After four summers in nearby Flat Rock, Daddy was known to everybody in Hendersonville, and half the town was out to see the parade. Mr. Justice, the local druggist and brother of Emily's doctor, called out, "Jordan, why don't you get out and let the pony ride?" Daddy was amused, but Emily felt the remark was disrespectful to her father and never liked poor Mr. Justice thereafter.

Before they reached the house, Daddy bought a couple of guinea hens from a street vendor. The next morning, they had eggs for breakfast and Daddy remarked, "The quickest dividends I ever collected."

After they had unloaded, Daddy told Nicy to look after Major, the pony. She replied, "I've already hitched him out in Hendersonville."

The regular cook was unable to leave Macon, so Nancy, who was an excellent cook, was relegated to the kitchen and Nicy, who was a poor cook, took her place as Emily's nurse. As it turned out, she was no better as a nurse than as a cook, but they got through the summer under the new dispensation.

Nancy and Nicy Flewelyn were born into slavery. Their father was body slave for a Mr. Flewelyn, who owned the Lanier Hotel. Mr. Flewelyn treated the girls with unusual kindness, and in later years they had only pleasant memories of their former master. Both girls remembered Wilson's troops occupying the city. When their father caught them on Mulberry Street watching the Yankee soldiers, he snatched them up and told them to go hide. After the war, they took the name Flewelyn, a common practice following the emancipation.

Nancy nursed Mother from the time of her birth in 1879, and twenty-two years later nursed Emily. She always referred to my mother as Baby and to my sister as Emily, continuing, at times, to treat Mother like a child. My grandmother died in 1889, when Mother was nine years old, leaving her youngest child in the care of Grandpa Brown, Mattiebrian (Mother's older sister), and Nancy Flewelyn. Consequently, Nancy occupied a very special place in the family. She went on looking after Emily until retirement in 1913, living with the family wherever they moved. The brick house in the backyard of our home on College Street was built for Nancy. It still stands.

Nancy was tall and held herself erect. She was always neatly dressed, very much a lady in manner, and sharp as a steel trap. She took complete charge of Emily, as she had my mother. She never thought Baby knew how to take care of Emily without her help. Every Sunday she took the child with her to Steward Chapel, the Negro Methodist Church, on Forsyth Street. Across the street was a drugstore that dispensed laudanum, which Nancy took regularly, as did countless other people, Black and White, for whatever ailed them. It was cheap and readily available. There was a very prominent white doctor in Macon who kept his wealthy patients happy on opium derivatives, year in and year out, although this was not spoken of openly. They were good patients and could afford both the doctor and the drugs. While Nancy bought her medicine, Emily ate ice cream at one of the little round tables so typical of drugstores throughout the land until modern times.

After her retirement, Nancy went to live with Nicy. Daddy gave her a pension, which was delivered every Saturday morning by Mother's chauffeur when he drove to the homes of the two women who did our household laundry. If for any reason the money was late arriving, Nancy walked to the big house to get her envelope. I still remember those occasional visits when I was a child. Martha and I stood in awe of her, and all the servants treated her with ceremonious respect. She worked for my grandmother and subsequently for my mother for more than thirty-five years, then lived in retirement for another thirty years. When she died in the early nineteen-forties, Nicy forgot to notify Mother or Emily until after the funeral.

Nicy and Nancy were as different as sisters can be. Nicy was short and fat, and as plain as Nancy was elegant, totally lacking her sister's dignity and refinement. She was married to Emmanuel Hunt who lived on North Avenue (now Pursley Street), in the Pleasant Hill district, where he raised hunting dogs. Their only son, Albert, drove a truck for Wood Peavey's furniture store. Nicy worked for Mother and Daddy only the one summer in Hendersonville.

One day, in Macon, Nicy slipped and fell getting off a streetcar.

Although not hurt, she took to her bed. When the insurance adjustor for the Macon Railway and Light Company, which Daddy owned, offered her ten dollars, she jumped out of bed exclaiming, "That's the best salve I ever had!" Every Christmas, for years, Mother took Nancy yards of gray outing and a large sack of grapefruit. The outing, available only from Dannenberg's basement, was for nightgowns; and grapefruit, which Nancy loved, was still a rare and exotic fruit.

The summer in Hendersonville was quite pleasant, with numerous guests, mostly mothers with children. Among them were Nettie Watkins Jones with her two sons, Hammond and Augustus (Mother's godson); Jonnie Holmes Sparks with Hazel; Auntie (Mattiebrian Brown Benton) with Rokie; and Daisey Bannon with Josephine. Other guests included Lawson Brown (Mother's only brother) and his wife Mamie Wylie Brown.

Jonnie came without her husband, Bobby Sparks, and worried about him constantly. Finally, Bobby telegraphed, "Fine as frog's hair." Emily and Hazel didn't know frogs had hair.

One warm afternoon, Hazel, Josephine, Rokie, and Emily went wading in a nearby creek, without Mother's knowledge or consent. A water battle ensued and the children got thoroughly soaked. Nancy was utterly disgusted that Nicy couldn't control the children. With Nicy, Emily had many privileges that Nancy would never have permitted.

Once, Augustus Jones bit Emily's cheek. Nettie sent him upstairs and told him he couldn't come down until he apologized. Finally, when he could stand the isolation no longer, he told his mother, "I'll apologize to G-Mother but I won't apologize to Emily"; and he was allowed to come downstairs in time for dinner. That day, Mother had canned peaches, his favorite dessert. When Augustus was served, he remarked, "It's a good thing I said it!" He died of tuberculosis in his early twenties, but his picture remained in Mother's bedroom, on the chest of drawers, alongside pictures of Daddy and her own children.

Auntie took Emily and Rokie to ride in the pony cart one fine day. When she touched the pony with the whip, to which he was unaccustomed, he lunged forward and threw the two children out the back of the cart. Auntie kept on riding, unaware that she was alone, until she heard them calling.

For Emily, the highlight of the summer was a motor trip to Mt. Hebron. There was a one-way, toll road to the peak, with traffic going up in the morning and coming down in the afternoon. When Mother, Daddy, and Emily arrived at the tollgate, no attendant was in sight, so Daddy instructed his chauffeur to get out and open the gate. As they drove through, a woman appeared from nowhere shouting, "I charges, I charges!"

Daddy, trying to reassure her, replied, "Keep your shirt on, we'll be back this afternoon."

The woman was joined by her grandson, a handsome lad of ten or twelve, who proceeded to explain that the road was narrow and cars could not pass, going up or coming down. Daddy was so struck by the boy's good looks and polite manner he offered to adopt him. "You come live with us in Macon, Georgia, and when you're old enough, I'll send you to college."

The boy showed no surprise and replied simply, "I'll have to think it over, but I'll let you know this afternoon when you come back."

When they returned around five o'clock, twin boys were waiting, each wearing his best clothes, each holding a knapsack. The first boy spoke, "This is my brother and I cannot leave him; but if you'll take us both, we'd be pleased to go."

Daddy responded, very seriously, "You're right, son. You shouldn't leave your brother, but I'm afraid I couldn't handle two boys."

In later years, when I heard the story, I wondered whether Daddy was serious or not; but Mother's reaction was never in doubt.

And so the long summer days in Hendersonville passed imperceptibly until September, when the caravan headed south.

Madame Nordica and Mr. Massee's Secret

In 1908, Mother and Daddy along with Emily and Nancy, were in New York at the time of the big parade celebrating the election of William Howard Taft as the twenty-seventh president of the United States. The parade lasted from mid-morning until after dark, passing the Holland House, where Mother and Daddy were staying.

At that time, Lillian Nordica, the great soprano, lived at the Holland House whenever she was in New York. She had recently married George Washington Young, a millionaire financier and speculator, with whom Daddy had financial dealings in connection with the construction of the hydroelectric plant near Jackson, Georgia. At the age of fifty, Mme. Nordica was beginning to wind down her glorious career, although some of her greatest triumphs here and abroad were still ahead. She was a woman of extraordinary beauty, always magnificently gowned. "She had become something more than a great singer: she was a national institution," wrote Ira Glackens, her biographer. She was a great lady as well as a great artist, and was always most gracious to my mother.

Like Daddy, Mme. Nordica loved good food. Her table in the Ladies Dining Room was located by a large window overlooking Fifth Avenue. Mother's table was discreetly located against the wall. One day, when Nordica arrived, Mother and Daddy were already in the midst of lunch. As she passed their table, she spied something unfamiliar and appetizing on Daddy's plate. After the appropriate greeting she inquired, "Mr. Massee, what is that you're eating?'

"It's a secret, Mme. Nordica," he replied, not wanting to tell her it was tripe.

"No, I'm serious," she continued. "I would like to order the same for myself, but I don't know what to ask for."

Mother was getting more and more nervous at the turn in the conversation, which Daddy was thoroughly enjoying. "Tell your waiter you want the Massee special," which she did, to her great satisfaction. Daddy thought that she never knew what it was she was eating, but I think it more likely she didn't care, so long as she liked it.

Enrico Caruso was an occasional guest of Mme. Nordica. Emily still remembers how he wound the spaghetti around his fork, then threw back his head and unwound the spaghetti into his cavernous mouth.

When the Taft parade got under way, Mme. Nordica invited Emily to sit with her for a good view of Fifth Avenue. Emily never heard Nordica sing but always remembered her great beauty and kindness.

Nordica died in Batavia, Java, on May 10, 1914, the most acclaimed singer ever born in America.

Emily Massee and Beth Cornell

on the Norfolk Line, 1913

In 1913, Daddy took Emily and her best friend, Beth Cornell, with him to New York on a business trip. Martha was less than a year old, so Mother stayed home all summer. Emily was thrilled because it was her first long trip without Nancy; and it was Beth's first trip to New York.

They stayed at the Holland House and had a wonderful time sightseeing and shopping. The first morning, they took a walk on Fifth Avenue and Beth got a cinder in one eye, looking up at the tall buildings. They went to the emergency room in Altman's, where the nurse in attendance removed it. Until I was born, the following year, both Emily and Beth called Daddy "Jordan."

When the time came to leave, Daddy gave the girls a choice, to stay a couple of days longer and go to the Coney Island amusement park, or travel as far as Norfolk, Virginia, by boat. They chose the boat.

Once on the boat, Daddy discovered there was a general on board, so he told Emily and Beth, "When we get to Fortress Monroe, there'll be a gun salute if they know I'm on board." So, when the boat approached the fort the girls were hanging over the rail in anticipation. As the twenty-one gun salute started, Emily and Beth went running for Daddy, screaming, "Jordan! Jordan! They saw you! They saw you!"

From Norfolk, they returned to Macon by train.

Years later, whenever Daddy told the story, Martha would get indignant: "How could they have been so dumb? They were twelve years old!" To Beth and Emily it was perfectly natural: if Jordan said it was true, it was true.

SUMMERS IN MACON,
1908-1914

The years from 1908 through 1914 were among the most eventful in the lives of my mother and father, but the summers were spent at home in Macon, rocking and fanning, trying to keep cool, just as Nancy had hoped. In 1910, the family moved from the Comer house on Orange Street to the McCaw house on College Street. They went to Atlantic Beach, near Jacksonville, Florida, for the last two weeks in May and the first week in June.

Martha Lawson Massee was born at home, September 24, 1912. Both the summer before her birth and the summer before her first birthday were spent in Macon. Mother, with the connivance of her beloved Dr. McHatton, managed to get Daddy out of town for the event. They persuaded him to take the Ideal Tour on the newly opened highway through the Catskill Mountains, with the assurance that he would be back in time for the birth of the new baby. Two years later, when I was due, Daddy realized that his presence was not required, and willingly took off for New York.

I, too, was born at home, October 9, 1914, the last of the three children. As a baby, I was desperately ill, the result of a milk formula that had agreed with Martha. In January, during the worst days of my illness, Mrs. John Comer's newborn baby, Hugh, was also very ill, which kept Dr. Jimeson, Macon's first pediatrician, busy commuting between the homes of his two best customers. Forty years later, Mother wrote to me of "those terrible days - I have never been the same."

Grandpa Brown died November 24, 1914, at the age of seventy-eight.

The summer of 1915, when I was not yet one year old, we all went to Asheville, North Carolina, for the first of four summers at Grove Park Inn.

HOT SPRINGS

In 1915, Daddy, Emily, and Brother Ray took off for Hot Springs, Arkansas. Emily was thirteen. Mother stayed home with Martha and me; I was just a baby. Daddy had planned to take Walter Odom, his personal valet, to look after him—he was totally incapable of looking after himself—but decided to take Brother Ray, the butler, instead, hoping that the hot baths would help Brother Ray's rheumatism. When they reached Memphis, the Mississippi River was ten miles wide, as a result of a recent flood. They changed trains there, which allowed ample time for breakfast at the station restaurant.

On the far side of the river, the tracks remained under water for several miles.

Going into Little Rock, they followed close behind a tornado. The travelers saw the path cut through the city. Emily was very impressed.

Hot Springs was all on one street, in a long valley. Looking out the windows of second or third floor bedrooms, guests could see only the side of an Ozark mountain. The town had professional gambling and horse racing, facts Daddy must have known before he agreed on the cure. Since Emily had nothing else to do, it was decided she, too, should take the baths. The travelers thoroughly enjoyed themselves until Daddy got lonesome for Mother. Whereupon, she agreed to join them.

Meanwhile, Emily in her spare time, took her first golf lessons. The golf pro's name was Willie Hore, and he was not much larger than Emily. The three were playing golf when Daddy had his second fainting spell. As he passed out, he called, "Catch me!" and fell into the shallow part of a water hazard. The two little people had considerable difficulty pulling two hundred sixty-seven pounds out of the water.

Pappy Bates had to go along to chaperon Mother when she went west to join Emily and Daddy. She had never been on a train alone except to meet Daddy in New York. On those occasions, Grandpa Brown put her on the train in Macon, where she locked herself in the drawing room and kept the door locked until she arrived in New York, except for the delivery of food served in her room. The compartment included an adjoining sitting room and two private baths. At each major stop, the station master telegraphed Macon that Mrs. Massee had arrived safely. The Macon car was transferred in Washington to a northbound train. When the train arrived in New York, Daddy met Mother at her door.

Going west, Mother and Pappy Bates disembarked in Memphis for breakfast, which was a great success. Pappy had his favorite breakfast food: fresh lettuce. When they had finished eating, Pappy asked to speak to the manager. He complimented him on the food and the service, adding, "I shall continue to patronize your restaurant." At the time he had never been farther from home than Atlanta in all his sixty-four years.

The augmented band of Maconites might have stayed longer in Hot Springs had not their sumptuous quarters been reserved months in advance by "a world famous guest." Emily recalls seeing the distinguished gentleman when he arrived in a wheelchair but cannot remember his identity—the only thing in her ninety-one years she doesn't remember. She thinks it might have been Andrew Carnegie. No doubt the hotel manager was surprised that Daddy had stayed so long. Due to their polite eviction, Daddy and his retinue arrived at the station even earlier than was his usual wont. Once there, he couldn't find the tickets. As he grew increasingly agitated, he said, "I'm supposed to be the sick one, now I've got to look after Ethel, Emily, Pappy Bates, and Jim Ray." Finally, he accused Mother of having left the tickets at the hotel, and a messenger was sent running back to the hotel. Eventually, he returned, saying the tickets were not at the hotel but the manager would be most happy to send someone to the city dump, since the trash had already been collected. Mother begged Daddy to let her look in his small suitcase, but he refused, "How could the tickets have gotten there when all the baggage was locked?" Only then did Daddy reluctantly agree to let Mother take a look. The tickets were right on top, where he had placed them after she packed. I might add that any object my mother ever packed was wrapped in tissue paper. Daddy was immediately restored to his usual jovial state, as though nothing had happened. Throughout this fracas, Mother remained calm and collected. Her proverbial serenity was both a blessing and a salvation. By then the train had arrived.

They reached Memphis and had breakfast, again in the railway station. This time there was no lettuce, so, after breakfast, Pappy Bates asked to see the manager, and told him, "I am not pleased with your restaurant, and in future I shall take my business elsewhere." Unfortunately, he never again got farther from Macon than Marshallville.

They all arrived, back in Macon several weeks after the initial departure and, despite the thrills, they were all glad to get home.

In 1917, Daddy returned to Hot Springs, taking with him Dr. Selden, a prominent eye, ear, nose, and throat specialist in Macon. Johnny was one of Daddy's closest friends. On Easter Sunday, Johnny, a staunch Episcopalian, announced that he was going to church and was very surprised when Daddy said he was going with him. He didn't know that Daddy was afraid of dying while Johnny was away. For years, whenever Daddy was asked why he didn't go to church, he would reply, "I went to church on Easter Sunday, 1917, in Hot Springs."

THE McCAW-MASSEE HOUSE

(Revised October 1997 in accordance with information obtained from Hazlehurst Smith Beezer.)

ROBERT HAZLEHURST PLANT
(1847-1904)

At the turn of the century Robert Hazlehurst Plant was undoubtedly the most successful man in Macon. The Plants had been prominent socially as well as in business since Robert's parents, Increase Cook Plant and Elizabeth Mary Hazlehurst, moved to Macon in 1837. Mr. and Mrs. R. H. Plant lived in a large wooden house on College Street, next door to the house of Thomas C. Dempsey. The Plant house was built in the 1850s by John Bennett Ross. Later it changed hands, and in 1891 Robert Plant bought it for his wife. Mrs. Plant was a daughter of John Bennett Ross and had lived in the house as a child. After Mr. Plant's death in 1904 the place was rented for two years, then sold to John T. Moore whose family lived there until it was destroyed by fire in November 1924. Four houses now stand facing College Street on the old homestead site, and an apartment house has recently been built on the rear of the property. Mr. and Mrs. Robert Plant had ten children, the oldest of whom was born in 1872, the youngest in 1896. It is said that the ten Plant children were allowed no social interaction with the twelve Dempsey children. The Dempseys were Catholic.

My mother could figure out the age of many people by remembering which Plant child they went to school with. She and Hazlehurst Plant were both born in 1879.

Robert Plant, like his father, was president of both the First National Bank and a small private bank. He started the Idle Hour Stock Farm in the 1890s, on property that is now the site of the Idle Hour Golf and Country Club. Here he located the second fastest one-mile track for harness horses in the country. Memphis had the fastest at the time, and Macon was next. He owned and trained some of the country's finest harness horses, and brought top-notch trotters and pacers here to run against his own horses. His horses raced with considerable success throughout the country.

Mr. Plant frequently rode out to his farm in a sulky to watch the horses run, from a large glass-enclosed cupola atop the trainer's quarters, returning to town in time for business. Young Tom Halliburton owned a small store at Vineville Branch. Every morning he stood in front of his store and tipped his hat when Mr. Plant passed. Eventually, Mr. Plant asked who the young man was, and when told gave instructions that all produce for the Idle Hour Farm was henceforth to be purchased from young Halliburton. That one order was the basis of Tom's success in business.

Robert Plant's sister Elizabeth married Mr. A. D. Schofield, head of the Schofield Iron Works. For some reason Mrs. Schofield fell out with her brother after the death of their father and never again spoke to him or any member of his family. Wallace McCaw, one of the most successful young businessmen in Macon, married two of Robert Plant's daughters. In 1893 he married Mary Ross Plant, who subsequently died. In 1897 he married Hazlehurst, her beautiful younger sister. Wallace and Hazlehurst built the house at 563 College Street, next door to her parents. They lived there until 1910, when they sold the house to my father and moved to Cincinnati.

During the 1904 crash, both of Mr. Plant's banks failed. They might have survived had he not been mortally ill. He hastened the end in order to prevent his investors from suffering. Though not required by law, Mr. Plant carried enough insurance to cover any losses resulting from his death. His life insurance totaled more than a million dollars, on which he was paying an annual premium of about $43,000. The New York Times obituary is worth reprinting in its entirety:

BANK PRESIDENT GAVE
HIS LIFE FOR CREDITORS

R. H. Plant's Suicide Makes $1,000,000 Life Insurance Available

CAPITALIST SHOT HIMSELF

I. C. Plant's Sons' Bank and the First National of Georgia Closed—
Dead Man's Famous Horses

Special to the New York Times

MACON, Ga., May 21.—A tragic sequel to the crash early in the week of the private bank of I. C. Plant's Sons and the First National Bank came this afternoon, when Robert H. Plant, the head of both institutions, committed suicide, thereby making available over $1,000,000 life insurance for payment on liabilities of about $800,000 of the two banking institutions.

That Mr. Plant deliberately sacrificed his life that the creditors should not suffer is believed by his most intimate friends and by the banking men who knew him here.

In the past twenty-five years Mr. Plant had accumulated life insurance, amounting to $1,015,888, on which he was paying an annual premium of about $43,000. As a result of his death the indications are that the creditors of the two banks will not lose a single penny. Many of the creditors are working people, whose deposits represented years of self-denial and saving. At least $800,000 of

Mr. Plant's life insurance is now made payable to his estate, and this amount, it is estimated, will fully cover his liabilities.

Mr. Plant had been ill for two months. When the banks collapsed ugly charges were circulated and much indignation was expressed because he failed to make any statements as to the cause of the trouble. During his illness, especially since the failure of his institution, Mr. Plant had been closely watched at his home in College Street here by his family and nurses for fear he would commit some rash act.

To-day he told his nurse that he wished to lie down, and the nurse left him to rest. Fifteen minutes later a pistol shot was heard on the porch. There the nurse found the capitalist, with a 38-calibre pistol in his hand, dead.

The bullet had passed through the right temple and out of the left, flattening itself upon the wall. Death probably was instantaneous. The Coroner was at once summoned, and upon the testimony of the nurse and of a physician a verdict of suicide was rendered. Mr. Plant leaves a wife and nine children.

Wallace A. McCaw, President of the McCaw Manufacturing Company and M. Felton Hatcher, a prominent attorney, are sons-in-law of the dead man.

The Plant banking institutions are the oldest in the city. After they closed last Monday the receiver of the private institution reported a deficit of over $344,000. The National bank examiner has as yet made no report as to the First National's affairs.

Mr. Plant, in addition to being identified with various manufacturing enterprises, was formerly largely engaged with the New York Life Insurance Company. He was known throughout the trotting world, and his horses for years have raced on the grand circuit. He owned Grattan Boy, Dulce Cor, Miss Willamont, and other well-known horses.

George H. Plant, Vive President of the First National Bank, is a brother.

A long article in the New York Herald Tribune is even more detailed with regard to Mr. Plant's insurance:

The following is the life insurance with which he expected to pay his debts and leave his family comfortable for the remainder of their lives:

New York Life.....................	$500,000
Equitable Life.....................	$115,000
Mutual Life.........................	$100,000
Penn Mutual.......................	$ 80,000
Union Central.....................	$ 50,000
Massachusetts Mutual..........	$ 50,000

Home Life...........................	$ 50,000
Washington Life...................	$ 30,000
Manhattan Life....................	$ 20,000
Mutual Benefit.....................	$ 20,000
Northwestern Mutual...........	$ 428
	$1,015,428

This insurance had been taken out during the last twenty-five years; $800,000 of it was payable to his estate, but nearly $50,000 of this was hypothecated, leaving $750,000 for his creditors.

In 1906, the Idle Hour Farm was sold at public auction to my father and John T. Moore. A corner of the property was subsequently sold to Mr. Dan Horgan for greenhouses forming the Idle Hour Nurseries. Some years later Mr. Horgan built a beautiful home there, designed by the distinguished architect Neel Reid.

On the day of Mr. Plant's funeral, Mrs. Schofield gave a lawn party, with Japanese lanterns strung across her front yard. She wanted it known to one and all that her brother's death did not concern her. Those who knew the truth of the incident chose not to remember, but years later young Andrew Lyndon coaxed the truth out of Mae Burke, who lived across the street and knew the Schofields well. Mae admitted, somewhat apologetically, "Yes, they did have a party that day, but it was only a party for young people."

After the Plant house was sold to John Moore, Mrs. Plant and seven of her children moved in with the McCaws, in a house with only four bedrooms. The Wallace McCaws had five children, but the last child was born in 1911, after they had moved to Cincinnati. The Plant children were housed on the third floor, which could not have been very comfortable although there were seven rooms, including a large ballroom. The Plants stayed for two years with the Wallace McCaws, until Mrs. Plant built a house down the street, a house later occupied by Mrs. Jack Lamar.

Margaret Plant, another daughter of Robert Plant, married Felton Hatcher, Daddy's associate in building the dam and hydroelectric plant on the Ocmulgee River near Jackson, Georgia. As children both Hazlehurst and Margaret were classmates of my mother at Mrs. Blue's private school, although Margaret was two years younger.

The Lawsuit in Tennessee

Shortly after purchasing the Idle Hour Stock Farm, Daddy fired a man who had worked for Mr. Plant. On several occasions the man threatened my father's life. The situation was so serious that Daddy hired a personal bodyguard, Jim Anderson, who was a brother of Mr. W. D. Anderson. Finally, the man followed Daddy to Tennessee – I think Tennessee was his native state – where he provoked Daddy into slapping him, in front of witnesses. Daddy was arrested but released on bond. On the advice of his lawyers Daddy refused to return to Tennessee for trial, and the governor issued a warrant for his arrest. The governor of Georgia refused extradition as did the governor of New York. In all other states Daddy was a wanted man. Under these circumstances he could continue his business trips to New York City but could not get off the train in any intervening states. To get from Macon to New York one had to change trains in Washington, D.C., but fortunately a passenger remained in his railway car which was transferred to another engine and track. The man suing Daddy had the case postponed time and again, until finally the case came to trial and Daddy was completely exonerated, but not until it had cost him a great deal in lawyers' fees. The Macon papers treated the whole affair to more attention than it deserved, turning it into the media event of the year. When news reached Macon of Daddy's vindication a brass band came and played in front of his house.

The only good thing to come out of the unfortunate episode was the association with Jim Anderson who went into the wholesale gasoline business and supplied us with gasoline and oil for many years. Daddy had a huge tank under the garage from which fuel could be pumped into the automobiles. Motor oil was stored in a smaller tank above ground. I was intrigued with the man who had been my father's bodyguard, a sort of gun for hire. Whenever I tried to get him to talk about the old times he would smile and say, "Ask your Daddy."

THE IDLE HOUR STOCK FARM PURCHASE

My father and John T. Moore, who was then his partner in the Bibb Brick Company, bought the Idle Hour Stock Farm from the Plant estate in 1906. The property was sold at public auction. Daddy and Grandpa Brown told my mother they were going to take part in the bidding just to help the Plant family, but I doubt that she believed them. It is more likely that she hoped her father would restrain her husband if bidding went too high. In any case, Daddy and Mr. Moore made the highest bid, and for the next five years took their trotters on the Grand Circuit, which included the top racetracks in the country. In an interview with Gertrude Smith Trawick for the Macon News in 1960, Daddy recalled:

Robert Plant had much finer horses than we did. I rather neglected the stock farm because at that time I was playing for table stakes in New York and I considered the Idle Hour a ten-cent limit game.

However, I did have two horses that raced on the Grand Circuit, and they were Gay Bingen and Emily B., the latter named for my daughter, Mrs. James F. Brown, Jr.

The Grand Circuit races started at Cleveland, included all the big tracks and wound up at Boston. One year Gay Bingen won a $12,000 purse in Boston, and right after the race someone offered me $30,000 for the horse. I didn't even bother to answer, because a horse that could win $12,000 in one race was worth lots more than that.

However, that same night Gay Bingen stepped through a loose board and broke a leg so she never raced again.

He sold the horse with the broken leg at auction, in the old Madison Square Garden, to the Russian government for breeding. Two of Gay Bingen's colts won the Russian Grand Prix. Prior to the accident, Gay Bingen had lowered the world record for horses in its category.

Daddy and John Moore had Axworthy trotting horses in their stables, and the stock farm staff included several trainers and a teenage blacksmith, W. C. Scott, who became better known as head of the trust department of the Citizens and Southern National Bank. I have a photograph taken in 1907 at the Idle Hour Stock Farm of Daddy and Emily seated in his seven-passenger, six cylinder Ford, the third car in Macon. With them are Stamper, the chauffeur, Edward Harrington, a New York promoter, and Mrs. Harrington. Some years later, at Grove Park Inn in Asheville, Henry Ford wanted to purchase the picture to use in his national advertising, but my mother was horrified at the idea of her daughter appearing in an ad. Mr. Ford said the car was the only model missing in the Dearborn Museum collection.

Years later Daddy lost his love of trotters and developed a passion for racehorses. He missed only three Kentucky Derbys in thirty-five years. Emily shared his enthusiasm and often accompanied him to Louisville, Belmont in New York, and Hialeah in Miami. In his later years he had as much fun placing two-dollar bets as he once had betting thousands. At a race in Miami not long after the depression, he ran into a Macon man who had made a fortune out of the failure of the Fourth National Bank, buying up deposits for two cents on the dollar, selling them when the deposits were redeemed for almost ninety cents on the dollar. The man said, "Jordan, I'm glad to see you're still able to place a bet."

Several times Daddy and Emily went to the races in Miami with the Sam Colemans. Mr. Sam would slip Daddy a ten-dollar bill to make a bet for him without his wife Edith knowing. When the horse won, Daddy had more fun watching Mr. Coleman's excitement than winning himself.

After the old Log Cabin Club burned, the Idle Hour Farm was bought for $30,000, in 1911, by a group forming the Idle Hour Country Club. To meet the purchase price, a cash payment of $10,000 was made and the remaining $20,000 was covered by first mortgage bonds. The property included 168 acres of land. Since Daddy was the president of the Macon Railway and Light Company, owner of the trolley line, it was stipulated in the agreement that the line, which terminated in Ingleside where the Alexander IV school now stands, would be extended to the new County Club. The extension terminated at the crossroads below the present swimming pool, the location then of the farm's big barn which was used for storage purposes. The present location of the club house was then the site of the stables and exercise ring for the horses. The two frame houses on the property were subsequently occupied by the club manager and the golf professional. One of the houses was for a time the home of the Dave Massees. Eden Taylor, Jr. and Jack Massee were the first and second presidents of the Idle Hour Country Club

In 1905, the Macon Railway and Light Company financed the building of a new theatre in the rapidly expanding amusement center at Crumps Park, along with other improvements, and the creation of a dance pavilion. In the summer there were plays every night, concerts in the afternoon, and other attractions, such as a shooting gallery, an electrical theatre, and a moving picture show. The park continued to be popular through the prewar years.

Mother and Daddy organized theatre parties and carried their friends in a private streetcar to Crumps Park for an evening of entertainment. Years later, when Mother, Daddy, and Emily were on a visit to New York, I took them to see the muchly acclaimed musical comedy "Lady in the Dark," starring the legendary Gertrude Lawrence. After the performance, Daddy sighed, "We used to put on a better show at Crumps Park for a quarter."

WALLACE EUGENE McCAW
(2 July 1871 - 4 October 1933)

Legend has it that Wallace McCaw went to Massachusetts Institute of Technology in short pants and graduated at nineteen, but a letter written to his mother the night before graduation is clearly dated June 1892, when he was almost twenty-two. At the time of his marriage to Hazlehurst Plant in 1897 he was one of Macon's most successful young businessmen. They built the mansion at 563 College Street—now 619—next to her parents on one side and Mr. T. D. Tinsley on the other. A one-story wooden house previously occupied the lot. Mary Callaway Jones, an early historian of Macon architecture, thought that the wooden structure was moved back and attached to the new brick house, but Emily Massee Brown remembers only a large wooden room on the rear. The lot was purchased from Nellie Dempsey

[2] Some of this information is taken from "A Brief History of the Idle Hour Country Club," originally prepared by Winburn Stewart, revised and updated by Pink Persons, Jr. for the club yearbook, November 1, 1967.

[3] For much of this information I am indebted to the History of Macon, Georgia, by Ida Young, Julius Gholson, and Clara Nell Hargrove (1950).

Needham for $12,500.

Work on the new house commenced in 1901, as attested by the cornerstone. We do not know when the McCaws moved in, but construction halted when they took up residence and was not resumed until my father bought the house in 1910.

Wallace McCaw was president of the McCaw Manufacturing Company, previously the Georgia Mills and Elevator Company, of Macon, Georgia, manufacturing lard substitutes, or compounds under the trade names of Flake White, Invincible, and Plantern. They were all cottonseed oil products. The company had successfully weathered the 1891-1896 depression. In 1909, Procter & Gamble, in Cincinnati, Ohio, constructed a hydrogeneration plant in Ivorydale for the manufacture of a new shortening, principally formulated from cottonseed oil, that could compete with the lard compounds being sold by the meat packing companies. Procter & Gamble purchased the McCaw Manufacturing Company in January, 1909, in order to acquire a complete shortening factory as a pilot plant for concepts which might emerge.[4] P & G purchased the McCaw business for $1.4 million. As part of the deal, Wallace McCaw was hired and moved to Cincinnati. Years later his daughter Margaret told Emily Brown that Procter & Gamble wanted Wallace McCaw at any price, but were also determined to acquire the franchise for his cottonseed oil products.

Within five or six years he was a director of the company and president of the Buckeye Cottonoil Company, a subsidiary company. He was a member of the Executive Committee of Procter & Gamble, in active charge of the Flake White Department.[5] Mr. McCaw served as a vice-president of P & G from 1919 until 1924. In 1910, P & G patented an all-vegetable shortening that had properties superior to all shortenings then on the market.

In 1928 Wallace McCaw was elected vice-president, director, and general manager of Colgate & Company, the first in 122 years not a member of the Colgate family. A truly remarkable man!

Daddy Buys the McCaw House

When Wallace McCaw departed for Cincinnati he left his wife in Macon to sell the College Street property. Mother and Daddy went immediately to inspect the house. They had been looking at houses ever since they moved into the Comer house on Orange Street, including the beautiful Cowles-Bond house, now known as Woodruff House, and the Cadwallader Raines house on Georgia Avenue. Neither house had central heat or adequate plumbing. Mrs. McCaw showed them all over the main floor of the house. When Daddy told her, "We like the house; we'll take it," she replied, "Jordan,

[4] See Eyes on Tomorrow, by A. Schisgall ("From Cotton to Food").

[5] Information from Wallace McCaw's testimony in a patent infringment case in 1916.

don't be so impatient. Wait until Ethel has seen the bedrooms." But Daddy was adamant, "We don't need to see anymore. We want the house."

Mrs. McCaw was insistent, "Jordan, you go back to your office, and I'll take Ethel upstairs. Then, if she still wants the house, you and I can close the deal." Fortunately, my mother liked the second floor.

In telling me this story, Daddy explained, "Boots, I had one helluva time. My BVD's had slipped down and I was just hobbling along, barely able to walk. I knew damn well I'd never make it up those front stairs."

"But Daddy," I asked, "Why didn't you tell Mrs. McCaw you'd like to ride on the elevator?"

"I thought of that, but suppose she had started walking down after we had seen the second floor? In those days you couldn't tell a lady that your drawers had dropped down, so I just decided to buy the house on the basis of what we had seen. Ethel liked it, and that was all I needed to know." The house was purchased in my mother's name for $50,000.

THE GOLDEN YEARS

The Big House on College Street, 1910-1932

THE HOUSE ON COLLEGE STREET, THE MOVE, AND ALTERATIONS

The plans for the house on College Street, which are now in the archives of the Historical Division of the Washington Memorial Library, show that the house was designed for Wallace McCaw by Alexander Blair, a Macon architect; but my father maintained that Mr. Blair was only the local architect in charge of construction, representing a Northern architect whose name is forgotten. This was borne out by his brother, Jerome Massee, who worked for Mr. McCaw and surpervised the actual building, on a day to day basis. He also handled the payroll. No one seems to have asked Hazlehurst McCaw about the architect, but since her death more than one member of the family has expressed doubt that Blair was the original architect. There is a legend in the family that the architect was none other than Richard Morris Hunt, of Biltmore house fame, although Hunt died in 1895. This supposes that the house was designed for Wallace McCaw and his first wife, Mary Plant, and that Hazlehurst Plant, his second wife, discarded the original plans and hired Alexander Blair to redesign the house, retaining only the façade and the front hall. The truth may never be known, unless relevant documents are found among the McCaw papers in Cincinnati. Even after the existing plans were drawn, Hazlehurst and her husband made significant changes. However, it should be noted that there are stylistic details common to the McCaw house and two other Macon houses designed by Blair in the first decade of the century: the house on College Street designed for Nicholas M. Block, c. 1900-1906, and the house on Vineville Avenue for Dr. Thomas N. Baker in 1908. The Block house was for many years the home of Sam Coleman, Jr. and his family. The Baker house was later occupied by the Jack Massees, who eventually sold to the Ralph Birdseys. It is now the Red Cross Chapter House. Several architects and historians are of the opinion that the McCaw house is too superior in design and detail to have been the work of Alexander Blair, but I disagree with that completely. To me the difference is one of cost.

The McCaw house was built by day labor at a cost of more than $50,000. Begun in 1901, according to the cornerstone, no one knows how long it took to build. The McCaws were living there at the time of Mr. Plant's death in 1904. When my father bought the house in 1910 the interior was not completely finished. Either Mrs. McCaw or my mother had the two rooms left of the front hall converted to one large room, leaving an extra chimney. The space behind the library, marked servants' hall on the Blair plan, was left unfinished by my parents. A laundry in the basement, with large zinc tubs, was used by the McCaws but not by the Massees.

The style of architecture is usually described as French Renaissance

Revival, or Beaux Arts, a far cry from the prevailing late Victorian, Queen Anne Revival. The exterior is built of imported oyster-white brick, the irony of which did not escape my father, particularly when he had to match the brick for the rear extension.

Broad white marble steps on the front and side led to a one-story verandah extending across the front of the house. My father had the wooden floor of the verandah replaced with red ceramic tile, a decided improvement. The roof of the verandah was supported by eighteen Doric columns, with balustrades between. A matching balustrade bordered the roof of the verandah. These are now entirely missing, along with all other ornamental woodwork on the exterior of the house. The Doric columns have been replaced with modified Roman columns, not fluted. The original columns of the porte-cochere, however, are still standing.

The hipped roof, originally of red slate tile, is punctuated by four dormer windows, and rising above the roof, in the very center, was the square roof garden. Only the flat base remains; the surrounding balustrade and approaching stair are gone. A forlorn water spigot is all that is left of a vanished Babylonian garden.

I have described in some detail the exterior of the house because most of the fine detailing is gone, but the basic structure remains strong, a house built to withstand change. The interior is in bad condition, but the damage is superficial and could be repaired easily. The ceilings in the front bedrooms have been dropped, completely altering the proportions. The baths have been divided to provide space for cooking facilities. Only a few of the 1910 light fixtures have survived; the rest were stolen by vandals. The new chandeliers are attractive but too small, especially the one above the main stair.

Every convenience that could be imagined at the turn of the century was incorporated in the original design. All doors entering the house were storm doors, with tile-floored vestibules, to keep out the cold air in winter. The front rooms, including the great hall, are separated by double doors that slide into the wall. When out of sight, as they always were when we lived there, the vista from one end of the house to the other was quite impressive.

The ceilings of the rooms on the main floor are sixteen feet. Inside, sliding shutters, in addition to the usual outside blinds, kept out the direct sun rays in hot weather. These shutters were all sold after we moved. The bedrooms had ceiling fans and alternate louvered doors that were stored in the basement when not needed. A large passenger elevator, run by hydraulic pressure, went from the main floor to the roof, three floors above. Each door to the elevator shaft had two knobs that had to be turned simultaneously. The upper knob was placed so high a child could not reach it. Even standing on a chair, a child would not be able to turn both knobs at once.

Little remains of the magnificence of the interior except the front hall and the oval dining room, and even there the varnish on the paneling has cracked and darkened with age. The hall is 17 1⁄2 feet wide and 37 feet deep. The staircase is the finest feature of the house. It was made in Chicago and brought to Macon by rail in three pieces, then assembled in place. A landing half way up the stairs opens onto an alcove between tall Ionic columns, with a wood-burning fireplace between large leaded glass windows overlooking the backyard. It is still a strikingly original concept. From the landing the stair divides to the right and to the left. On the second floor a balcony connects the hall on the right to the hall on the left.

The oval dining room has always been the most beautiful room in the house. The walls are paneled in red mahogany up to the tray ceiling. A large vault for storing silver is concealed in one wall. The elaborate mantelpiece is especially fine. Each of the four mantelpieces on the main floor matches the woodwork of the particular room. The carved oak mantel in the library was also very fine.

The rooms on all three floors were connected to the service oven by speaking tubes with whistles. There was also a house telephone from my mother's bedroom to the butler's pantry. As children, Martha and I were addicted to speaking through tubes, and took delight in startling the butler with the whistle, although Mother discouraged their use as unsanitary.

Wine closets were located in the basement and in the hall adjacent to the billiard room. Champagne was stored in the basement closet, along with German beer in ceramic bottles – I still have two – and imported mineral water which was favored by no one.

Behind the dining room were the butler's pantry, where the silver and china and crystal were washed, the kitchen hallway where the commodious, hotel-size ice box stood, the locked pantry, and two stairs: one to the second floor, one to the basement. On the stair to the second floor was a broom and mop closet with sink. The kitchen and the servants' back porch were in a wing on the back of the house, on the Tinsley side. It may be a minor detail, but I think an important one, that beneath the front door alcove there were two closets: one for the butler, and one for the downstairs maid.

Before Daddy added the extension on the rear, the second floor consisted of four bedrooms, each with a walk-in closet and a separate bath. Daddy had the plumbing replaced with more modern equipment, except for the Chippendale tub with overhead shower in Grandpa Brown's room. The bedrooms opened onto a long hall extending almost the entire width of the house, with a stair to the third floor on the Tinsley's side.

My father told me that he commissioned Curran Ellis to design the exterior, but the plans are marked:

Blair, Kern, and Adams – Architect
673 Cherry Street
Macon, Georgia

The main purpose of the extension was to provide Daddy with his own sleeping quarters. Emily was the only child at the time so it wasn't to escape the noise created in later years by Martha and myself.

In addition to his bedroom, there was an unheated sleeping porch, a dressing room with cedar lined closets for suits and coats, and floor to ceiling drawers for other items of clothing and his own towels and linens. Only Daddy was allowed to use a bathmat; the rest of us used a clean Turkish towel folded. We all used one towel for the body and a linen towel for the face. An elaborate dressing room is fairly common today, but in 1910 it was quite a novelty. Next to the dressing room was the master's bath room, containing a specially made, 7' x 4' porcelain tub, a basin, an enclosed toilet, and a marble shower in a separate alcove, with needle sprays on two sides and the usual sprinkler above. When I was allowed to bring my toys and play in his tub I thought I was in heaven, especially since Martha was not allowed there.

When the tub arrived the extension had been completed, but the tub was too large to go through the doorways. A hole was made in one wall and the tub lifted by pulley and installed. I have often wondered how the subsequent owner got it out when Daddy's quarter was turned into a six-room apartment.

In the mid-twenties, Daddy bought two antique beds, an elaborately carved West Indian four-poster bed for himself and a low Honduran brown mahogany bed for Emily. Richard Ross, Daddy's valet, complained that the bed was too high for him to put on Daddy's shoes and socks, so Daddy decided he would swap beds with Emily. The bed that Emily got was identical to one owned by Mary Callaway Jones which was lost when her Pratt-designed house at Clinton, Georgia, burned; but someone had lowered her bed by cutting four inches off each post! When Daddy bought his bed it still had ropes to support the feather mattresses, and the low bed had a piece of heavy canvas stretched across the frame to hold a straw mattress and a feather mattress. Mr. Henry Muecke, Macon's leading antiquarian, built box springs and mattresses for both beds. He couldn't understand why Emily said the bed was so hard she couldn't sleep, until he discovered she was sleeping on the mattress made for someone more than twice her weight. A similar bed is in the Lady Pepperell house in Kittery, Maine. The other furniture in Daddy's bedroom was chosen for size not beauty. His room was so far from the front rooms no one could hear him snore at night. He slept so soundly he never heard the local morning cry of the peacock Mrs. Paul Willingham kept in her yard two doors away. One Winter I moved into Daddy's sleeping porch for the healthy fresh air. In those days, the air outside was clean! I got so cold I moved back to my own room long before Spring. The sleeping porch had windows on three sides with split bamboo shutters that rolled up and down. The two beds were cast iron and there was no other furniture. All very Spartan. I don't think my father ever slept there.

On the first floor, beneath my father's suite, was a huge room always known as the nursery, plus a bath, a closet, and a sun porch. When the wing was built the contractor thought the main furnace would heat the entire house, but it didn't, so a separate furnace was installed, which had one advantage. During those weeks in the Fall when the weather was uncertain, only the rear furnace was used. Both furnaces were hot air, burning coal at first, later crude oil, and finally natural gas. When the additional furnace was installed the fire place in the nursery was closed, although the mantel was left standing. In the mid-twenties Mother had Mr. Muecke build a bookcase there to hold the increasing number of books belonging to the children. The elaborate mantel was carried off to Brother Ray's house in the Pleasant Hill district. When I started high school, the nursery became the family room. There we installed our first radio and the big electric phonograph. The room was panelled in oak with horizontal beams across the ceiling. My father once said to me, "I hope your mother doesn't decide those beams should go in the other direction." There was an upright piano for the children, but as we grew older we practiced on the baby grand in the library. I got so tired of practicing I improvised pieces, thinking no one except my governess would know the difference, but once Mother called from upstairs, "Can we get back to Chopin now?"

The living room, in the front of the house, was so large it contained two sofas, a large library table, two tall secretaries, a desk, a grandfather clock, and two tilt-top card tables – all without crowding. Until the Oriental rugs arrived there were four rocking chairs, but they were moved to the nursery out of sight. Mother was less concerned with the fashion than with the fact that on deep pile rugs rocking chairs tend to move with rocking.

I remember when the Oriental rugs arrived from Altman's. The New York store sent a decorator from Brown's in Atlanta to be sure they were properly laid! The decorator persuaded my mother to move all heavy furniture off the rugs, except for the dining room table. The rugs remained in pristine condition, but the living room was never as beautiful again.

The layout of all the rooms was planned with remarkable foresight for everyday convenience and for elaborate entertaining. The entire third floor was intended only for entertaining, complete with a billiard room, dining room, and fully equipped pantry. Food was brought up from the first floor on a dumb-waiter. During the years we lived in the big house, the third floor was used periodically for sleeping quarters for my nurse, Anna Lockhart, and later for my German governess, Fräulein Alwina Eichler. One room was used to store empty boxes, suitcases, and trunks, including the wardrobe trunks containing Mother's trousseau, trunks so large the Railway Express would no longer accept them. Next to that was the Santa Claus room for storing gifts for next Christmas. Emily had her own storage room, and finally there was the ballroom or billiard room. I barely remember the huge billiard table, with a low-hanging lamp above it, and counters or cords stretched across the ceiling. That room had its own lavatory, for men only, and the original lighting fixtures, which utilized both gas and electricity. When no longer used for billiards, the room was used for storing rugs during the summer months. The rugs were laid flat, separated by newspapers – moths are said to be illiterate – chinaberry tree leaves, and crushed mothballs. To this day I love the smell of mothballs. Grass rugs were put down in place of the wool. The gold draperies were taken down, along with the lace curtains, to be replaced by white cotton. The heavy velvet portieres were also stored. Those portieres were brown on the outside and blue on the inside. Years later I took them to New York. All the sofas and chairs were covered with off-white linen slipcovers. I hated to see the change, but it shouldn't have mattered since we went to North Carolina every summer to escape the heat.

In the yard back of the house there was a red-brick garage, built as a stable and big enough to house many horses and carriages. The building extended across the entire back of the lot. It included a heated room for the chauffeurs, with toilet and shower inconveniently located on the other side of the garage. There was another toilet for the other male servants. The black female servants used the facilities in Lula's house. There was also a large storage room. The garage was demolished after we moved, but Lula's house was converted into a separate apartment.

I have spent so much time discussing the house on College Street not only because it was outstanding, but because it so perfectly accommodated my parents' way of life. That house was almost as great an influence on my development as the people who lived there. Only the Johnston-Felton-Hay House was as well-designed for convenience, comfort, and formal entertaining – and possibly the houses designed by Alexander Blair for Nicholas Block and Dr. Thomas N. Baker. I am told that others have been built recently, but I have not seen them.

The house now belongs to Dr. Peter Holliday III[6] who has done wonders to prevent further deterioration. Dr. and Mrs. Holliday live next door in the beautiful ante-bellum house occupied in my childhood by Mr. T. D. Tinsley and his family, of whom I shall have more to say later.

[6] The house has since been purchased by Dr. and Mrs. Walter Rizzoni.

Daddy's Illness

After the move to College Street there were indications that Daddy's health was deteriorating, but the symptoms were largely ignored in the light of his superabundant vitality, until he began having blackouts. One day while playing golf he keeled over and fell into a waterhazard with only Emily and a caddy no bigger than she was to drag him out. Had the water been deeper they could never have managed. Apart from excess weight the local doctors could find nothing wrong with him. Only doctors insisted that he had dizzy spells but did not become unconscious. As though to prove the doctor wrong, Daddy passed out in his office. When he came to, the doctor was peering into his eyes. "Well, Doctor, was I unconscious?" "You were indeed," the doctor conceded. Finally, he and Mother set off for Johns Hopkins Hospital in Baltimore, then regarded as the finest medical facility in the country. He was placed under the care of Dr. Barker, an outstanding internal medicine man.

After numerous examinations, Dr. Barker decided that Daddy would have to go on a diet. The very word frightened Daddy since he loved to eat. The doctors assured Daddy that if he stuck to the diet he could lead a normal life and probably live to a ripe old age. "But if you don't you may drop dead at any time, today, tomorrow, a year from now – who knows?" After mulling that over, Daddy said, "I'll give you my decision at five o'clock tomorrow afternoon." It was a choice that in his eyes required serious consideration. That same evening when the nurse brought him a delicious T-bone steak for dinner, he queried her, "Tell me about this diet. What would it be like?" When the nurse told him he was already on the diet he said, joyfully, "Lead me to it." The next day he told Dr. Barker that after serious consideration he had decided to go on the recommended diet. Every night he had a steak for dinner until finally he asked the nurse if he could have a piece of Smithfield ham instead. "Why certainly, Mr. Massee," she said, but when she brought his dinner the next night, the piece of ham wasn't much bigger than a fifty cent piece. After that he stuck to beef and chicken, and of course seafood, for which Baltimore was famous.

Prior to his incarceration, Daddy smoked about twenty cigars a day, Romeo and Juliets, pronounced Ju-li-ets` with the accent on the last syllable. When Dr. Barker discovered this he warned, "Massee, you'll have to cut down on the smoking. I can let you have four cigars a day." Horrified, Daddy responded, "Doctor, if I can't have but four I don't want any," but the doctor warned him that cutting out smoking completely wouldn't be easy. Daddy never smoked again as long as he lived, not even when the smoke around him was so thick he could hardly see the poker cards. So, he decided to chew tobacco instead, which the doctor thought wouldn't harm him. When Mother arrived at the hospital that day he said, "Old Dear, you certainly can pick 'em," since it was she who had chosen Dr. Barker in the first place. Gentlemen no longer chew tobacco, but in those days Southern gentlemen did. From then until he died Daddy chewed Humbug Chewing Tobacco, a very expensive brand. The only acceptable gifts on Christmas or birthday were Humbug or Roger and Galett violet toilet water. He called it his fruitcake. In the mid-thirties, Anne Rogers, his trained nurse, told the salesman in the tobacco shop on the corner of Cherry Street and Third that she wanted a box of fruitcake. She was told to try the grocery store. When she told him that Mr. Jordan Massee told her that was where he bought his fruitcake and that he said no one else in Macon carried it, he realized what she wanted. Years later the manufacturer went out of business because men who chewed tobacco couldn't afford Humbug. The president of the Southern Railway – my father was on the board of directors – sent a letter to all conductors to buy boxes of Humbug anywhere the railroad stopped long enough. Daddy cut back, slightly, for fear the supply would give out before he did, and he no longer shared with anyone. My mother for many years regretted her choice of doctor. Just before Daddy's death, he requested that the last box of Humbug be put in the coffin with him, "for the journey, just like King Tut."

The dentist at Johns Hopkins Hospital sent Daddy to an extractionist to have a tooth pulled. Now there was nothing in the world Daddy was afraid of except a dentist. The extractionist was a Frenchman and so small he had to stand on a platform to pull teeth. The next day the dentist discovered a small piece of bone that had broken off when Daddy's tooth was pulled, and said he would have to schedule an operation to have it removed. About that time a general blew in and insisted the dentist take a quick look in his mouth since he was leaving for France in about an hour. The dentist asked Daddy to please sit in the waiting room for a few minutes while he took care of the emergency. The War was just over and generals still came first. From the waiting room was heard the dentist saying, "It's just a little piece of bone from when you had your tooth pulled, nothing to worry about, it will work itself out." When the general left so did Daddy. To this day the record states, "Examination incomplete."

It wasn't long before Daddy and Dr. Barker were swapping stories. Daddy especially enjoyed the doctor's story of the Mormon who brought his wife all the way from Utah for treatment. When he arrived he claimed to be so poor he wasn't sure he would be able to afford treatment, but he did want the best. Dr. Barker assured him the bill would be adjusted to what the man could afford. When the woman was dismissed the man's bill was unusually high since the hospital had discovered the man was a millionaire. The man protested, saying, "But Doctor, she's not even my favorite wife."

Daddy never felt sick while he was at the Baltimore hospital and set up a running poker game in his room. Dr. Barker finally complained that the young doctors and interns spent most of their time looking after Daddy. Daddy regarded it as a precaution in case his bill was too high. During the weeks that he was there, Mother stayed in a hotel and came to the hospital, which was located on Broadway in the eastern part of the city, by taxi. One day, feeling economical, she took the streetcar instead. From the window she spotted three Meissen vases in an antique shop. She got off the streetcar to inspect the vases and persuaded the proprietor to hold them until she returned with her husband. As soon as Daddy was dismissed she took him, by taxi, to the out of the way shop to see the vases. Seeing how much she wanted them – "We need them for the dining room mantel" – he bought them and had them shipped to Macon, but not before telling his wife, "Ethel, next time don't try to save money by riding on a streetcar."

THE REMEDY

Following my father's visit to Johns Hopkins Hospital in Baltimore, his weight dropped from 267 to 167. This led to the following correspondence:

VALDOSTA, GA.,
Feb.28th.1919.
Mr. W. J. Massey,
Macon, Ga.,

My dear Sir:-

Mr. Clem Phillips gave me your name and address and told me I could write you for the Formula that you used to reduce your weight. He said he was a good friend of yours and that you would give me this valuable information for the asking. Mr. Phillips is a traveling man who makes shirts to order and I suppose that you remember him alright. He says you was once a very stout man and that now you are some 80 pounds lighter than you once was.

I am 32 years old and I weight around 260 pounds. I am always in good health and my weight is never in my way now but I would like to reduce a little because I am afraid that it will get in my way if I allow my weight to remain what it is now.

I want you to write me your remedy and you find enclosed a self addressed envelope for your reply. I am also willing to pay you for your trouble too.

I do not care to do something that might injure my health later, but if you have a good safe sound remedy, please write me at once and send me a bill covering your charges and I will upon receipt of same remit check covering.

Hoping to hear from you soon and with a good reply, I am,

Yours Very Truly,
[N. N. Langdale]

March 1st, 1919.
Mr. N. N. Langdale
Yellow Pine Variety Co.,
Valdosta, Georgia.

Dear Sir:-

Your letter of February 28th received by me today. Mr. Phillips informed you correctly. It cost me about $25000.00 to get off about eighty pounds and if you will send me a certified check for half of this amount I will send you the program.

Yours very truly,

Politics

Daddy was drawn somewhat unwillingly into local politics, as a means of protecting the interests of the Macon Railway and Light Company, which he owned. The number of paved streets grew slowly in the early years of the century, along with the even slower increase in the number of automobiles. During the period when Judge Lawton Miller served as mayor of Macon, 1908-09, paving increased rapidly, but primarily on streets with a streetcar track. Under the law the owners of the tracks were responsible for the cost of paving between the tracks and one foot on each side, which constituted a substantial part of the total cost. Streets without track were neglected by the administration. So Daddy decided to change the mayor by backing his business partner and next-door neighbor, John T. Moore. No expense was spared to get Mr. Moore elected, including parades on Cherry Street with elephants and a calliope rented from the resident circus, as well as the loudest brass band available. Cotton Avenue was abuzz with professional gamblers, most of whom were backing Miller. They gathered on corners, shouting, "Where's Massee now with all his money?" Just then Massee drove into Cotton Avenue standing in his open car, tossing a larger roll of bills, shouting back, "Right here ready to take your bets." The crowd not realizing that the bills were dollar bills except for a few on the outside of the roll, immediately changed sides, shouting, "We want Moore! We want Moore!" My mother said, "I would have to vote for Judge Miller; our families have been friends for years." Daddy didn't worry since at the time women were not allowed to vote!

During the heated campaign, it was rumored that the incumbent mayor had threatened to fire any policeman who voted for John Moore, if re-elected. When Daddy heard about that, he called together all the streetcar conductors and told them, "I'm not going to tell you who to vote for, but I will say this, that if Judge Miller is re-elected, I'll be out of a job and so will you." That day a reporter from the *Macon Telegraph* called Daddy at home during dinner, and if there was anything he hated it was being interrupted while eating. When he reluctantly went to the phone the reporter asked if it was true that he had threatened to fire any streetcar conductor who did not vote for Mr. John Moore. Daddy answered, "I don't like making statements to your paper; every time I do so I am misquoted." The earnest young reporter assured him, "Mr. Massee, I give you my word that you will be quoted verbatim, et literatim, et punctuatim." "All right, here's your statement," Daddy said. "You can take a running start and go plumb to Hell!" The next day, Mother packed her bags and took Emily to the mountains until the election was over. Judge Miller fired fourteen policemen and firemen, and Daddy fired fourteen streetcar conductors. They simply swapped jobs. John Moore was elected and served through 1913, during which time the city benefited by numerous improvements, including the paving of many streets where there was no streetcar track.

While John Moore was Mayor, Daddy served as Mayor Pro Tem whenever Moore was out of town. On one occasion a black man who worked for the city was arrested for stealing a mule. Daddy ruled that the city had too many mules and dismissed the case.

It should be recalled that Lawton Miller was Daddy's lawyer when he sold the steam plant on the Ocmulgee River to the Georgia Public Service Commission. In 1913 Daddy and John T. Moore sold the Idle Hour Stock Farm and the 160-acre tract at Rivoli, which they had purchased from the Plant family, to the group that formed the Idle Hour Country Club. Mr. Moore and his large family continued to live next door in what had been the Plant house until it burned.

I find it amusing that John Moore, before he became mayor, entertained a group of Macon businessmen to build a plant for making pulp for paper from okra stalks. The process worked but it was found that growing the okra was too expensive. Anyhow, okra belongs in vegetable soup.

THE LAW

"The law is a ass—a idiot," Mr. Bumble

Many of my father's stories concerned the law, and some of his best friends were lawyers: Judge Felton, Judge Lawton Miller, Roland Ellis, Bob Hodges, and above all, Felton Hatcher. They weren't always on the same side in litigation, but that never altered their friendship. Judge Miller once said, "Jordan, you have greater knowledge of the law and less respect for it than any other client I've ever had." His ethical values were so much higher than the law required, there was seldom any conflict. Differences arose only in matters that he believed were not constitutionally within the jurisdiction of any branch of government, such as gambling, drinking, fishing, hunting, and fast driving. He was not averse to a little political chicanery, so long as it was within the limits of local custom. His standards were based on expediency rather than morality. He paid the highest wages of anyone, far in excess of prevailing standards because he believed it paid off in the long run. That is not to say he lacked disinterested virtues, for he had many. He gave generously, but when he lent money he expected to be paid back, with interest. He borrowed money freely whenever needed, but with substantial collateral, which meant no risk to the bank.

Once when I was a small child, he borrowed ten thousand dollars from a large Macon bank. When the thirty days were up, he went by the bank to have his note renewed. The president of the bank, Mr. R. J. Taylor, hoping to embarrass my father, said, "I'm sorry, Jordan, the bank is not prepared to extend the loan. We must have our money by five o'clock." Daddy drove to Atlanta, where he borrowed the money, and was back in Macon before the bank closed, no small feat in those days of dirt roads and slow cars. When he paid the note, Mr. Taylor said, "I'm curious, Jordan, how did you manage to raise that much cash on such short notice?" "That was no problem," Daddy replied, "when I went home to dinner I told my wife I needed ten thousand dollars, and she took it out of Emily's pig bank." With the exception of his father-in-law, Daddy regarded all bankers as crooks and had facts and figures to prove it. But I've gotten away from the law and lawyers.

Growing up in Massee's Lane, Daddy's closest friend was a black boy his own age, named Cuff Anderson, the son of Grandmother Massee's cook, Aunt Epsey. They were inseparable. They played ball, fished, swam, and hunted together until Daddy moved away. Cuff continued to live on the plantation and was forever getting put in jail for gambling. Daddy would take time off from work and drive to Marshallville to get him out of jail, but he was getting tired of this. The next time, when it began to look serious, he took Roland Ellis with him. Mr. Ellis advised Cuff to plead guilty, feeling certain he would be fined and then released. "No, Sir," Cuff protested, "I ain't never pleaded guilty to nothing, and I ain't going to start now." Daddy lost his temper and told him, "Then you can rot in hell for all I care." Turning to his lawyer, he added, "Let's go, Roland, if he has no more sense than that he should stay in jail until he learns better."

Mr. Ellis said, "No, Jordan, don't be so impatient, we must stay and see that Cuff gets a fair trial; everyone deserves that much." So they stayed. When Cuff swore that he had never had his hands on a deck of cards in his life, the prosecutor reached for a deck of cards that had been brought from the scene of the crime, and flashed the bottom card in Cuff's face. "What's that?" he shouted. Cuff grinned from ear to ear and said, "Lawd, that's my Mammy's picture." It was the queen of spades. The judge gave Cuff a lecture and dismissed the case.

When Jim Brown first heard the story, he said tactlessly, "Mr. Massee, the Queen of Spades is not black;" but Daddy wasn't concerned with minor details. He didn't need to be told what any card look like, having handled many a deck before Jim was born.

Years later, Cuff Anderson became the preacher in a large Baptist church in Chicago.

For some reason the story of Cuff always reminded Daddy of the time when Judge Emory Speer tried a man for drunkenness. Judge Speer gave the culprit a long lecture on the evils of alcohol and imposed a stiff fine. The man responded, "Your honor, I enjoyed the sermon but bedamn the doxology."

On another occasion while Daddy was serving as mayor pro-tem, Mr. George S. Jones, Sr. protested an open saloon at Vineville Branch, on the grounds that his eight little children had to walk past it. The case was postponed for a week. At the second hearing, Mr. Jones referred to his nine little children. Daddy said, "I thought last week you said you had eight children." Mr. Jones replied, "Both statements are correct, your honor."

Early in this century, Mr. Willis Sparks came within an inch of becoming the biggest man in Georgia, but his venture failed. He was a very arrogant man and totally humorless. One day, coming out of Brown's Bookstore on Second Street, he encountered a group of small black children playing on the sidewalk, blocking his passage. Waving his stick in the air, he shouted, "Out of my way!" The children scattered in fear and trembling. Emily excused him because he was extremely nearsighted and afraid he might trip and fall on the children, but my father was not of the same opinion.

When called for jury duty, Mr. Sparks asked Judge Speer for a military exemption, as he was a member of the Macon Volunteers. "Take your seat," Judge Speer said sternly, "If we have a war I'll release you." While serving on the jury, Mr. Sparks made the judge nervous by rattling something in his pocket. Finally, Judge Speer said, "Mr. Sparks, what is that you are rattling?" Mr. Sparks took five silver dollars from his pocket and showed them to the judge, who said, "Give four of them to the marshall and you may continue rattling the rest as much as you choose."

Judge Speer lived in a beautiful Greek Revival house in Vineville, known to subsequent generations as the Sanford Birdsey home. He rode into town every day on his horse, followed by a servant on another mount. After arriving at the courthouse, the servant took both horses back to Vineville.

One day, Judge Speer sentenced a white man convicted of murder to two years imprisonment. The next case was a black man caught stealing a case of hair tonic, which he probably thought was alcohol. The judge pronounced him guilty and sentenced him to ten years in jail. Roland Ellis, who was sitting in the rear of the court room, rose and said, "Your honor, this is one hell of a court of justice: two years for homicide and ten years for Herpecide."

Grandpa Brown had a lawyer, Mr. Ed Johnson, whom he called "Honest Ed," or "Country Ed," depending on whether or not his efforts had recently benefited my grandfather. Grandpa had a violent temper and often in the middle of the night he would think of someone whose banknote was overdue, and he would phone Mr. Johnson then and there. "Ed, I want you to sue him; I want you to sue Hell out of him before breakfast!"

It was said that Mr. Brown never made a bad loan, but he did conduct one transaction that he regretted. An old countryman came in with a sack of silver coins for deposit. The coins were counted and placed in the vault. About six weeks later the countryman returned and asked for his money. Mr. Brown opened the vault and took out the coins, still in the same sack. "Do you wish to withdraw all your money?" he asked. "No," the man replied, "I just want to see if it's all right." No record was kept of what Mr. Brown said.

Daddy had lots of other stories about lawyers, some of which will appear in a different context. Judge Felton deserves a whole book to himself, and I shall refer to him from time to time, whenever his path and my father's crossed significantly. Of all the judges and lawyers, the most important in my father's life was undoubtedly Felton Hatcher, especially during the planning and construction of the hydroelectric plant on the Ocmulgee River at Jackson. His devotion to Mr. Hatcher and his admiration for Mrs. Hatcher knew no bounds. He told me at the end of his long life that he had known only four great ladies: my mother, Isabelle Thomas Johnston, Rietta Etheridge Callaway, and Margaret Plant Hatcher.

Ethel Brown Massee

Here lies a most beautiful lady,
Light of Step and heart was she:
I think she was the most beautiful lady
That ever was in the West Country.
But beauty vanishes; beauty passes;
However rare, rare it be;
And when I crumble who shall remember
This lady of the West Country?

Walter De La Mare

People who never met my mother expect more than an introduction, while those who knew her, however intermittently, insist on a permanent likeness of the person they knew. It would take an Edith Wharton to satisfy both groups. My mother was a very private person who didn't even like to have her picture taken. She would prefer a Boldini portrait capturing the style while concealing the character. The best that I can provide is a series of snapshots of her, alone and with others, at various times in her long life. It is up to the reader to assemble the pieces like a jigsaw puzzle to form his own picture, even without all the pieces.

I have my own theories, none of them Freudian, of how anyone becomes someone, but I haven't the slightest idea of why my mother was the person she was. Without cause and effect we must rely on the meager information provided by faded photographs. I know next to nothing about her mother, Emily Lawson Brown. My mother spoke of her as a saint. I know much more about her older sister, Mattiebrian Brown, and her nurse, Nancy Flewelyn, as will be seen in subsequent chapters. Her childhood was apparently uneventful. She was sickly and, according to cousins, spoiled. Her father gave her whatever she wanted, including a squirrel in a cage with a wheel. Her closest friend as a child, and throughout her entire life, was Martha Hunt, who became Mrs. George Cornell. As babies they went out together in a carriage, and played together constantly as children. The Hunt family lived across a narrow lane, beside the First Baptist Church. Her other close friend as a child and as a young lady was her cousin Odille ("Dilse") Taylor.

When Mother was around eight years old her father told her he was going to put her on an allowance like her sister and brother. Her response was revealing, "No, Papa, I'd rather keep my money with yours," which is what she continued to do until her marriage. After the death of her mother, Mrs. Oliver came to run the Brown household, and with her the two Oliver boys, Hugh and James. She seems to have cared better for Hugh, who must have been pious even as a boy, but adored James. There were other childhood friends, such as Irene Winship, North Winship's aunt, but I know little about them.

For my mother, there were none of those long trips to North Carolina or Virginia that punctuated the lives of her parents and grandparents. She seems to have traveled no farther than Hawkinsville to visit Brown and Lawson relatives. She must have enjoyed those visits since in the early twenties she named her summer home in Asheville, NC, Pine Retreat which was the name of the Lawson plantation where her mother was born. It is safe to say she was never a silly child, neither her father nor Mrs. Oliver would have tolerated that, nor did Nancy tolerate any misbehavior. She was taught not to sit on the edge of the bed and to keep her possessions in perfect order, habits she never outgrew.

Throughout her adult life she was described as a great lady, meaning an Edwardian lady, elegant, gracious, and perfectly groomed at all times. She was only five foot four inches tall but seemed taller due to her remarkable carriage. Even in old age she held herself erect without appearing stiff. When my nurse Anna Lockhart saw a picture of her taken around 1917 she said, "Madam, you are so graceful." She was always beautifully dressed, whether in a Worth gown in 1912, or in a simple black dress from Goldman's on Cherry Street in 1947. She was very soft spoken and never raised her voice. If she was ever angry no one knew it. She smiled a great deal but seldom laughed out loud. She had the most perfect skin I ever saw in an adult which was attributed to never using soap and water on her face. She wore no makeup except for rice powder, although earlier in the century she used liquid white powder. When I was a small boy she sometimes wore a single black "beauty spot" pasted on her cheek, in the shape of a star or a crescent moon. She carried these in her gold mesh handbag, and when we went driving, which was often, Martha and I enjoyed decorating our faces with many beauty spots. I associate them with veils. In the teens, women often wore hats with veils, when they weren't wearing feathers. Later, in the twenties, Mother wore a pair of silver foxes around her neck in cold weather. Vonceil Brown, her great-niece asked, "Aunt Ethel, is that a dead dog?" Above all, I associate the scent of white heliotrope with my mother, the only perfume she ever wore. In her handkerchief drawer she kept heliotrope sachet. To this day, whenever I smell heliotrope I recall my mother, like Proust with his Madeleine.

Her dark brown hair was worn in a pompadour, which was especially becoming, until around 1919, when women started wearing their hair held close to the head by hair nets, one of the ugliest fashions ever perpetrated on the female sex. It lasted until the mid-twenties when women started cutting their hair short, in the manner of Irene Castle. Mother had hers cut in Paris in 1926. She was so embarrassed she refused to go to the opera that night. For the rest of the summer she wore a hat, until we got back to New York where she could have it trimmed more becomingly. In old age she wore it short, shingled in the back, almost white by then, naturally curly, admired by all. None of the clothes worn in the twenties were becoming to women in their prime. Those fashions were flattering only to young women like Joan Crawford and Louise Brooks, called flappers.

Every morning Mother dressed for breakfast, but as soon as Daddy left she changed for a house dress made of a blue denim-like material with large mother-of-pearl buttons down the front. Fifty years later, her granddaughter, Emily Bonner, used those buttons on a shower curtain she designed. Mother spent the morning in the housedress supervising every detail of the housework. When she went to the kitchen, which she seldom did, she wore a turban to keep the smell of cooking out of her hair.

Her friends envied the way her satin petticoats rustled when she walked. As was the custom she wore more undergarments than women today can imagine. Worst of all was the corset which had to be laced up the back. My mother had a passion for shoes, but her feet were so narrow no one else in the family could wear her shoes. Fifteen minutes before Daddy arrived home for dinner she changed from the housedress to something more suitable to the downstairs. He saw no reason why she wouldn't wear her nice clothes for housework and thought that most of the work should have been left to servants. Once he came home early and caught her on the top of a ladder cleaning the prisms in the living room chandelier. Each of the ladder's four legs was held by a servant. He glanced at her and said to me, "If that woman had one more servant she'd work herself to death." Sometime he would pretend to be angry with her for not letting a servant carry out some chore, but no one took him seriously. Everyone knew he thought she was perfect. He often said to her, "Old Dear, you're a lot of trouble to yourself." The house except for the kitchen was kept immaculate. When she complained about the kitchen, her sister said, "Ethel, you can have a clean kitchen or a good cook, but you can't have both."

For my father, the entire day revolved around the mid-day meal, which was served at two o'clock. This left the afternoon free for my mother to receive callers or play bridge. I don't recall many callers; they were not encouraged.

My mother's dress and manner were so formal many people thought she was cold and unapproachable, but nothing could be farther from the truth. It is true she was not given to demonstrations of affection, except with her children or grandchild, but she was always understanding, even compassionate. I saw her cry only twice: when we left the Big House and at her sister's funeral. She had a coterie of young ladies who regularly sought her advice on matters of the heart. These included Cathleen Jacques, Ann Willingham Jordan, Aleen Connor, and many others. I suspect she offered more support than advice.

Mother went into mourning when her brother died and she never again wore colors, only black, gray, or white – with the exception of a beautiful pleated Grecian style gown of pale shades of rose and gray with white. It goes without saying, she never wore liquid fingernail polish, not even colorless.

She loved music and dragged my father off to many an opera. Shortly after her marriage she started collecting phonograph records, some of which Daddy enjoyed. She loved shopping, especially in New York, and kept a file on things to buy. At a family gathering at Sea Island in the 1940s, most of us agreed that Daddy and Martha were the most democratic. She protested, saying, "I know all the girls who work at Woolworth or Kress by name." Even I thought that was pretty funny, since her visits to the dime store were like Queen Mary at a country fair.

For the weekly grocery shopping, with Lula the cook and the chauffeur, she wore white cotton gloves and picked the okra pod by pod to be sure they were small enough. Even the ears of corn had to be individually inspected.

In my lifetime, Mother was seriously ill only once when she had a dangerous fever during a national epidemic. She was never in very good health but complained of nothing, took almost no medicine. She was never a patient in a hospital. Maybe that's why she was so fond of hospitals, "They're so clean and smell like Lysol." She usually accepted with resignation the ways of God towards men, but when her nephew, Lawson Brown, died, she seriously questioned Divine Wisdom.

Although she could not cook, she did make fabulous egg-nog, orange marmalade, and dark chocolate fudge. She enjoyed good food, which she ate in small quantities. I remember how much she relished the bluepoint oysters in New York and the food at the Crillon in Paris.

She wasn't very good at sewing but crocheted beautiful afghans and made washrags by the hundreds by binding together two squares of cheesecloth. Whenever a friend went on a trip she gave her a cake of fine soap and two washrags, one for the face and one for the body. At the end of her life she told Emily to buy more cheesecloth and colored threads since she might give out. When she died, Emily found almost six dozen washrags under her bed.

No description of my mother would be complete without mention of her magnificent jewelry. After the depression, when Daddy could no longer afford diamonds and sapphires, she collected silver jewelry set with semi-precious stones.

After Grandmother's death, Nancy Flewelyn had as much to do with training Mother as her sister Mattiebrian or Mrs. Oliver did, which is why Mother trusted Emily to her, or, later, trusted me to Anna Lockhart, freeing her to be with Daddy. All three relationships went far beyond the traditional white child-black nurse association.

Mother and Daddy's Friends

The Jack Massees

My father probably had more friends than any other man in Central Georgia but only one was very close, his brother Jack. On the other hand, my mother, although perceived as a very private person, actually had a surprising number of very close friends, namely: Martha Hunt Cornell, Odille Taylor Preston, Jonnie Holmes Sparks, Nettie Watkins Jones, and Rietta Etheridge Callaway. To this list, I should probably add Rosa Snowden and Mary Seymour Jones. Four couples qualify as close friends of both my parents: Jack and Gene Massee, Lawson and Mamie Brown, Felton and Margaret Hatcher, and Bobby and Jonnie Sparks.

Oliver Jerome "Jack" Massee, Jr. was six years younger than my father. As a boy Daddy was closer to Marion, his older brother. He and Jack became close after the younger brother's return from Eastman Business College in Poughkeepsie. From then until Jack's death in 1932, they were inseparable. Daddy brought Jack into the Bibb Brick and Tile Company, where they complimented each other. Daddy was the consummate salesman, and Jack the perfect plant manager. Jack said, "I'd rather stand under the pump on the coldest day in January and let the water run down my back than ask any son-of-a-bitch to buy our brick," to which Daddy replied, "And I'd swim to Forsyth just for the fun of landing a big job." Daddy had a remarkably even disposition, while Jack had a violent temper. According to Daddy, "When it came to cussing, Jack was a connoisseur: he could toss a handful of peas into the air and cuss them individually before they hit the ground." He pronounced the word kŏn-nô'-shȧ, imitating Jack. They never tired of each other's company. Once, in telling a story, Jack said some man made a fortune in the retail jewelry business. Daddy corrected him, "Jack, you've got the facts right but the details wrong: he lost a fortune in the wholesale jewelry business."

When Jack announced to his parents that he was going to get married, his father said, "Jack, I hope you're marrying a girl who can truthfully say, 'Our father and mother who art in heaven.'" Daddy added, "Instead, he married half of Americus." His wife Eugenia Glover ("Gene") was small and chic. The only way she could get clothes that fit was to make them, or re-make them, herself. According to Emily, no mean seamstress herself, Gene could copy a dress from a photograph in Vogue magazine so perfectly no one could tell that it was not professionally made. No other woman in Macon, except my mother, was as beautifully dressed in the 1905-1925 period.

The Jack Massees purchased the house on Vineville Avenue designed in 1908 by Alexander Blair for Dr. Thomas N. Baker. The 28-room mansion was built on 4 1/2 acres of land. When the Massees moved to the Massee Apartments in 1924, the house was sold to the Ralph Birdseys, who sold the front of the lot, on Vineville Avenue, for two filling stations. The house is now the home of the American Red Cross. The house was set way back from Vineville Avenue, with a large front lawn, where Jack sometimes allowed his cow to graze. If the neighbors complained it is not recorded. Uncle Jack loved homemade ice cream, which he had Gus churn daily. Gus moved with them to the Massee Apartments to fire the furnace. The Vineville Railway station was just behind the Massee house, where one could conveniently get on or off the train, saving considerable time since trains on that line had to back into the downtown station.

Uncle Jack, like Daddy, spent a great deal of money on clothes, but they looked better on Jack due to his magnificent physique. Both had plaster casts of their feet at Hannon in New York so that they could order shoes by mail and be sure of a perfect fit. Each pair of shoes before delivery was manipulated by hand until soft. Their summer suits were made by Terry and Jut in New Orleans. They both wore fine Panama hats, which Mr. R. J. Taylor, the richest man in Macon, envied but felt he could not afford. Once when Daddy felt obligated for some political favor, he had Neel's deliver an identical hat to Mr. Taylor. Mr. Taylor returned the hat to the store in exchange for a three-piece suit, two shirts, and a silk tie. Every year Daddy and Uncle Jack bought identical twin-six Packards. At the earliest possible opportunity, Jack would drive Daddy's car for comparison, and every year he would say, "Brady, I hate to tell you this but your car is a lemon." Daddy always replied, "You're right, Jack, your car is better than mine," which satisfied them both.

Despite the loss of one leg, Jack was an inveterate golfer, often playing 18 holes, although two holes on the back side were better suited to mountain goats. There were no motorized carts then; the players walked. They preferred a foursome, often including my mother's cousin, Peter Taylor. Peter was the first president of the Idle Hour Country Club; Jack Massee was the second. Daddy's valet, Walter Odom – later Richard Ross – accompanied the foursome, with a thermos bottle of ice water and plenty of towels. After the game, the valet helped Daddy shower and dress.

The Massee brothers and Peter Taylor attended an exhibition match given by four professional golfers. The eighth green was a hard one, and all four players hit balls that touched the green then bounced into sand traps. Jack, who was a little high, borrowed a club from one of the players and in a loud voice said, "Let me show you how to do it." He took a quick swing and made a hole in one! Other players have done the same on that green, but not under such auspicious circumstances.

After a long hot day at the brickyard Jack would come to the office for a cold shower and to hear a detailed account of Daddy's activities for the day. Apart from Grandpa Brown, it may have been the best audience Daddy ever had. When Uncle Jack lay dying, in 1932, he called for "Brady," and died holding Daddy's hand. Mother and Aunt Gene were also close – they belonged to the same bridge club in 1905 – but saw less and less of each other after the twenties.

The Jack Massees had two daughters: Virginia in 1903 and Sims in 1908. Virginia and Emily were lifelong friends, and Sims and Martha were friends as girls, frequently wearing identical clothes. Sims visited Martha in Asheville, first at the Von Rook house, and later at Pine Retreat, when she kept a framed picture of Logan Lewis on her dressing table. The Jack Massees spent the summer at Grove Park Inn the year it opened. They preferred to stay in one of the charming cottages rather than in the main building. Aunt Gene had considerable difficulty controlling Sims, who had her father's temper. One day Gene was going out and told Sims she could not go but Sims got in the car and refused to get out. About that time Uncle Jack appeared unexpectedly on the scene. When Sims saw him she practically fell out of the car, but it was too late. Jack carried her screaming into the cottage and submerged her in a tub of cold water, clothes and all. As a child Sims looked like her father and was tall for her age. But she stopped growing and when I saw her a few years before her death she was as small as Martha Massee.

Jack and Gene had a more serious problem with Virginia when she fell in love with Bill Adams. Very late one night, Jack asked Daddy to accompany him on a visit to the Adams home, now the 1842 Inn. Daddy knew it would be useless trying to dissuade Jack from going at that hour. After they had rung the bell for a long time, Mr. Adams finally came to the door, in his nightshirt. "What's the matter, boys?" he inquired. "I want to see Bill," Jack replied. "What did you want with Bill at this hour?" the old man asked. "I want to kill him," Jack said emphatically. "Oh, Jack!" Mr. Adams sighed, "I hope you won't do that." Eventually, Virginia and Bill Adams were married, in the Massee home, on Vineville Avenue. For some reason, Mother was unable to attend the wedding – Martha must have been ill – so Daddy and Emily went without her. Aunt Gene disapproved so much of the match she locked herself and Sims in her bedroom and refused to attend the ceremony. Uncle Jack was completely helpless and left Emily to run the show. Neither Daddy nor Mother ever felt the same towards Gene after that. They knew that Bill Adams had a drinking problem but thought that if Virginia was determined to marry him, her parents should have made the best of it, which is precisely what Jack did. He gave the couple a small house on Nottingham Drive and put Bill to work at the Bibb Brick Company. My only memory of Bill Adams is when he took me fishing in one of the lakes formed when an abandoned claypit filled with rainwater. While we were fishing Daddy and his chauffeur arrived to see what luck I was having. I had just hooked a large fish when the line got tangled in the branches of an overhead tree. "Don't let him go, Boots; hold on to him," Daddy hollered, wading out into the water up to his waist. Bill and the chauffeur tried to stop him but he was determined not to let that fish get away. I shall never forget the look of pride when he climbed out of the water holding my fish. Bill and Virginia had one child, Betty, born in 1923. After Virginia's second marriage, to Jimmie Cook, Uncle Jack and Aunt Gene legally adopted Betty, a lovely child with beautiful red hair.

Sims Massee married Kennan Rand and moved to El Paso, Texas. Aunt Gene spent the last years of her life with Sims in El Paso and died there in 1957. Sims returned to Americus after the death of her husband. Her mother was born there, and Betty lives there with her husband, Fred Horn. They have three daughters.

Isabelle Johnston

My mother considered Isabelle Johnston one of the most beautiful women she had ever known, which is borne out by the portrait of her by Nagel. Daddy always referred to her as one of the four great ladies he had known. After the death of her husband, Richmond Johnston, Isabelle moved to Atlanta with her two daughters, Pam and Isabelle. They lived in a lovely Georgian style house, surrounded by boxwood. Martha and I went with Mother several times to call on Isabelle Johnston. Later, I took to going alone, when in Atlanta for a concert. On one visit, Isabelle called over the banister to me in the hall below, "Look out for the dog, he bites." I replied, "He just did." Fortunately, the dog was too old to inflict much damage.

Pam Johnston raised longhaired dachsunds, which were quite rare at the time. She gave one to Aunt Aileen who by then lived in Winter Haven, Florida. Later, Pam invited the Dave Massees to bring the dog to Atlanta for the annual dog show, as her guests. Her favorite dog could not win the prize as best of breed unless there was competition. So Aunt Aileen and Uncle Dave visited Pam and entered their dog in the show. To Aileen's great embarrassment, the dog Pam had given them won the prize. The judges were puzzled when the owner questioned their judgment.

The Englishes

Before the Coca-Cola barons took Atlanta, old Col. English was a force to be reckoned with. He lived in a large mansion in what had once been a nice residential area. Gradually the business section expanded, leaving his house surrounded by concrete paving and shops, but Col. English refused to move. One day he was sitting on his verandah high above the street when he noticed a motorist parking in front of his house. The Colonel told an elderly servant who was sweeping the porch, "You see that man?" pointing his finger. "Well you go down there and tell him I don't allow anyone to park in front of my house." Reluctantly, the old family retainer went down the front steps and spoke to the man in the offending car. The man got out of the car and walked away, while the servant returned to his sweeping. Col. English said, "Did you tell that man what I told you to tell him?" "Yes, Sir, Boss, I told him." "And what did he say?" "I can't tell you that, Boss," was the reply, but Col. English persisted, "God Damn it! I asked you a question and you better answer." The old man did answer, "He say, 'You go tell that old son-of-a-bitch he don't own Atlanta anymore.'" One can only guess at what the Colonel said then, but his son Harry loved telling the story. Bar whiskey was only 10¢ a drink in those days, but Old Man English's favorite bartender served him in a "Groover," a large beer glass.

The sons of Col. English carried on the family business manufacturing brick and hollow tile. Harry English's wife Florence was one of the most colorful members of Atlanta society. She was a good-looking woman, small and expensively dressed. In the twenties, when the fashions were not flattering to women over thirty, Florence continued to look sensational. She and her husband built a beautiful house on West Pace's Ferry Road, designed by Philip Schutze – now the home of Ann Cox Chambers. I often called on Florence when I was in Atlanta. I remember her in a short sequined gown, descending the semi-circular stair in her front hall, dressed for a dinner before the opera. Mother said she looked like an angel until she opened her mouth. Her speech was colorful to say the least.

Harry and Florence English were friends of both my parents and the Jack Massees. I have an amusing photograph, taken at a Florida beach resort, of Daddy and Emily; Bobby, Jonnie, and Hazel Sparks; Virginia Massee; and Florence English. The ladies are wearing more clothes than at an evening dance, with shoes, stockings, and hats. My mother is nowhere in evidence. She was sitting on the hotel verandah, well protected from the sun, holding the ladies' jewelry.

Florence and Harry English usually spent the summer at Grove Park Inn, in Asheville, North Carolina, but one summer they went to the Greenbriar instead. Florence reported, "Well, I got that out of my system." During the Winter, Florence would often drive down to Macon. She always stopped at the office on Broadway to speak to Daddy before going to dinner with the Jack Massees. I remember her at our house only once, sitting on the sofa, no doubt telling Mother some outrageous story. On another occasion, she told Mother and Daddy, "I used to hate Harry's younger brother but when he got married I realized I didn't need to worry anymore; the Lord had taken him." The last time that Emily saw her was at the races in Miami, "She looked like an aged follies girl in white fox, with too much make-up and too much jewelry."

The Lawson Browns and Judith Wiley

Lawson Brown was my mother's only brother. Born in 1872, he was seven years older than she. He was strikingly handsome, with dark hair, olive complexion, and large brown eyes, and my mother adored him. He was full of fun and liked to tease her as a child. He fought in Cuba in the Spanish-American War. Afterwards, he married Mary Adelaide "Mamie" Wiley, daughter of Col. Charles M. Wiley, Ordinary of the Bibb County Court for thirty years. They had one son, Lawson Brown, Jr., who was born in 1903. My mother and father were deeply devoted to both Lawson and Mamie Brown. Until my father's death, he carried a pocket knife given to him by Mamie.

I know very little about my Uncle Lawson or his devoted wife. They lived in a house on College Street which was remodeled for them by Neel Reid. Lawson had an automobile agency and sold my father a Locomobile limousine which cost $5,173 in 1909.

Lawson's sudden death in 1912 was a terrible shock. Mamie never recovered from his death and died in 1915. Emily said she died of a broken heart. Lawson Brown, Jr., lived with his grandfather, Col. Charles M. Wiley, and the Colonel's daughter-in-law, Judith Gambrell Wiley, who gave up her job in Texas as a nurse to keep house for Col. Wiley and raise Lawson, Jr. The boy had smallpox but Judith nursed him through it. In the First World War she returned to nursing and served in France at the front. After the armistice she was sent to Asheville, N.C., to recuperate. One day she was walking down the main street with a general who was impressed with her record. By chance, she noticed, in a photographer's window, a picture of Daddy with his three year-old son. She sat down on the curb and cried. The general phoned my father and told him the story. Without delay, Daddy drove to Asheville to see Judith. It wasn't long before she was released from the hospital and was back in Macon. Whenever Martha or I was ill Judith donned her uniform and took her turn administering mustard plasters. For years she taught Sunday School at the First Baptist Church. Although no blood kin, she was regarded as a member of our immediate family. After Lawson was grown, she worked in the ordinary's office and would surely have succeeded Col. Wiley had she not been a woman, but continued her work under Walter Stevens. She and I were good friends for many years despite the age difference, or possibly because of it. She accompanied me to Atlanta to hear Luarezio (?) Bosi in La Traviata and brought sandwiches and dark fruit cake for the journey. We were stopped by a policeman in Jonesboro, who said, "You left your tickets in Macon, but your father says there will be someone at the door to let you in."

Judith was an ardent prohibitionist as had been her father, Dr. J. B. Gambrell, one-time president of Mercer University. Her husband, Sid Wiley, who died young, was an alcoholic, but eventually Judith completely erased that from her memory. She had a small car and once a week would pick me up after work for a swim at the Ike Winship lake. We both enjoyed swimming and, even more, standing under the waterfall. By the time my family moved to the little house on College Street, Judith, who always talked a lot, had become a compulsive talker. Once an interesting woman she now told stories in such detail no one except my mother could stand it, and no one could believe half the stories she told. It's something that seems to happen only to women who are alone and live vicariously through others. Judith lived through my mother and through Mrs. Walter Lamar, and of course through her Sunday School pupils.

She was a highly intelligent woman whose mind gradually atrophied, which may or may not have had anything to do with her final illness. For some years Judith rented a room in Dr. and Mrs. Miller's home on the corner of Georgia Avenue and College Street, which cannot have been very convenient since there were no cooking facilities. Finally she moved to the Massee Apartments where she had one room and a kitchen-dinette. Her large bed took up almost the entire room. When she became ill, she lay there in a coma, oblivious of everything around her, kept alive by blood transfusions insisted upon by her sister in Dallas. There was no living will then, and no doctor willing to pull the plug.

Judith Wiley was one of those women who spend their lives in the service of others more fortunate than themselves, never complaining, seldom rewarded. When Col. Wiley died he left her nothing, assuming, I suppose, that Lawson would care for her. Unfortunately, Lawson's wife, Vonceil, disliked her, and even Lawson favored my mother who never meddled in his affairs, and who was certainly more glamorous. When Mrs. Lamar died she left Judith nothing. Fortunately, Mr. Lamar left her a small amount of money, which seemed to Judith like a fortune.

Lawson Brown and Vonceil Grace, from Florida, were married in our house on College Street. Finally, Mother had a bride to come down that beautiful stair. Their son, Lawson III, died as a child, but a daughter, Vonceil II, survived and lives now in Florida.

Judith Wiley was a good woman, but like many Baptists she was bigoted. She treated Blacks well and was liked by them, but she spoke of them patronizingly, as though they were children. She seldom had a good word for any Catholic although her own mother was born into that faith. Even with those faults, when she gets to heaven Job will get up and let her sit down, as my father said of Mrs. Jack Lamar.

When Lawson Brown, Jr., was dying, Judith and Mother went together to see him in Florida. Both were profoundly shaken by his death. Mother usually faced death with equanimity, but she could not accept her nephew's death as a part of any divine plan. She kept asking, "Why Lawson? Why Lawson?" until finally I said to her, "Stop crying, Mother. That way lies insanity." She stopped asking perhaps not to God.

Bobbie and Jonnie Sparks

After the death of Lawson Brown, Mother and Daddy depended more and more on Mr. and Mrs. Robert Sparks for companionship. Bobby was the younger brother of Mr. Willis Sparks, and Jonnie was the daughter of Dr. Holmes. They lived conveniently around the corner, on the Washington Avenue side of the block. For years they played cards at our house several evenings a week: hearts or setback, also known as High, Low, Jack, and the Game. Daddy insisted he couldn't handle more than five cards at once, although he frequently played Rook ("Methodist Bridge") with Mother, Martha, and me. No matter how often Bobby came to the house, he always brought small gifts for Martha and me. Jonnie was a good pianist and could play all the popular tunes by ear. Without Mother, they occasionally took Hazel and Emily to Recreation Park for swimming. Once the two men persuaded Jonnie to come down the high slide by promising to catch her at the bottom, which they didn't. They were pleased as boys with their prank. When Martha and I were finally christened, Jonnie Sparks and Johnny Selden were my Godparents. Until Hazel Sparks married and moved away from Macon she was one of Emily's closest friends.

Jonnie and Bobby, and Mother and Daddy attended the same social functions, including the Saturday night dances at the Country Club. The next day Mother and Jonnie spent at least half an hour on the phone discussing in detail the events of the previous night in code: "Did you notice what the small blonde was wearing? I thought the skirt was much too short for a woman of her age." Emily figured out that the small blonde was always Ann Hines. They thought the telephone operator might be listening to their conversation. Perhaps she was: there was no radio or television in those days, and the society pages of the newspapers carried no local gossip. Mother never talked on the phone to anyone else more than those minutes.

Once Bobby brought me a small black cat which I promptly named "Mother," instead of "Daddy," which would have been more appropriate. He was the last pet, apart from goldfish, to stay overnight in the big house, until he grew accustomed to sleeping on the porch of Lula's house.

Every Winter the adults went to Homassasa, Florida, fishing. The accommodations were primitive, and one year they had to share a bath, which Mother and Daddy had to go through the Sparks' room to reach. Mother spent most of the night going back and forth to fetch water in a pitcher for a bird bath. Each time, Jonnie would say, "Turn over, Bob, Ethel's passing through."

Bobby Sparks was in the coal, ice, and ice cream business, and he brought Martha and me our first Eskimo Pies. When I was about nine years old I had a birthday party, to which I invited the three Smith boys from across the street and Horace Wright. Martha was the only girl. For dessert, Bobby sent a huge tray of fruits such as grapes, bananas, oranges – all made of ice cream or milk sherbert in different flavors. After dessert, we retired to the front yard to catch lightning bugs, which we put in glass jars with perforated tin tops. Anyone who has ever caught lightning bugs will recall the smell.

Occasionally Mother and Daddy took Martha and me to Atlanta on the train. We boarded the train at the big terminal station at the foot of Cherry Street, and when we passed the Vineville station, Bobby would be on the platform waving. A lot of fun went out of our lives when Bobby died in 1932, at the age of sixty. Jonnie continued to call on Mother frequently in the forties, much to Daddy's annoyance. Whenever he saw her approaching he would say, "Here comes that damned old Sparks woman," and move to the rear of the house. When Hazel's husband, Parker Highsmith, died in 1945, Hazel and her two sons moved back to Macon. Hazel herself died of cancer in 1952, leaving Jonnie to raise the boys. Jonnie kept her slender figure but was careless in her dress. Mother used to say, "The Lord did so much for Jonnie, she should do her part." Until Mother became bedridden, she and Jonnie would sit on the front porch drinking Coca-Cola, poured over real ice and served with cheese biscuits or tomato sandwiches, depending on the time of day. Once confined to her bed, Mother refused to see any of her old friends again. Recently, when I went to Riverside Cemetery to get vital statistics, I stopped at the office and asked where the Robert Sparks lot was located. The man in charge took me to the door and pointed, "See where that power lawnmower is, the Sparks lot is right there." I said, "Suppose the next time I come here the lawnmower is not there, how will I find the Sparks' lot then?" The man didn't even smile, but I thought I heard Bobby chuckling.

The Newspaper Crowd

After Mother and Daddy moved into the big house in 1910, they entertained a great deal and took an active part in Macon's social activities, but after our return from Europe in 1926 they began to see fewer and fewer people, "and them few seldom," except in Asheville, where guests filled the house all summer. I think Mother and Daddy were bored. They were certainly ready for the newspaper crowd. Mr. W. T. Anderson was more than a newspaper man, he was a public figure. In 1914 he became owner, editor and publisher of The Macon Telegraph; and in 1930 he bought the Macon News, thereby owning, with his brother Peyton Anderson, all of Macon's newspapers. From then until 1940 the Telegraph and News enjoyed a golden age. The Andersons employed a group of journalists unequaled in the Southeast, headed by Mark Etheridge as managing editor of The Telegraph. W. T. Anderson married Elizabeth Griswold Anderson, whom my mother called Cousin Lizzie although not kin.

I first encountered Mr. Anderson during the Macon Centennial, in 1923, when he served as master of ceremonies at the celebrations in Central City Park. Without benefit of electrical amplification, his booming bass voice carried to every seat in the grandstand. Only Creature's Band was louder. He was already a crusader for causes, alerting the public to the dangers of soil erosion, and the advantages of growing soy beans. Above all, he did everything in his power to benefit the Black population, especially in the field of education. One day in the late twenties Daddy brought Mr. Anderson home to dinner. When he saw the Persian rugs, he lay down on the floor, in front of the living room fireplace, and rolled like a barrel all the way into the dining room. He was a large man who loved to eat. A friend's cook once said of him,

"That man eats like there ain't no God." He became a frequent guest at our house. Sometimes he invited himself, calling to say, "Miss Ethel, tell Lula to put my name in the pot." He ruined so many neckties spilling soup, it became a regular joke. Only once was he late to dinner. At 2:15 Mother said, "We won't wait any longer," and started for the dining room. When we got there Mr. Anderson was already in his regular seat, wearing a golfer's rubber cape. We all liked Mr. W. T. immediately, especially Martha and I since we regarded him as on our side politically. Through him we met the famous Susan Myrick! She came to the house one afternoon to pick Daddy up, before meeting Mr. Anderson at the paper. When she arrived, Martha and I were lying on the floor of the balcony overlooking the front stairs. From that vantage point we could see reflected in the mirror anyone entering the front door. She was wearing boots and riding habit. We were as thrilled as if we had seen Priscilla Dean. Soon she was a regular guest. When some of Mother's friends expressed surprise, Mother told them, "It's all right. Cousin Lizzie receives her."

Several times we had Sunday dinner with the Andersons in their home in Shirley Hills: Mother, Daddy, Martha, and I. It was there that I first heard the magical sound of Mary Garden's voice, but that is a story for a later chapter.

Susan Myrick had been for several years athletic instructor at Lanier High School for Girls, before joining the staff of The Macon Telegraph. At first she ran an advice to the lovelorn column – called Fanny Squeers. Later she worked on the paper in many different capacities, but was best known as farm editor. Her friends called her "The Blue Lupin Queen." She was not a beauty, but had a good figure. Her skin had been exposed to too much sun and rough weather. She was an interesting woman, well read, loads of fun, and full of energy.

At Daddy's request, Mother had a formal dinner party for Mr. Anderson, Marsh and Willie Snow Ethridge, and Sue Myrick. She used silver place plates, silver goblets, and the finest china and crystal. Lula oudid herself in the kitchen, and I was in charge of drinks. A good time was had by all, but Mother was fearful of what Willie Snow might report in her column, despite Mr. W. T.'s promises. She did not write about the dinner party but did quote my father from time to time, always out of context. After leaving The Telegraph the Ethridges moved to St. Louis, where Mark was editor of The Louisville Courier Journal, one of the most respected papers in the country. The last time I saw them was at the home of Terry Murray in Brooklyn Heights. Mark had retired and they lived in Scarsdale. Willie Snow continued to write books about her experiences. One day she was walking to the station to catch the train when she realized she probably wouldn't make it. She went up to a well-dressed woman getting into a car and introduced herself, adding "I have an appointment with my editor in Manhattan and I'm afraid I'll be late. Will you please give me a lift to the station?" The woman asked what time her appointment was, and when Willie Snow told her, said, "Hurry, you can make it," and drove off. But my favorite story is one Mark liked to tell. One day when he was trying to read, Willie Snow said, "I'd like to give a party for all my friends, but I would have to invite at least a hundred people." Mark stopped her and said, "You don't know a hundred people. If you can list the names of one hundred people you know personally, I'll give you ten dollars." That evening Willie Snow said, "Mark, you owe me ten dollars; here's a list of a hundred people and I know them all." He willingly gave her a ten dollar bill, and it was several days before she realized that she had been tricked into silence for a whole afternoon. They were a study in contrast: Mark was dignified and quiet; Willie Snow was loud and funny. Daddy thought her very funny, as did her many readers; but I don't think Mother was amused. She always referred to her three children as "the unholy three."

Mother became devoted to Susan Myrick. After she seldom entertained anyone except Adele Smith or Angus Domingos, she was always delighted when Susan dropped by for a Coca-Cola. "The Myricks are highly regarded in Milledgeville, which, as you know, is much older than Macon." That was a line fraught with meaning. After Martha's death, Susan purchased what remained of her house on Oglethorpe Street, facing Tatnall Square. The inside was gutted but the brick walls remained intact. Susan engaged a good contractor to restore the house, and that is where she lived after her retirement, painting watercolors. I called on her once when I was in Macon, and was surprised to learn that she had turned into a conservative, bigoted old lady. I prefer to remember her as a leader of the avant-garde and one of the first liberated women in Macon. Margaret Mitchell said of her, "She totes her own load."

Harry Stillwell Edwards[7]
23 April 1855 – 22 October 1938

Among Mother and Daddy's friends, I have deliberately saved until last Harry Stillwell Edwards, Macon's most acclaimed writer since Sidney Lanier. He was a close friend from almost the beginning of the century until his death in 1938. The relationship was such that he insisted on being called "Uncle Harry," and always addressed my father as "Nephew." Emily, Martha, and I all called him "Uncle Harry." His article, entitled "Dreamer," which appeared in *The Macon Telegraph* on Sunday, June 8, 1919, is the best thing ever written about my father.

Harry Stillwell Edwards was born in 1855. He married Miss Roxie Lane in 1881. In 1885, Mr. A. R. Lamar was editor in chief of the

[7]For information on the life and achievements of Harry Stillwell Edwards, I am deeply indebted to The History of Macon, Georgia, by Ida Young, Julius Gholson, and Clara Nell Hargrove; from the Press of Lyon, Marshall & Brooks, Macon, GA, 1950.

Telegraph and Messenger, and Edwards associate editor. They wrote such brilliant and vigorous editorials that the *Telegraph and Messenger* became one of the leading newspapers in the South. In March, 1896, Harry Stillwell Edwards won the $10,000 prize in The Chicago Record mystery story compilation, with Sons and Fathers, which he wrote in forty days. The novel created a sensation. Most of the prize money was spent on bicycles for every member of his large family. In 1887, Mr. J. H. Campbell bought controlling interest in The Telegraph and the paper became more conservative. Lamar and Edwards both resigned.

In 1900, the nomination of Mr. Edwards for Macon postmaster was bitterly opposed by Senator A. O. Bacon. Objections were finally withdrawn and the appointment was confirmed. At some point, when he was out of office, Daddy took him to the White House to see President Theodore Roosevelt, hoping to get him reappointed. The president was sympathetic to their request and gave them a card of recommendation, addressed to the appropriate members of his administration. While they were in the oval office the president asked, "Massee, what line of business are you in?" Daddy informed him that he was building a hydroelectric dam on the Ocmulgee River to provide cheap electricity in central Georgia. President Roosevelt led them to a window and pointed to a young couple playing tennis. "That young man playing tennis with my daughter Alice is from Macon, Georgia." It was North Winship. Some years later, Daddy encountered Teddy Roosevelt at a fund raising party in Atlanta. Mr. Roosevelt came up to him and said, "Massee, how's the dam?" That was a remarkable feat of memory considering the number of people Roosevelt met every year, and there were no aides then to provide such information; anyhow, he was no longer the president of the United States.

Harry Stillwell Edwards was still postmaster during the construction of the new Federal building and remained in office until 1913, when President Woodrow Wilson replaced him, on the advice of Senator Bacon.

President William Howard Taft visited Macon in November 1909. According to my father, Judge Felton, Harry Still Edwards, himself, and a Black ex-senator from reconstruction days were the only registered Republicans in Bibb County. Nevertheless, President Taft was warmly received and given an elaborate meal at the residence of Judge C. L. Barlett. Judge Felton, Mr. Edwards, and my father were supposed to ride with the president in an open carriage with two facing seats. When President Taft and Judge Felton were seated there was no room left, so Daddy and Mr. Edwards had to follow in another carriage. Taft and Felton each weighed 320, and Daddy was not far behind. Only Mr. Edwards was slender.

Harry Stillwell Edwards' popularity as a novelist continued. In 1907, The White Spider was published. Princess Gagarin, wife of the

Russian Consul General in Beirut, was granted permission to translate the novel into Russian. Mr. Edwards was elected to membership in the National Institute of Arts and Letters in 1912, believed to be the only Georgian so honored.

In 1914, Edwards opened the Holly Bluff Country Club at White Elk, a year after the Idle Hour Country Club opened at its present location. The Holly Bluff property was chosen in 1917 as the site of Camp Wheeler, for training soldiers. Mrs. Ellen Washington Bellamy appointed Harry Stillwell Edwards to the board of trustees to control the planning and building of the Washington Memorial Library – actual construction commenced in 1917.

For many years, Edwards continued his column at the paper, called "Coming Down My Creek," but his most popular story remains Eneas Africanus, which has gone through many editions and is still in print. When a group of bankers who were interested in investing money in the Jackson Dam project asked my father how they could obtain copies of Eneas Africanus, Daddy took them to J. W. Burke & Company, where they bought many copies. One of the bankers asked if there was any possibility of getting the author to sign his copy. Seeing Edwards walking on the other side of Cherry Street, Daddy said, "I think that can be arranged." The author stood signing books, leaning on the fender of Daddy's car. Later Henry Ford was quoted as saying it was his favorite American story. Shortly before the death of my sister Emily, she gave her last signed copy of Eneas Africanus to two friends of mine from London who were visiting Macon for the first time. Periodically, there is talk of a Broadway musical based on the story.

When I was taken as a child to see Harry Stillwell Edwards, parts of a wooden bridge soldiers had built across the large lake at Holly Bluff still remained. Uncle Harry always came down to the dam even when it was only Fraulein, the chauffeur, and myself. He made me feel he was just as glad to see me as he would have been had it been my father. Near the end of his life, he posed for a clay bust by Marshall Daugherty. I consider it the best of Marshall's bronze portraits of prominent Maconites.

My father was never a joiner but was once persuaded to attend three meetings of the Rotary Club on a trial basis. At the first meeting, Mr. W. D. Anderson spoke on good citizenship; at the second, Bill Dunwody spoke on salesmanship; and at the third, Harry Stillwell Edwards was blackballed when his name was submitted for membership. Daddy never went back.

Both my parents had many friends; others will appear in subsequent chapters.

NEW YORK TRIPS

At least twice a year, Mother and Daddy traveled by rail to New York for shopping and theatrical entertainment. They stayed at the Holland House not only because it was conveniently located but because of the food, which Daddy thought the best in New York. Shopping centered around Altman's, on Fifth Avenue at 34th Street, and Lord & Taylor, farther up the Avenue – with visits to F. A. O. Schwartz for toys, after Martha and I had joined the family. Most people read the New York Times for the news, but my mother subscribed to the Sunday edition to follow the advertisements. When she arrived at Altman's, she was assigned a special clerk who guided her from one department to another, avoiding duplication of sales slips and shipping instructions. These women probably had far wealthier customers but they were devoted to my mother because of her kindness. On returning to Macon, Mother never failed to write the store manager complimenting certain sales persons. I have noticed that rich women pride themselves on how considerate they are to clerks, but I have known only two who actually were, my mother and Alice Astor. Which reminds me of the time someone said to Dorothy Parker, "You'll have to admit Clare Boothe [Luce] is kind to her inferiors," to which Mrs. Parker replied, "And where does she find them?"

While Mother was shopping at Altman's, Daddy was in the manager's office, swapping stories. Once he asked the manager to give him a letter of introduction to the manager of W. J. Sloane, "My wife wants some oriental rugs." The man pulled out a ledger to prove that all of Sloane's finest rugs were purchased from the Altman collection. "Stick with me, Mr. Massee, and I'll save you a lot of money." Daddy described what was needed for the big house, but it took Altman's about four years to acquire a matching set of rugs. They were all Persian Sarouk, dark blue with red and gold patterns. Only the rug for the library was different, with dark blue and gold designs on a Chinese red background. In addition to the four large rugs, there were those runners and an assortment of scatter rugs, all in matching colors.

Only Emily had the patience to accompany Mother to Lord & Taylor when she was buying gloves. She insisted that Emily bought gloves two sizes too large. On one trip, they took a taxi from the Biltmore Hotel to the end of the island because Mother had read about a place that cleaned long white evening gloves cheaper than in mid-town; at least that was Daddy's story, no matter how many times Mother protested that they cleaned them better downtown.

My father had two heroes, Teddy Roosevelt and Edward Henry Harriman, the financier and railroad magnate. One day when Daddy was in New York alone, on business, he was in the New York Stock Exchange when someone pointed out Mr. Harriman, so when he left,

Daddy followed at a respectful distance. At Maiden Lane, Harriman turned and entered a jewelry story so Daddy followed, curious to see what such a man would buy. Mr. Perry, co-owner of the shop, came up to Daddy and asked if he could help him. "Boots, I couldn't very well say I was following Harriman, so I bought a platinum and diamond horseshoe for your mother. She seemed to like it." I asked Daddy why he admired Mr. Harriman so much and he told me, "He bought up railroads, one by one, planning to turn them all over to the federal government. All utilities and public transportation should be government-owned." When Harriman died in 1909, his influence extended to over 60,000 miles of track, but his methods excited the bitterest criticism, culminating in a stern denunciation from President Roosevelt himself, in 1907. He was the father of William Averell Harriman (1891-1986), governor of New York and United States Ambassador to the Court of St. James.

Daddy bought so much jewelry, Mr. Perry arranged to sell him anything in the store at wholesale, plus 10 percent. The mark-up on jewelry is usually 100 percent or more.

After the Holland House closed, Mother and Daddy moved to the newly constructed Biltmore Hotel, which was conveniently located near the theatre district. I never tired of hearing Mother talk about the New York theatre she knew in the first quarter of the century. They saw everything short of Shakespeare and burlesque, even going over to see Henry Irving and Ellen Terry. Their preference was for "plays about our kind of people," which meant sophisticated drawing room comedy with John Drew, Henry Miller, a young John Barrymore, and above all, Ethel Barrymore. My mother thought her performance in Declasse' was the finest thing she ever saw in the theatre. They also went to see the meteoric Allah Nazimova in everything from *A Doll's House* to *Bella Donna,* before returning to Elsie Ferguson, the exquisite Billie Burke, and Grace George. Mother was so impressed with a gown Grace George wore she wrote the actress asking permission to have it copied. Miss George wrote her a charming note saying she would be flattered. Mother had Hickson copy the dress from her picture taken in the gown. Of course they went to see Maude Adams whenever she appeared, including Chanticleer, by mistake. After the performance, Daddy said, "Old Dear, you certainly can pick 'em." Another dreadful mistake was Maeterlinck's *The Blue Bird,* of which the young Tallulah Bankhead remarked, "There's less here than meets the eye." For melodrama they had Mrs. Leslie Carter and Olga Nethersole. Then there were the unique performances: Florence Reed in *The Shanghai Gesture,* Jeanne Eagles in *Rain,* Laura Hope Crews in *The Silver Cord,* and Guy Bates Post in *Omar The Tentmaker.* They particularly enjoyed George Arliss in *Disraeli,* Otis Skinner in *Kismet,* William Gillette in *Sherlock Holmes,* and George M. Cohan in anything. They watched young performers at the beginning of their careers: Ruth Chatterton, Leonore Ulric, Helen Hayes, Katharine Cornell, and Judith Anderson; but never forgot Julia Marlow in her pre-Shakespearean days, the enchanting Laurette Taylor, beautiful Jane Cowl, the great Pauline Lund,, or the Lunts. They seldom went to musicals unless to see Fritzie Scheff. Mother took pleasure in the fact that Ethel Barrymore, Nazimova, and she were born in the same year, 1879. Of all the distinguished performers in a later generation, my mother preferred Katharine Cornell, but Daddy didn't like her in *The Barrets of Wimpole Street.*

When Daddy was in New York alone on business he ate at various restaurants, including Rectors and Luchow, but when Mother was with him they always ate at the Holland House, later at the Biltmore. When people told him about some restaurant where the food was better than at the Crillon, the Rome Excelsior, or the Biltmore, he assumed they were not big tippers, or didn't know the difference.

Mother especially enjoyed the cold weather, even the snow. They both watched the growth of the city from 14th Street to 57th and beyond. When they got home there were stories to tell and gifts to distribute, and Grandpa Brown was waiting to hear Daddy tell about it all. Daddy once told me he wanted to move to New York but Mr. Brown talked him out of it.

ESCAPADES

It all happened in 1921 or 1922 when Dorothy Blount spent the winter in Macon with her aunt, Mrs. Walter Lamar. Her parents hoped that the formidable Miss Dolly would help keep Dorothy out of trouble. Dorothy had been married to a highly eligible young man in Baltimore, with the approval of both families. She was ravishingly beautiful, and as smart as she was good looking. She herself told Emily the details of the elaborate ceremony. After the marriage vows, the bride and groom walked down the aisle, down the church steps, and onto the sidewalk. Suddenly, Dorothy turned and addressed the gathering, "I hope you're all satisfied," and sped away in a waiting taxi, without the groom. The marriage was annulled.

Annie Camille Lamar, who will figure prominently in this story, was the great-niece of Mr. Walter Lamar. She and her siblings lived with their grandmother, Mrs. Jack Lamar. Around the time of Dorothy Blount's marriage, Annie Camille ran off to Jacksonville, to marry Garnet Star, taking her friend, Kitty Birdsey, as chaperon. Mr. Warren Roberts was her uncle by marriage. His wife, Camille Lamar Roberts—another great beauty—was the niece of Mr. Walter Lamar. Annie Camille's marriage ended in annulment, or divorce. One can guess why she was not included in Mrs. Lamar's plans for Dorothy. Annie Camille was only one of the many reasons why my father said, "When Mrs. Jack

Lamar gets to heaven, Job will get up and let her sit down."

When Dorothy arrived in Macon, Miss Dolly made elaborate plans to keep her busy. Lula Comer was engaged for French lessons for Dorothy, Emily Massee, Anna West, and Queenie Wise. Professor Joseph Robinson, who taught English at Mercer University, was employed to give weekly classes in modern poetry, to which a wider audience was invited. All their combined efforts were to no avail.

Virginia Massee entertained a group of young ladies at bridge, in Dorothy's honor. One foursome comprised Dorothy Blount, Annie Camille Lamar, Genna Low, and Emily Massee. Throughout the game, whenever Dorothy and Annie Camille were not partners, they whispered to each other. Genna and Emily had no idea what they were whispering about. The next day, half of Macon knew.

Dorothy Blount, Annie Camille Lamar, Terry Adams, Ben Willingham, and Jim Harbin ran off together. No one ever found out who was paired with whom. It did become known that Jim Harbin was the odd man out, but not why he was included in the escapade at all. Terry Adams was the most attractive of the four surviving Adams brothers. Mamie Adams, who subsequently married Bobo Murray, was his only sister. His brother Bill later married Virginia Massee. At the time of the runaway, Terry was married to Ann Willingham. Ben Willingham was the husband of Anne Townshend Bowdrie Willingham, and the brother-in-law of Terry. (Years later, Ben Willingham, Jr. referred to his mother as Mrs. Alphabet Willingham.) Jim Harbin was a ringer for the Mercer football team. Jack Massee had once locked up Virginia to prevent her from eloping with Jim Harbin.

Once again, Warren Roberts was sent to bring the culprits home. This time he elicited the help of Dr. John A. Harris, Mr. Walter Lamar's brother-in-law, a remarkable man in his own right. He lived in New York City and had devised the first electric traffic signal. At his own expense, he installed his signals on Fifth Avenue. As a result, he was awarded a contract for signals at all intersections on important streets. The Harris device was operated from a wooden tower ten or twelve feet high, where a traffic cop ordinarily stood. The operator manipulated the red and green lights in accordance with the specific needs of ongoing traffic.

Mr. Roberts learned from the ticket seller that the fugitives were headed for New York. That is all he had to go on. He and Dr. Harris telephoned every respectable hotel until they located the youngsters, and persuaded them to return home. I take for granted Dr. Harris' authority but feel certain that it was Mr. Warren Roberts, with his extraordinary tact and diplomacy, who achieved this brilliant stratagem. He had plenty of experience with Annie Camille and would have more with Valeria, her beautiful younger sister, when she ran away to get married and married the best man instead of the groom.

Ann Willingham Adams and Anne Townshend Willingham, the deserted wives, had both sworn they would never speak to their errant husbands again, but welcomed them back with open arms upon their return. Each husband explained to his wife that he had gone along just to look after his brother-in-law.

Years later, Dorothy Blount, who in her youth could have had almost any man in Georgia, or Maryland, married or single, was reduced to marrying Emory Winship, who was old enough to be her father. Mr. Winship had inherited a portion of his first wife's considerable fortune. Subsequent scandals are best left buried in old newspaper files.

Annie Camille later married a nephew of Mr. Walter Lamar.

Any resemblance to characters in Cosi fan tutte is purely coincidental.

PAPPY AND MARIE BATES IN MACON

I don't know exactly when Pappy and Marie Bates moved from Marshallville to Macon, but it must have been around 1900, when Daddy started the Bibb Brick Company. Pappy was the head bookkeeper for more than twenty-five years. At the office, he wore a lightweight black jacket and a skullcap and sat on a high stool before a huge slant-top desk. The ledger books were kept in a walk-in iron vault behind him.

As far back as I can remember, Pappy and Marie had an apartment on the second floor of the Old Cannonball House on Mulberry Street, which was conveniently located near the Methodist Church. Pappy had regained his religion and Marie had never lost hers. His knowledge of the Bible was prodigious. Once Daddy disagreed with a friend over the source of some quotation. Daddy maintained it was from the Bible; his friend felt equally sure it wasn't. So he told Pappy to stop work and find the quotation, even if he had to re-read the Bible from cover to cover. That wasn't necessary. Pappy found the passage with little difficulty and proved Daddy right.

Martha and I enjoyed going to see the Bateses at the Cannonball House. We were allowed to play with their stereoscope, for which there were many pictures of scenic wonders and famous monuments. Pappy and Marie must have been of my grandparents' generation, and were probably in their late seventies when we were five or six. They were certainly the oldest people we knew, and they looked it. Marie was covered with tiny wrinkles and wore clothes that had not been fashionable since 1900. All of her dresses had high collars, lots of lace, and swept the floor. She favored lavender, gray, and white. Like Pappy, she was tall and very thin. Both were humorless, although they seemed to enjoy Daddy's funny stories, probably like children, for the wrong reasons.

Whenever Mother and Daddy went to New York, which they did every winter for two or three weeks at a time, Pappy and Marie Bates came to stay with Martha and me, and to look after the household. Their duties were rather light since Mae Farmer, a qualified trained nurse in starched white uniform and cap, also moved in for the duration, in case Martha or I got sick. I don't think Marie had anything to do with the actual running of the house, which ran itself, so thorough was Mother's planning. Pappy handled the finances, with the same meticulous care he lavished on the books at the brickyard. Lula was always careful to provide him with fresh lettuce, which he ate for breakfast, and to save his dinner until the evening meal, since he didn't come home from the office in the middle of the day. When Mother and Daddy returned from one trip, Pappy said to Daddy, "Jordan, your cook took such good care of me while you were away, I took the liberty of giving her a substantial tip. I hope you don't mind."

"Of course not, Pappy, I think that was very nice of you; and I'm sure she appreciates it."

When Daddy went over Pappy's expense account, he found the following item: "Tip to cook...$5.00."

During that visit, Martha had a crying spell because, she said, "I'm so lonesome." When Miss Farmer pointed out that in addition to herself, Mr. and Mrs. Bates were there, and numerous servants, whom she called by name, one by one, Martha sobbed, "I want my own people."

Meanwhile, Anna Lockhart and I went about our daily routine in perfect harmony. I knew that Mother and Daddy would be back soon, bearing gifts from Schwartz and, especially for me, six pink bananas, a rare and exotic fruit that I thought grew in New York. Of course, I was not allowed to eat one unless it was scraped. Until we children were grown, Mother continued to believe that bananas were inedible unless scraped. When Emily went off to school in Baltimore, she was admonished to eat no bananas unless they were scraped. Consequently, she ate no bananas.

I recall only one occasion when I created a disturbance during my parents' absence. One night at supper Miss Farmer said I couldn't have any more cheese straws. I stated emphatically, "My mother begged me to eat cheese straws at night."

Marie Bates was hard of hearing, which sometimes made communication difficult. One day I was over at the Wrights' house playing with Horace, with Walter Odom to keep an eye on me. Although I had been told to be home by five o'clock, Horace and I were having such a good time his mother suggested I phone Mrs. Bates and ask if I could stay a little longer. I got Marie on the phone but couldn't make her understand who I was or what I wanted. So I hung up and ran across the Moore's front yard to our house. When I got there, Marie was still talking on the phone, hearing nothing.

The most memorable of their sojourns was when they took Martha and me to the state fair at Central City Park. The annual fair was a great event in our lives. Mother and Daddy usually took us, but in their absence, Pappy and Marie Bates went in their place, which must have been a great relief to my mother who hated the crowds and the dust. We were also accompanied by Daddy's chauffeur and Marylu Tanner, the replacement for Anna Lockhart, who was recuperating from a broken leg. We had a wonderful time, all of us.

A singular item on that expense account caught Daddy's eye immediately: "Merry-go-round...$22.00." Pappy explained, "I couldn't let the children ride alone, so I had Marylu go with them. They rode for a couple of hours before I could get them off."

I think Mother and Daddy derived as much pleasure from that twenty-two dollars as Martha and I did, to say nothing of Marylu.

In later years, when Pappy and Marie Bates were too old to assume the responsibility, Beulah Wright Fagin came to stay with us whenever Mother and Daddy were in New York. She was a dear sweet soul. We were happy with her and she was in Paradise.

The Jordan Massees and Religion

"The Almighty has His own purposes. ... Men are not flattered by being shown that there has been a difference of purpose between the Almighty and them."
—Abraham Lincoln

Daddy and Religion

I don't think Daddy had any religion at all, although his ethical values were extraordinarily high. He may have felt that there was a divine will in the universe, but without comprehensible purpose. If the will of God was beyond human understanding, why bother about it. His opposition to organized religion was total. He maintained that the biggest crooks sang the loudest on Sunday. He knew them.

As a child he must have sat through many a long and tedious sermon in the Baptist Church his parents forced him to attend, but that is not what he chose to remember. There was one incident at church he did recall with pleasure. The wife of the preacher wanted a new hat decorated with a long white ostrich plume, which she had seen in Macon. Her husband told her that the hat was too expensive, he could not possibly afford it. So she sold their old mahogany bureau and with the money bought the hat. The next Sunday she purposely arrived late to church in order to make a grand entrance. Her husband stopped in the middle of his sermon, and said, "Ladies and gentlemen, please rise; here comes the lady with the bureau on her head."

Sometime later, another Baptist preacher pointed out to his congregation how wise it was of God to create all of us different. "If we were all alike, every man would want my wife," he explained with obvious pride. An old man in a back pew called out, "If they wuz all like me, none of them would have her."

Preachers came and left with great frequency in those days. Maybe they still do. My grandfather invited one of them, who was a good friend, to Sunday dinner. "Well, O. J.," he replied, "I'll be pleased to accept unless one of my rich parishioners invites me." They both knew it was a joke, but my father didn't and resented the remark.

A visiting preacher came to dinner one Sunday. As in all rural communities the food was all placed on the overloaded table and passed from one diner to another if out of reach. There was always plenty of everything. The preacher kept helping himself to the hard butter sauce, which was intended for the dessert, spreading it generously on one biscuit after another. Of course my grandmother was too polite to point out the error, and kept a stern eye on her five children to be sure there was no snickering. Finally, the preacher said, "Mrs. Massee, that's the sweetest butter I've ever tasted."

Lastly, there was a Baptist preacher in Marshallville who received a call from a much larger church in Macon. While he was in his study praying to the Lord for guidance, his wife was upstairs packing. Isn't that a metaphor for gender difference: the men always praying for divine guidance, while the women are upstairs packing?

Long after Daddy had left Marshallville, the Baptist Church burned to the ground. Grandmother Massee phoned Daddy at once. This was a call not from the church but from his mother and he responded as her favorite child. He took the church building committee to Vienna, where they saw a church they liked. He obtained the blueprints and found a good contractor. Then he donated enough brick and hollow tile for the building. I am sure that both parents were proud of their oldest son, Marion, who remained a pillar in the Baptist Church, but when they wanted help they turned to my father. When Daddy died we received a beautiful letter of condolence from the Baptist Church in Marshallville paying tribute to his generosity, which had not been forgotten.

As a little boy, Daddy went fishing one day and returned with a string of minnows. His mother, humoring the child, as parents are wont to do, said to him, "What kind of fish are these?" "Baptists," he replied. She inquired further, "Son, why do you call them Baptists?," and he answered, "Because they spoil so soon after taken out of the water." She wore him out.

When I was about that same age, Martha and I had a heated argument over religion. Being a tattletale, she ran to Daddy screaming, "Jordan doesn't believe in God!" Although he didn't seem especially concerned, he told her, "Then he's a damned fool," and went on reading his afternoon paper. The incident tells us little if anything about his religion, but much about his attitude towards his children.

My Mother and the Church

Like my father, Mother was brought up a Baptist, but she never liked that denomination. She felt that religion was a very private matter and that any public expression was distinctly in bad taste. However, she was far more tolerant towards other people's religious practices than my father was. After she got married she went to her father, in trepidation, and announced, "Papa, I have never been happy in the Baptist Church; I wish to become an Episcopalian," and waited for the anticipated explosion. To her surprise, he replied, quite calmly, "Daughter, I think that is a wise decision. You will like the Episcopalians: they have almost no religion at all."

She joined Christ Church, where she remained, at least nominally, a member for the rest of her life. Long after the church had stopped having private pews, with each family's name engraved on a brass plaque, she continued to sit in the same place and took a dim view of any outsider who invaded her pew. Every year she made a substantial contribution, which my father paid quite willingly until the church started asking for a definite commitment in advance, like income tax today. He resented that.

I don't know how it was before I was born, but when I was growing up, Mother attended church regularly only during Holy Week.

What did she really believe? With the passing of the years, she cared less and less for the church as an institution and disapproved of every effort to modernize the Episcopal Church. She was not wedded to the past, but she thought that the church, like the theatre, was better in the old days. She was neither High Church nor Low Church, and was not attracted to the Church of England. She agreed with her own church on such matters as divorce, but only because the church agreed with her. Yet, she believed in transubstantiation. She loved the ritual of the church, so long as it remained strictly impersonal. She certainly denied the authority of the church. As a grown woman she had chosen the Episcopal Church because it provided a dignified way to be christened, confirmed, married, and buried, although any personal reference to the deceased, in the burial service, was offensive.

She felt that religion was primarily a matter of faith, not dogma, and that all rational explanations were futile. Hers was an attitude of resignation more than acceptance. Only once did I ever hear her question the Will of God, and that was when her nephew Lawson Brown died. She kept asking, "Why? Why him, at his age?" I told her, "That way madness lies," and she said no more, although nothing had been resolved.

She was painfully aware of those less fortunate than herself. Her kindness and sympathy knew no bounds. My father helped everyone he could and left the rest to Teddy Roosevelt; while my mother lived by a standard she never demanded of anyone else. By being true to herself, she became quite unwittingly an inspiration to all.

Many people knew my father, and knew him well; whereas only a few intimate friends and members of the family ever really knew my mother, although she was widely admired and genuinely loved. Perhaps in the final analysis love is the highest form of knowledge.

The Second Generation Goes to Church

On Good Friday, Martha and I were given the choice of going to school or accompanying Mother to church. Given that choice I unhesitatingly opted for church. I had no idea the Seven Last Words would be so long. I spent most of Bishop Mikell's interminable sermon trying to figure out how so many words could be counted so few.

Martha and I were only required to attend Sunday school, although when Martha was big enough, she would often go to church with Mother, she was so reluctant to be parted for an hour or so. I started out at St. Paul's, which was only half a block from our house. Miss Theo Tinsley was my teacher. Every Sunday we were given a little four-page pamphlet containing a biblical story suitable for small children. Thanks to my nurse, Anna Lockhart, who read the story to me over and over during the week, I was letter perfect by the next Sunday. I liked the stories of the Garden of Eden and of Noah and the Flood, but I took a dim view, even then, of Abraham and the sacrifice of his son, Isaac. All of it seemed very remote and not very romantic. Anna's zeal extended far beyond the stories we were given to study. When barely four years old, I could recite the Lord's Prayer and the Twenty-Third Psalm without faltering. On our daily walks, Anna would stop people on the sidewalk to hear her little boy perform. I was a willing victim, not because I liked showing off in public, but because I wanted to please Anna and thereby receive my reward, usually a banana. Just before we got home, Anna would say, "Now if you tell your mother about that banana, she'll punish you, then I'll punish you again." I had no intention of revealing our secret since I knew that my mother thought bananas were bad for children, and that Martha got none.

One day Anna and I were half an hour late getting home from one of our excursions to Pleasant Hill. Dinner was already in progress.

Anna said to Mother, "Madam, don't be angry, I can explain. As we were coming down College Street, so many white ladies stopped us to admire the beautiful little boy, we couldn't get through the crowd." Daddy said, later, that when Mother heard that, she showed her eye teeth and all was forgiven. Anna always called me "King the Beauty," a nickname which haunted me in later years.

After Daddy had paid an especially large lawyer's fee, he announced one day during dinner that when I grew up he was going to send me to Harvard to become a lawyer. Well, that was too much for Anna, who was waiting on table. She chimed right in and said, "Oh! Mr. Massee, I always thought my baby would grow up to be a Baptist preacher." Obviously, neither had reckoned on the baby.

I remember very little about St. Paul's except for one stained glass window depicting the Holy Ghost as an angel with wings but no face. Instead of a head the figure had a disc, like a moon, without features. That enigma is still there.

After about a year, I was transferred to the Sunday School at Christ Church, where I was immediately promoted to a higher grade due to my advanced knowledge of the Bible. Anna walked me to church every Sunday morning, except in very bad weather, followed by Martha and her nurse. We had as little to do with them as possible. As soon as Sunday School was over, Anna and I walked to the Negro Baptist Church, on the corner of New Street and High Street, where we attended morning service for the grown-ups. In return for my patience and good behavior I was sometimes allowed to go up and down the center aisle with one of the silver plates, collecting nickels and dimes and quarters. The fact that Brother Ray was a deacon may have contributed to this special dispensation. Above all, I remember the "shouting" in the aisles when the more faithful were overcome with the Spirit of the Lord. I had never seen anything like that at St. Paul's or Christ Church, where religious fervor, if any, was more discreet. I also remember the glory of the singing, which was a far cry from the choir at Christ Church which consisted mainly of members of the Luther Williams family.

For years I thought I was the first integrated Southerner, until I learned that Emily had attended the same church with her nurse, Nancy, thirteen years earlier. Even as late as the thirties, an elderly woman would occasionally stop me on the street and say, "I know you. You used to take up the collection at my church when you were a little boy."

One such encounter was somewhat different. A very old woman stopped me in front of the little house on College Street. "Ain't you Mr. Massee's son?," she asked. When I acknowledged that I was, she continued, "Well, how is that pretty little blonde wife of yours?" I told her that she had confused me with Mr. Dave Massee's son, Drew, my first cousin, and added, "His wife is fine." I simply didn't have the heart to tell her that Drew had had five or six wives since that pretty little blonde she remembered.

PROMINENT MACON FAMILIES

The Callaways

My father always wondered how Merrel Price Callaway married three of the most beautiful women in Georgia. The answer was simple: he was very handsome and he was an aristocrat.

Merrel was born in a beautiful red brick house on Pine Street, a house in the Greek revival style of Bulfinch, which was not characteristic of Macon. Later the house became the entrance to the Middle Georgia Hospital, eventually to be torn down when the hospital was enlarged. When he married Annie Crutchfield, the sister of Rose Crutchfield, they built an imposing house on College Street. It was said that when his wife died, Merrel was so grief-stricken he tried to throw himself into the open grave. Nevertheless, he soon married the exquisite Rietta Etheridge, one of my mother's closest friends. They sold the College Street house to Mr. James Porter and moved to New York, where Mr. Callaway became the executive vice-president of The Guaranty Trust Company, thereby proving that an honest man can become a successful banker. Rietta bore him three children, including my beloved Henrietta. Finally, in his old age, M. P., as his children affectionately called him, married Hazlehurst Plant, daughter of Robert Plant and widow of Wallace McCaw. In her youth she had been a great beauty, and at the time of her second marriage there were still traces of her patrician good looks. She was a devoted wife, and they lived in Savannah until his death in 1957. Mr. Callaway had given Henrietta his summer house in Darien, Connecticut, and visited his daughter there from time to time. Whenever Miss Hazlehurst measured her husband's medicine Henrietta was afraid she would get the wrong bottle since the old lady's eyesight was not what it once had been.

Merrel Callaway had two sisters: Kate Malone and Mary Callaway Jones, as she always referred to herself. Mrs. Malone taught me in the fourth grade at Gresham School—pronounced Gres-sam by the old-timers. She was very strict and consequently a very good teacher. Mary Callaway married Dr. Frank Jones, a leading chiropractor, and they lived in Clinton, Georgia, in Lowther Hall, the most beautiful of the Daniel Pratt houses in the Milledgeville area. Like my mother, Mary collected antiques at a time when most Southerners got rid of them. The furniture was all nineteenth century but was called Colonial. One of her most beautiful pieces was an elaborately carved four-poster bed, identical to my sister Emily's bed, evidently both were intended for some huge bedroom. Unfortunately, someone had cut four inches off the legs of Mrs. Jones' bed to make it more accessible. My Grandfather Brown had done the same with his own bed. Almost all the furniture was lost when Lowther Hall burned to the ground. After the loss of that wonderful house, Dr. and Mrs. Jones moved back to Macon, where Mary continued her research into the history of architecture in Central Georgia, barely recognizing the Johnston-Hay house built in the mid 1850s, which was already too late.

In addition to her pioneer work, Mary Callaway Jones joined forces with Dolly Lamar in her tireless effort to instill in every child a love and reverence of Robert E. Lee and Sidney Lanier. In that Great Cause she elicited the help of many friends, however unwilling, chief among whom was Alice Burden Domingos, who was too kind to say no. Mrs. Jones was instrumental in having a bronze plaque placed on the Second Street building where Lanier had practiced law in offices on the second floor. When the two ladies went down to unveil the plaque and place a floral wreath on the door, a distraught woman came running down the stairs screaming, "Don't put that up, he's not dead yet," referring to her husband, not the poet.

When Paul Bigelow first moved to Macon, Mary Callaway Jones offered to take us on a guided tour of Milledgeville, with Roy Domingos driving. She sat on the front seat directing Roy and lecturing Paul on life in the Old South. Whenever we passed a lone chimney near the highway, she turned to Paul and said, "Burned to the ground by the Yankees," as though he were personally responsible. However, it was not to Mrs. Jones but to Sue Myrick that Paul owed his first lesson in the preservation of architecture in Central Georgia.

Daniel Pratt (1799-1873) was a remarkable architect-builder from New Hampshire who built many houses in the Milledgeville area between 1821 and 1831, before moving on to Alabama where he designed numerous buildings in what was to become Prattville. All of his houses were in the neoclassical style popular in New England early in the century. For a history of several of these houses, see *Antiques Magazine,* September 1972.

Dr. L. C. Lindsley, who taught chemistry at Georgia State College for Women, in Milledgeville, was the brother-in-law of Sue Myrick. He was obsessed with the architecture of Pratt and eventually owned three houses he designed: Westover, where he and his family lived; the Gordon-Blount house, near Haddock; and a third house, nearer Milledgeville. He had three little girls and said he would leave each of them a Pratt house. Alas, it was not to be.

One hot Sunday afternoon, Sue drove Paul and me over to see Westover, which Dr. Lindsley was slowly and laboriously restoring himself by hand. He had just spent his entire salary from the preceding year acquiring two period chandeliers for the ballroom, and, according to Sue, could not afford to live in the house for another twelve months.

The ballroom was the first room I had ever seen that had been stripped down to the original paint, revealing the marbleizing and artificial woodgraining. All the rooms were painted in bright colors, not the expected white. When we were there, the Lindsleys were living in the slave quarters to the rear of the big house, a one-story brick building with dirt floors. There were no screens on the doors and the chickens wandered in and out as they chose. Dr. Lindsley explained that he could not move back into the main house until the children were old enough to be taught to keep their dirty hands off the walls and woodwork. When we left, Paul said, "That's the best introduction to Faulkner anyone could ever have."

Subsequently, Westover burned, and, after Dr. Lindsley's death, the Gordon-Blount house was sold to Mrs. William N. Banks, who moved it approximately a hundred miles to its present location near Newnan, Georgia. Except for an inappropriate colonnaded portico on what used to be the rear, it is the most beautifully restored and furnished house this side of Charleston.

The remarkable Mary Callaway Jones collection of photographs of Central Georgia architecture, containing many pictures of buildings no longer in existence, is now housed in the Washington Memorial Library in Macon.

NUTS PER CAPITA

Andrew Lyndon and I never tired of swapping stories about eccentrics. I maintained that Macon had produced more nuts per capita than any other town or city in the United States. I had to admit that we knew more about Macon and its skeletons in the closets than about other parts of the country. Everyone knows that the Deep South and New England encouraged individuality more than other regions. Only recently has conformity become the norm in all parts of the country. Now it's difficult to distinguish one rebellious youth from another. The same role models prevail everywhere; but it was not always so. There are more diverse groups than there used to be, but within each group the individuals are all alike. Perhaps differences are more subtle than in earlier times. There is a new trend to maintain, or revive, ethnic differences, but these are all group differences, not individual.

In Macon's past, the evidence of strong individuality is overwhelming. Just a few years ago, I heard a story that confirmed my opinion. I could hardly believe that I hadn't heard it before, nor had Andrew. Emily and Roy Domingos both insisted they thought we already knew the story, which goes as follows:

Mr. and Mrs. E. Y. Mallory, Sr. lived in a large house on Vineville Avenue, near the home of Richard Burden. The Mallory children and the Burden children played together. As girls, Alice Burden (Mrs. I. L. Domingos) and her sister Octavia Burden (Mrs. Tom Stewart) were allowed by the Mallory children to peep through the key hole of the secret bedroom in the Mallory house. That room was kept locked at all times and only Mrs. Mallory had a key. Once a week she would let herself in to dust the furniture and change the bed linens. Later, Mrs. Domingos and Mrs. Stewart discovered that the room was kept in readiness for the second coming of Christ. Unfortunately, no one seems to have found out how the Mallorys knew that the Messiah would appear in Macon and take up residence in their home, but how happy they must have been in their private knowledge.

The case of Mrs. Scott, a Holy Roller, is simpler. Her contact with the Holy Family was direct and frequent. The local branch of this strange religious sect was centered in Cross Keys, on the outskirts of Macon. When I was a child, there were still houses and public buildings there with large crossed keys painted or embossed on the eaves, which I found puzzling since I thought the keys of St. Peter belonged to the Pope, but such is the universality of Christian symbols. Every Saturday afternoon a group of Holy Rollers would gather on the corner of Third Street and Cherry to preach in unknown tongues. Sometimes they were joined by Rufus Mosely, Macon's only genuine saint, but more of Mr. Mosely in another chapter.

Mrs. Scott owned and operated Lakeside Amusement Park, which was located just beyond Cross Keys. It was very popular with Maconites for swimming and boating during the long, hot summers. In the late 1920s, only a few adventurous males swam publicly in topless bathing trunks, in the European fashion. By 1930 the custom prevailed, even in Macon. Sometime after that Mrs. Scott announced, on divine authority, that there was to be no more topless bathing at Lakeside. When the public transferred its patronage to Recreation Lake, the rival amusement park, Mrs. Scott announced that she had misinterpreted the divine order, which was intended to apply only to women. It was certainly a surprise to everyone that any woman had even contemplated going swimming at Lakeside topless.

I used to go swimming at Lakeside quite often with Susan Myrick. I had a new bikini, brief even by 1990 standards, which I had ordered from Hawaii. We decided I should launch it at Lakeside in order to shock the natives. We swam out to the last float, which is quite a distance from the shore and bathhouses, and were lying on the wooden float sunbathing when the lifeguard arrived in his row boat. He held up a pair of bathing trunks and said to me, "Mrs. Scott says for you to put these on, but don't take your own off. Put these on top of what you've got on now."

A year or two later Mrs. Scott was taken ill, so ill that her family had her hospitalized, which she protested vigorously since she didn't believe in doctors. She grew steadily worse in the hospital and refused to take any medicine. Finally, Mr. Mosely was called in by the family to reason with her. This was no time for unknown tongues. In his gentle manner, Mr. Mosely explained that God had created doctors to keep His children healthy, and that he felt sure Jesus would want her to take the prescribed medicine. Mrs. Scott sat up in bed and said, "Not at all. I spoke to Jesus this morning and He never once mentioned any medicine." To Mrs. Scott there was nothing strange or mysterious in the ways of God.

MISS DOLLY

On the death of his father, Walter Lamar inherited a fortune in stocks and bonds. At the end of the year he tried desperately to balance his accounts, which he found especially difficult since he had never done a day's work in his entire life. In frustration, he turned to his wife and said, "You know, Dolly, I'm almost sorry Papa died."

Mrs. Lamar, "Miss Dolly," was a highly visible character in Macon for two or three generations. She was extremely well born and highly ambitious. At a time when ladies in high society avoided publicity at any cost, Miss Dolly actively sought it. Somewhere around 1920 she appointed herself Queen of Macon Society and had friends on both newspapers to back her claim. She thought the title was hereditary. Dolly pleased herself, but didn't always please everyone else.

As President of the Daughters of the Confederacy, she was tireless in her efforts to keep alive the Southern mythology, especially if Robert E. Lee or Sidney Lanier was involved. Single-handedly she got the Georgia poet into the Hall of Fame. She refused to acknowledge that the Confederacy had lost the War Between the States or that society was any less grand in 1930 than in 1900. Truth to tell, high society in Macon died around 1927, but Miss Dolly was blissfully ignorant of the fact. With it all, she was a kind woman, despite a peculiar blindness to the needs of those who served her most loyally.

In the mid-twenties, when radio was in its infancy, Dolly was broadcast from Richmond. Mr. Lamar stayed at home glued to his new radio. After several preliminary speakers, a voice was heard introducing "Our Distinguished President of the Daughters of the Confederacy, Mrs. Walter D. Lamar, of Macon, Georgia." Miss Dolly rose to the occasion, and began, "Ladies and Gentlemen..." At that moment, Mr. Lamar turned off his radio and said, "Oh! shut up, Dolly!"

On another occasion, Mrs. Lamar was again asked to speak in Richmond, this time in commemoration of Robert E. Lee. Addressing a large audience, Miss Dolly began, "Ladies and Gentlemen, I am here to talk about the greatest of all Americans, Abraham Lincoln." There was a loud gasp from the audience before Miss Dolly realized her terrible mistake. The incident was reported in Time magazine under the heading "Slip of a lass," and much later was immortalized in the Modern Library edition of the writings of Dr. Sigmund Freud. In a footnote, Dr. Brill, the translator and editor, stated that in moments of stress, or under the influence of alcohol, sometimes the truth will out.

In the early thirties, Mr. and Mrs. Lamar made a trip to the Near East, where they acquired a beautiful oriental rug for their dining room. Miss Dolly was disappointed because their large table covered the center medallion of the rug, so she cut a small hole in the middle of the rug in order to run a wire up to a concealed light bulb under the table, thereby illuminating the medallion.

My father couldn't stand Mrs. Lamar and got tired of reading about her in the local newspapers. One day he phoned his friend, Mr. W. T. Anderson, who owned the Macon Telegraph, and said, "Bill, if you don't stop mentioning Charles Lindbergh and that damned old Lamar woman in every issue of your newspaper I'm going to cancel my subscription." Mr. Anderson replied, "I'm sorry, Jordan, but if I did I'm afraid I'd lose many more subscriptions." Both Lindbergh and Mrs. Lamar were good copy.

Once a week Mrs. Lamar and her mother, Mrs. Blount, played bridge with Mrs. Roland Ellis, Sr. and her mother, Mrs. Hobson. Mrs. Blount was always accompanied by her other daughter, Miss Fanny Blount, who was not overly bright. During one game, Fanny kept interrupting, "Mother, this morning...." Mrs. Blount kept saying, "Hush, Fanny, we're in the midst of a most difficult hand." Finally, when the hand was over, Mrs. Blount turned to her daughter, and said, "Now, Fanny, what were you trying to tell me?" Fanny replied, "I wanted to tell you that I went shopping this morning."

When the Community Concerts started coming to Macon, my sister Emily was active in selling subscriptions, which were all of five dollars for the entire series of four concerts. Fanny Blount's name was on Emily's list of calls. After Emily had explained what a wonderful series was being offered, Fanny said, "I'd like to join but I'll have to ask Mr. Scott if I can afford it." Mr. Scott was the long-suffering head of the trust department of the C & S Bank, which handled the Blount estate. Fanny was delighted when Mr. Scott approved the expenditure and she continued to subscribe every year, with Mr. Scott's consent.

After Emily gave up soliciting subscriptions, Ruth Grace took over her list. She called Miss Fanny and was informed, "Oh! no, I only buy tickets from Emily Massee." Ruth had to get Emily to phone Fanny and assure her that it was all right to place her subscription through Ruth. Fanny Blount was not the only subscriber who refused to buy tickets from anyone except Emily. Mr. Lamar was another.

Miss Fanny played the violin, after a fashion. Once she was invited to play for a club, of which she was a member in good standing. She asked my friend Roy Domingos to accompany her on the piano. Roy went dutifully every afternoon to practice. All through rehearsals, Fanny kept talking to herself, "Now, Fanny, you can do better than that. Yes, Fanny, that was pretty good." Anyhow, the musical interlude was well received.

After Mrs. Blount's death, Fanny continued to live in the large Blount house on Orange Street, quite alone, until Mrs. Clara Ophelia Bland, a poor relation, persuaded Fanny that she shouldn't live by herself, and moved in with her. Well, it proved to be a most unhappy arrangement. At times, the two ladies didn't speak. Miss Fanny bode her time until one morning just after breakfast, Clara Ophelia went out on the front porch to fetch the morning newspaper. Seizing the opportunity, Fanny locked her out. Clara Ophelia finally had to go to a neighbor's house and phone Mr. Scott, who came at once and talked Fanny into allowing her cousin back into the house. But the arrangement didn't last much longer.

For years, before all that happened, Clara Ophelia Bland augmented her meager income by selling Christmas cards. Every year she would call on my mother, who felt sorry for Clara Ophelia, but not sorry enough to buy the sentimental cards she sold. One year Mother was upstairs when Clara Ophelia arrived. She instructed Marylu, the maid, to tell Mrs. Bland that she was unable to see her, that she appreciated her calling, but had already ordered her cards from Tiffany. Marylu in conveying the message told Clara Ophelia, "Madam says she's sorry but she gets all her cards from Tifton."

Clara Ophelia also wrote poetry. When she had collected enough poems for a slender volume, she decided to publish them. She asked Professor Robinson, who taught English at Mercer University, to write an introduction. He told her that it would be more prestigious if she could get Dr. Fred Jones, the recently appointed head of the English Department, which she promptly did. Dr. Jones was too new in town to refuse.

No one seemed to know much about Mr. Bland, from whom Clara Ophelia had been divorced years before. As an old lady, Clara Ophelia attended some sort of function in Milledgeville at the Old Governor's Mansion, which was being used as the home of the president of the women's college. She found herself seated next to a stranger who introduced herself as Mrs. John Bland, to which Clara Ophelia responded, "I am the first Mrs. John Bland."

Some of the best stories about Dolly Lamar concern her running battle with the Schofields, who lived next door. These will be dealt with in the following chapter.

THE SCHOFIELD GIRLS

The Schofields
Riverside Cemetery Macon, Georgia:

Alonzo Dee Schofield
(January 3, 1857-November 8, 1936 married
Elizabeth Wilson Plant
(December 30, 1859-September 2, 1950)

Their two daughters:
Elizabeth Plant Schofield
(January 4, 1881-April 10, 1965)
Gladys Schofield
(June 17, 1893-August 18, 1976)

Even before they died, the Schofields were legendary, having attained the status of fictional characters. I have selected stories told to me by eyewitnesses, usually members of my own family, or Calder Payne, a frequent guest at "The Two Magnolias," the Schofield home on Georgia Avenue. Calder loved a good story but he loved the truth more. I am also indebted to Susan Myrick, who in a 1951 letter first informed me of the Alpha Delta Pi party. Before setting down these incidents, I had Henry Muecke, something of an antiquarian himself, drive me to Riverside Cemetery to obtain vital statistics. While Henry was parking his antique car, I proceeded to the Schofield burial plot where I was viciously attacked by hordes of fire ants. By the time Henry joined me, I was dancing an Irish jig on Elizabeth Schofield's grave. Even in death the Schofields brook no invasion of their privacy.

It has been a long time since anyone knew the cause of the Schofield-Plant feud. My mother said the Plant girls of her generation were ignorant of the facts, too young to have been aware of what transpired between their father, Robert H. Plant, and his older sister Elizabeth Schofield. My father thought the trouble started when old Mr. Increase Cook Plant died in 1892. Apparently, Elizabeth thought her husband Alonzo Schofield should have been made president of at least one of Mr. Plant's banks, due to his business experience as founder of the Schofield Iron Works. The family thought otherwise, and Robert Plant succeeded his father as president of the First National Bank. I doubt that my father heard any part of the story from Mr. Schofield whom he disliked as much as he admired Mr. Plant. In any case, from the death of Increase Plant until the death of Gladys Schofield in 1976, no member of the Schofield family ever spoke to a Plant again. Not only did Mrs. Schofield break off relations with her brother, but with all Plants unto the third and fourth generation. I have already told how

Mrs. Schofield gave a lawn party at the time of her brother's funeral, a story which took forty years to verify. Even people who had reason to dislike the Schofields could be strangely reticent. It was one thing to repeat funny stories, another to reveal the awful truth.

After the death of Wallace McCaw, his widow Hazlehurst Plant McCaw eventually returned to Macon. Shortly thereafter she attended a dance at the Idle Hour Country Club, not unaware that the club house and golf course were built on the site of her father's stud farm and race track. Seeing Mrs. Schofield seated alone on a sofa, she sat beside her and introduced herself, "Aunt Elizabeth, I am Hazlehurst." Mrs. Schofield did not reply and turned her back on her niece. By that time talk of the Schofield malice was rampant, and I doubt that any other member of the Plant family risked being snubbed. They probably realized that life was more pleasant outside the inner circle.

It was a nuisance for any hostess to avoid inviting Schofields and Plants to the same party, but none admitted the inconvenience. As long as the old lady was alive, the three Schofields moved in a body and were so entertained.

The twenty years prior to Mr. Schofield's death in 1936 were an Indian summer for the Schofield family. Mr. Schofield had become a kindly old man, resigned to life with his wife and two daughters who doted on him. While no longer wealthy, they were able to maintain the house on Georgia Avenue with dignity and to entertain occasionally. They believed their home was the hub of Macon society, unaware that no one else shared their faith. They even managed a trip abroad every two or three years, which added to their prestige, since prior to the second world war, only the Burkes went to Europe every summer. They always returned with something to startle the natives. One year it was a "Winker" for their motor, which was rather useless since they drove an open car and could indicate a turn to the right or left manually. Another year it was a motoring costume for Mr. Schofield, complete with goggles and a beret, the first seen in Macon outside the movies. The costume met with considerable approval at a time when the highways were mostly unpaved and the dust was horrendous. Inevitably they imported a Parisian taxi horn with a rubber ball which they squeezed vigorously when passing less fortunate motorists. From one trip they brought the Ellsworth Halls a gadget for measuring distances in centimeters; unfortunately, the Halls didn't own a car. It was the last period in which the Schofields could afford to be kind.

Their greatest import was Tommy France, said to be the first long-haired schnauzer in America. He was not allowed in the Pullman car, so Elizabeth and Gladys took turns riding from New York to Macon in the baggage car. Soon after his arrival in Macon, Tommy France acquired his own engraved visiting cards so that he could make formal calls with his mistresses. In this age of collectibles, one of those tiny cards would fetch a pretty penny.

On returning from one of their trips to England, Mrs. Schofield and Elizabeth referred to Gladys as "Glaaadys" (as in glade), rather than the familiar "Gladys" (as in glad). The new pronunciation was introduced at a formal party given in the Schofield home. No explanation was forthcoming, so it was assumed that the change was the result of research in the Old Country. Roland Ellis, Jr. lost no time in pointing out that "Glaaadys" is the Welsh word for pumphandle. "Glaaadys" immediately became "Gladys" again.

Once a week the Schofields drove to Atlanta to buy bread and other delicacies not available in the provinces. Today that would hardly be worth mentioning, but in the early twenties it was quite out of the ordinary.

After Mr. Schofield's death the trips to Europe were considerably curtailed. One summer the Schofields called to wish the Burkes, who were sailing from New York in a few days, "Bon Voyage." When the Burkes arrived at their hotel, they found a telegram from Mr. Burke, "The Schofields sailed from Hoboken this morning." No previous mention had been made of their impending voyage.

Elizabeth Schofield was a beautiful young woman and would probably have married well had she not been mean as hell. For several years she was a private secretary in Washington, an unusually good job for a woman at that time. After her father's retirement she returned to Macon to manage his affairs. Gladys was always homely, but she was a gifted landscape architect, responsible for some of Macon's loveliest gardens. During the war Elizabeth worked at the Warner Robins assembly plant, as did my sister Martha. Gasoline was strictly rationed but Bill DeVaughn managed to get extra rations for Elizabeth, thereby establishing a bond between the Schofields and the DeVaughns. Martha admired Elizabeth and Gladys for the way they worked so hard. Later, they admired Martha's courage in the face of greater adversity than their own.

Few people except the Massees and Maude Comer were permanently acceptable to the Schofields. It was easy for Maude, she was Gladys' best customer, and easy for Mother and Daddy because they almost never saw them. At the beginning of the season the Schofields called on Mother, leaving the appropriate number of cards. A few days later, Mother returned their call. She included Daddy's card although he never accompanied her. Around 1937, Mother decided the whole procedure was ridiculous and made no more calls except in case of death.

People knew they were being ostracized by the Schofields when invitations were not forthcoming, but they seldom knew why. The Jim Browns, the Walter Graces, and the Bobo Murrays were inseparable, and it was a great inconvenience when they were not in or out of favor at the same time. Finally, they were returned to favor simultaneously.

When Jim and Walter approached their hostesses at the end of the party, Elizabeth positively fawned on them. "It's so good to have you in the home again!," then turning to Emily and Ruth she added, "You, too." Bobo and Emily thought it better on the outside. It didn't seem to matter much to Mamie Murray. As the only daughter in the Adams family she had other things to worry about.

When I returned to Macon in the mid-forties, Maude Comer had a garden party at Mrs. Lassiter's, in the Jordan-Dunlap-Stevens home on College Street, now Beall's Inn. The guests were seated at small tables in the garden. This had the advantage that guests could avoid other guests if they chose. The food was excellent, the best in Macon. I sat with Mother and Harry Marshall. At one point, Mother said to me, "You must go over and pay your respects to Mrs. Schofield." When I introduced myself, Elizabeth said, "Mother, you remember Jordan." It was a statement, not a question, but obviously the old lady did not remember Jordan. By this time Elizabeth was beside herself. She ordered one of the waiters to fetch a chair for Mr. Massee, then continued addressing Mrs. Schofield, "Jordan has come back to us from New York." With a few more hints, the years of forgetfulness began to fade—too many, too quickly. "My husband always spoke so highly of Jordan," she mumbled. When I took my leave of the Schofields, Elizabeth said, "The home is closed for the summer, but we are receiving on the terrace." As I departed, Mrs. Schofield bowed in the direction of my mother. Heads of state do not visit other heads of state, which is why we have ambassadors.

Visits on the terrace were trying. Sitting under the scuppernong vine was to be devoured by mosquitoes. Like the Schofields, I am impervious to mosquito bites but poor Emily positively attracted insects of all varieties. Martha had to confess that she was dangerously allergic to mosquitoes, and after that the Schofield girls always sent her a small basket of freshly picked scuppernongs. Each guest was provided with two English biscuits, a slice of cheese, and a glass of homemade wine. It isn't possible to eat scuppernongs with decorum, but I can't remember what we did with the pulp.

A long-time friend of the Schofields was T. Willie Hooks who owned the Lanier Hotel, where he lived. Mr. Hooks had a drinking problem and whenever he was on a binge the hotel staff was instructed to say he was in Siberia. Friends knew what that meant and others didn't need to know. Once when he was in Siberia, a large churn of homemade strawberry ice cream arrived from the Schofields. One of the waiters put it in the hotel freezer, where it remained for a couple of weeks. When Mr. Hooks recovered, he was informed of the gift. "Oh, my God," he said, "Return the churn at once." Unfortunately, the churn was returned still containing the strawberry ice cream. T. Willie was excommunicated, and only his irrepressible high spirits got him back in the Schofields' good graces.

Several years later, Mr. Hooks gave himself a birthday party in the dining room of the Lanier Hotel. In the midst of the festivities, Mr. Robert Woodruff arrived on his way to Atlanta after a fishing trip in Florida. He knew nothing of the party and was embarrassed when T. Willie insisted he join the celebration. Having little choice, Mr. Woodruff graciously accepted. While another place was being set, T. Willie led him around the long table introducing him to the other guests. When they came to Gladys Schofield, he said, "Gladys, I'd like for you to meet my friend Bob Woodruff." Without even looking up Gladys replied, "I do not wish to meet Mr. Woodruff." Trying to treat it as a joke, Mr. Hooks continued with the introductions. When they came to Elizabeth Schofield, she stopped eating, put down her knife and fork, and said in a loud voice, "I do not care to meet Mr. Woodruff either. His father was a crook and I assume he too is a crook." Mr. Woodruff was the head of Coca-Cola and known to everyone present as one of the finest men in Georgia.

The day after the incident at the Lanier Hotel, Ruth Taylor called on Mother. It was a warm summer afternoon and we sat on the porch listening to Ruth describe the party. After she left, Mother said, "I can't believe Gladys and Elizabeth would do such a thing, they're such nice people." When Mother retired, I said to Martha, "Is she calling Ruth Taylor a liar?" Martha's reply summed it up, "Of course not, Mother knows the story is true but doesn't wish to acknowledge it."

I have written elsewhere of the elegance with which May and Martina Burke entertained. At one particularly lovely party, Elizabeth Schofield turned to Emily and said, "Our mother always said it's better to have white waiters in black jackets than black waiters in white jackets." Lady Bracknell had spoken.

Among the regulars always welcome at "The Two Magnolias" were William and Calder Payne, who kept the girls informed of the latest Macon gossip. Always welcome until Calder did something, or said something, that offended the Schofields and had to be excommunicated. Shortly thereafter, William called. When he entered the living room, Mrs. Schofield said, "Young man, you should be strung up by your thumbs from the nearest oak tree." Entering just in time to prevent a lynching, Elizabeth said, "No, Mother, this is William not Calder."

Working for the Schofields could be hazardous. During the war, their old family retainer asked Gladys what would happen if the Russians took over. Gladys told him to stick his arm in the freezer and keep it there until she told him to take it out. When he could stand the cold no longer, he pleaded, "Miss Gladys, my arm hurts. Can I take it out now?" She agreed but warned him, "That's what it will be like for your folks when the Russians take over." A few years later Gladys blamed all the world's troubles on "the atom bum."

The Schofields could be counted on to provide some comment on any occasion. They dealt in personalities rather than ideas. Like most people to the manor born, they made no distinction. Usually their malice was canceled by their charm, but not always. And there were many degrees. They seldom had a kind word for Kathleen Jacques, but the barbs were fairly innocuous. Kathleen ran the Sunday School at the First Baptist Church and the Schofields, like my mother, thought so much religion was in poor taste. When Kathleen had a fall in church, the Schofields quickly spread the word that Mrs. Jacques had taken a nose dive from the pulpit and broken her arm. When Kathleen appeared with her arm in a sling, it was assumed the Schofields knew what they were talking about. She and her husband lived in a beautiful tudor-style house on Nottingham Drive. When Elizabeth heard that Kathleen had pneumonia she said, "I'm not surprised, she lives over there on the river bottom." As the wife of Randolph Jacques, Kathleen was spared more serious attacks.

Frances Gurr McLanahan enjoyed no such privilege. On one of Andrew Lyndon's visits to Macon, Elizabeth asked, "Andrew, tell us about Mrs. McLanahan. Of course, we never knew her when she was here, but we understand she sees people in New York. How can that be?"

In the mid-forties, Macon elected a new mayor, which was good news to everyone but the Schofields. Elizabeth immediately asked Martha, "Who are these people who have taken over City Hall? In the old days, Judge Lawton Miller considered it an honor to serve as mayor." The question was purely rhetorical.

Mr. and Mrs. Walter Lamar lived next door to the Schofields. "Miss Dolly" was a lady in the Southern tradition, and not even a Plant could look down on a Blount or a Lamar. The Schofields were not alone in resenting Dolly's claim to be the first among equals. They did not like Dolly and were not amused by her pretensions. They tolerated her, praising Mr. Lamar while ignoring his wife. "Miss Flew" Johnston had been no shrinking violet when she dominated Macon society, but even at her silliest acted with more decorum. Mrs. Lamar was something new, a woman to the manor born whose name appeared in print every day, often on the front page. The Schofields disapproved but there was nothing they could do about it—yet.

The trouble began one summer morning when Mrs. Lamar hired the Davey tree surgeon to trim some dead limbs from a tree on the edge of her property. He came to Mrs. Lamar's back door and reported that a woman next door had ordered him to stop, insisting that the limb would fall in her yard and crush the rose bushes. Recognizing the voice of authority, he stopped, pending further instructions. Mrs. Lamar emerged to discuss the matter with Elizabeth and with Gladys who had joined her sister in the fray. Again, Elizabeth insisted that the dead limb would fall on her rose bushes and when that happened she would sue both the Davey tree people and Mrs. Lamar. With considerable diplomacy Mrs. Lamar suggested that Elizabeth and Gladys show the tree man how to cut the limb properly, which they were delighted to do. As might have been predicted, the limb fell in the Schofields' yard and crushed the rose bushes. By all accounts, Mrs. Lamar withdrew, leaving the Davey tree surgeon to fend for himself as best he could; but he was no match for the Schofield girls, and pretty soon he was at the back door again to inform Mrs. Lamar that the two women had picks and were pulling down the buttresses that held the wall. It was obvious to him that if they continued the entire wall would collapse on their property which was several feet below the Lamar's level. This time Dolly went into action. First she explained to Gladys and Elizabeth that although the wall was on Lamar property, the buttresses had been built on the Schofield side with the permission of their late father. The Schofields were adamant, "We know of no such agreement, do you have it in writing?" Meanwhile they continued to demolish the nearest buttress. In desperation Mrs. Lamar returned home and took out an injunction to prevent the Schofields from endangering her wall. A date for the court hearing was set, but nothing further was heard of the matter until the Burkes gave a party several months later. During the first lull in the conversation, Elizabeth made an announcement: "I'm sure you all want to know what happened. We lost the case by default. A lady does not appear in court." The explanation seemed logical but it was not the end of the matter by any means.

In 1951; the Alpha Delta Pi's, created as the Adelphian Society of Wesleyan College, met to celebrate living for a century. The Delta Pi's, clad in tea gowns, stockings, and girdles met and did the usual things women do at conventions, including attending a tea at Dolly Lamar's. The Schofields had their sprinkler on in front of their house so that Mrs. Lamar's guests had to cross the street to avoid getting soaked. The heat was intense and the entire Lamar yard was crowded with small metal tables, each with an umbrella for protection from the sun. Everything got off to a good start, with plenty of extra help pouring ice tea and lemonade, and there were individual hand fans, borrowed from the Mulberry Street Methodist Church. There was not a cloud in the sky.

Meanwhile, Elizabeth and Gladys had their yardman make piles of pine boughs and straw all along the wall separating the Schofields and the Lamars. When this was done, the man was instructed to pour gasoline on each pile. Promptly at four-thirty fires were ignited. As the flames soared, the yardman added an old rubber inner tube to each pile of burning rubble. It was a scene right out of Dante's Inferno. The smoke, the heat, and the stench were unbearable, and the Delta Pi's were forced to seek refuge in Miss Dolly's house. The windows and doors had to be kept tightly closed, although there was no air conditioning. The house was large but not large enough to accommodate so many Delta Pi's, to say nothing of the servants.

After the debacle, the two households stopped speaking, until Elizabeth and Gladys came over bearing gifts one Christmas morning several years later. Elizabeth spoke for the Schofields, as usual, "Dolly, our families have been friends for generations and it is absurd for us to stop speaking over a slight misunderstanding." Not to be outdone in Christian charity, Mrs. Lamar responded in kind, "I certainly agree. I was hoping you might call and I have a small gift for you under my Christmas tree." It was one of her famous plum puddings. A few days later, Mrs. Lamar received a note of thanks, delivered by the Schofields' servant. It read, in part, "As old friends we think you would want to know that the person who baked your plum puddings this year used elderberry wine instead of brandy." By that time, Miss Dolly was too old and too tired to continue the feud. Anyhow, there was more fun to be had from telling the story of the plum pudding.

Occasionally, though not often, the Schofields could laugh at themselves. One day Mrs. Schofield ran into her childhood friend Minnie Bass Burden. The two ladies were wandering around Rose Hill Cemetery, waiting for their children to finish distributing flowers. When Mrs. Schofield admitted she was suffering from gout, Mrs. Burden said, "Elizabeth, you drink too much!" Both ladies thought this was very funny.

The Schofield women could be charming and gracious, and visits to their home were not always painful. They were invariably kind to me, and whenever they spoke of my parents or Martha it was with genuine affection. After Daddy's death, Elizabeth and Gladys came to the Browns' house on Arlington Place to pay their respects. The two Emilys were not pleased with me for inviting them to come in and sit down. Neither the Schofields nor the Massees were about to indulge in an Irish wake, so the conversation was kept light. When I mentioned that Daddy had always filled his prescriptions at Chichester's Pharmacy near Mercer University, Gladys was overjoyed, "Did you hear that, Lizzie? Jordan favored Chicester's. I always told you they were the best!" Elizabeth didn't seem to care. Gladys had taken over. By 1965 she had become increasingly abusive of Elizabeth, as though in retaliation for all the years the older sister had the upper hand. The years after Elizabeth's death may have been the happiest Gladys ever spent.

When Gladys could no longer care for herself, her niece, Elizabeth Schofield Walton, from Jacksonville, took over her affairs. She obtained power of attorney and wisely had Gladys moved to a nursing home. The contents of the house were sold and the property was put on the market in order to pay expenses. Gladys meanwhile revoked her niece's power of attorney and placed her affairs in the hands of a group of people who planned to purchase and rezone the house and to build a row of town houses in the rear. Eventually, Gladys would be moved into one, rent free for the rest of her life. There was even a plan to have a portrait of Gladys for the main house. She had finally become the grande dame of Macon to a group of people she would not have spoken to a few years earlier.

Meanwhile, she remained in close contact, by phone, with Eugie Coleman Payne, although she never forgave Calder for notarizing the original power of attorney. She told Robert Quinlan that Calder had behaved very badly but that Eugenia Coleman might make something out of him yet! In May 1976, the Macon Telegraph published a delightful interview with Gladys, "Remembering the Way It Was;" and she appeared in a BBC documentary discussing "Life in the Good Ole Days," a subject she knew a lot about. Gladys Schofield died in 1976 at the age of 82.

The Walter Lamar house was torn down to make room for the ugliest apartment building in Macon. Even the Blount home on Orange Street was demolished, but the Schofield home, with its unique English basement, survives, beautifully restored. The hundred-year-old scuppernong vine is gone, but the garden contains many rare trees and oriental shrubs planted by Gladys Schofield and her mother. The legend of the Schofields lives on. Not long before Carson McCullers died, she called me in the middle of the night to ask, "What was the name of those girls in Macon?" I knew which girls she meant.

Under One Roof

Burden Smith & Company, also known as The Empire Store, was the best retail dry goods store Macon has ever known. The store was founded by Mr. Richard F. Burden (1851-1937), who remained president until his death. Mr. Burden came to Macon at the age of sixteen, from Jones County, and became a prominent influence on the business and religious life of the city. He married Amelia Maria ("Minnie") Bass, whose father was president of Wesleyan College for twenty years. Their three children were Eugene Bass Burden, Ann Octavia (Mrs. Thomas J. Stewart), and Alice Cobb (Mrs. Isaac LeRoy Domingos). They had four grandchildren: I. L. Domingos, Jr. ("Roy"); Ann Maria Domingos; Alice Burden Domingos; and Richard Burden Domingos. The four Domingos children, and Richard's wife Mary, have been like brothers and sisters to me.

For many years my mother traded with Burden Smith & Company. Not only was it the best store of its kind in Macon, it was home-owned and home-operated, which pleased my father. Mother was sure no one but Mr. Lord carried such fine linens. Her special favorite, however, was Mr. Dan Coffee, who would accompany her from one department to another. Only the linen department was independent of his supervision. In that time, customers with good credit ratings paid their bill only twice a year. Mother and Daddy always went together to the store to settle their account, and Mr. Burden was always most cordial. He had a favorite expression, "to be sure, to be sure," which amused Daddy, who always referred to him as "To-Be-Sure-Burden." Once, when they paid their bill, Mr. Burden said, "Jordan, I want you to know how much I appreciate Mrs. Massee's business. She is next to my best customer."

Daddy thought that the statement was provocative, so he asked Mr. Burden, "Who is your best customer?"

Mr. Burden replied, not as a joke, but quite factually, "The Insane Asylum in Milledgeville," which amused both Mother and Daddy.

Everything went along beautifully—Mother was pleased with Burden Smith & Company and Burden Smith was pleased with her—until a year or so later, when Daddy fell out with Mr. Burden. An underpass at the foot of Poplar Street had been proposed, which would have been highly beneficial to the Bibb Brick Company, as well as to other manufacturing plants on the other side of the railroad tracks running parallel to Broadway. The underpass would have provided easier access to the brickyard, saving trucks hauling brick and tile several miles. Mr. Burden opposed the construction on the grounds that it would be an unnecessary expenditure of public funds. Daddy resented this bitterly since he felt that Mr. Burden would not be affected personally one way or the other, and instructed Mother not to trade at Mr. Burden's store anymore.

Mother didn't like this at all, and told Daddy, "That will upset my list of pallbearers."

Daddy's response was "Well, old dear, having Mr. Coffee would have been inconvenient anyhow. He would have interrupted the procession to spit." Mr. Coffee chewed tobacco. (So did my father, later, much to my mother's regret.)

Reluctantly, Mother moved to Doody's, the rival store, on the corner of Cherry Street and Second. Martha and I were delighted with the change. Doody's had a row of stools with revolving tops, all along the counters. While waiting for Mother to make her purchases, we would try to get the stool tops all revolving simultaneously. No doubt the management had given orders that Mrs. Massee's children were not to be inhibited. I was also fascinated with the cash basket, which was raised by a pulley and shot across the ceiling to the business office on the mezzanine at the rear of the store, a primitive forerunner of the pneumatic tube system of a later date.

One day, Daddy bumped into Mr. Burden on the Cherry Street sidewalk. Mr. Burden said, "Jordan, I do hope our little political difference won't interfere with Mrs. Massee's patronage!"

To which Daddy replied, "Mr. Burden, if my wife ever sets foot inside your store again, your two best customers will wind up under one roof."

By this time, Mr. Burden's son-in-law, Tom Stewart, helped manage the store. With great charm and tact he calmed Daddy down, and Mother was allowed to return to her favorite store. Everybody was happy again—under Mr. Burden's roof.

The Mid-Day Meal

The midday meal was of great importance in our house, partly because my father loved good food and my mother prided herself on providing it, and partly because it was the occasion that brought the entire family together: Mother, Daddy, my two sisters—Emily and Martha—and myself. It must have been equally important to the many servants, black and white, as a period of rest between the morning chores and the rather less strenuous afternoon duties. It was also the time, during their own meal, when they could socialize. Furthermore, they all liked to eat.

Our immediate family ate in the mahogany paneled, oval dining room, the most beautiful room in that extraordinary house. The large table was round, except when extended with extra leaves for guests, and was always covered during meals with a monogrammed, white damask tablecloth. The silver napkin rings that had belonged to my grandmother were no longer used since my mother insisted on fresh napkins for every meal. There were enough leaves to extend the table to seat twenty-four, but the room was not long enough for the full extension. Lawson Brown, Mother's only brother, had made for her a large round wooden top, in two hinged pieces, which could be placed on the regular top to accommodate twelve without crowding. When not in use, it was stored in an empty room on the third floor.

My mother sat on one side of the table, directly opposite my father. Martha sat on one side, with her back to the double door opening to the music room. Emily and I sat across the table from Martha, Emily next to Daddy. When Emily was away at school in Baltimore, I sat alone on that side, between Mother and Daddy. Before I was born, Grandpa Brown chose that seat because from that vantage point, he could see through the music room—it was the library then—into the huge front hall, in case anyone came in while the family was eating, a rare occurrence indeed. Guests seldom arrived unexpectedly in those days.

Walter Odom, who had been Daddy's personal valet until a stroke left him partially paralyzed and curtailed his activities, sat in the telephone room to answer the phone. Neither Daddy nor Mother would go to the phone during meals, but Emily and Martha couldn't be deprived.

There were usually four servants waiting on the table during dinner. This did not include the cook, who never left the kitchen, but consisted of the butler (James Ray), Daddy's new valet (Richard Ross), the upstairs maid (first Annie Lee Bailey, later Marylu Tanner), and my nurse (Anna Lockhart). Anna stood behind my chair and waited on no one except me, unless Daddy needed more ice water and the others were too busy to fetch it.

Daddy was always in particularly good humor at dinner, entertaining us all with his funny stories. Sometimes, he would even play a game with me, in which we would alternately clap a hand on top of the other's, getting faster and faster, until I was proclaimed the winner. Whenever Martha and I got into a noisy altercation across the table, Daddy would say, "Ethel, speak to your children." We were never punished in his presence. Mother kept several fresh peachtree switches in a vase on the mantlepiece. If things seemed to be getting out of hand, Brother Ray would place one of the switches, referred to as Dr. Peachtree, on the table next to Mother's plate. The threat was usually enough to restore peace. Martha was a nervous, high-strung child, difficult to control. Occasionally, she got into an argument with Mother, in which I was not involved. As a last resort, Mother would march her off to the nursery, which was out of hearing, to settle their differences. Only once or twice was I ever taken from the table and subjected to the Dr. Peachtree remedy.

I was much less of a problem as a child than Martha. When Mother said no, I knew she meant it, whereas Martha argued with her until she got into trouble. At the age of five I expressed what was to remain my basic philosophy throughout life: "Anything for peace's sake." Well, almost anything.

My only problem was spinach, which I hated worse than the devil hates holy water. Following doctor's orders we were given spinach every third day. I used to count the days, which were otherwise much alike to me at that age. I looked forward to asparagus day, and tolerated carrot day since a slice of carrot can be swallowed whole with a sip of water, but spinach day was fearsome. I would wait until the spinach got cold, then send it back to the kitchen. Then again it was too hot. Or there was too much grated egg on top, or not enough. Often I would still be sitting at the table, all alone, for more than an hour after everyone else had finished eating and left the dining room. I was not allowed to leave until the spinach was consumed. Even Anna was not allowed to stay with me. After Marylu had joined the staff, she would sneak back, unbeknownst to my mother, and eat the spinach for me, bless her heart. Doctors at that time believed that spinach provided children with necessary iron. It was with considerable chagrin that I read, many years later, that spinach is no better than any other green vegetable. If only my mother had known that, much misery could have been avoided, hers as well as mine.

Whenever the adult conversation took a direction Mother didn't like, she would remind Daddy that "Little pitchers have big ears." At no other time was the social scale so much in evidence as at dinner. While the family was eating, the two white chauffeurs were served in the butler's pantry. (In later years, my mother preferred a black chauffeur.) Daddy's driver wore a business suit, while Mother's always wore a uniform, with a visored cap when driving.

After my German governess replaced Anna Lockhart, she was served at the same time, in the nursery, which was half a city block from the kitchen. If Fräulein was served more than she thought she would eat, she immediately returned some of it to the kitchen, having been brought up not to waste food, in the German fashion. That annoyed the black servants for some reason or other, although usually they got along quite well with her.

After the white folks had all been fed, the black servants gathered together in the kitchen for their meal. The food was exactly the same, regardless of who you were or where you sat, except when taste dictated otherwise. I recall that the black servants preferred catfish to shad, and country fried steak to small filet mignon, but my father preferred country fried steak, too.

In the kitchen Old Cook Lula sat alone at one table which was about an inch higher than the big table which was pushed up next to it at meal time. Brother Ray sat at the head of the big table, surrounded by the other servants. Being a deacon in the Baptist Church, Brother Ray always asked the blessing, which was never done in the white dining room, nor in the butler's pantry.

Once a week, the regular servants were joined by Matt Cheney, an amazon of a woman, who performed heavy-duty work, like washing windows. On days when Matt worked for the Horace Wrights, two doors from our house, she would run across the John Moore's backyard to us for dinner. The food was better. Matt Cheney had marital problems, and despite her unusual size and strength frequently got the worst of it in her periodic fights with her husband. She would arrive late at night, long after Daddy had gone to bed, and she and my mother would sit in Mother's bedroom, which I shared, discussing her problems. I pretended I was fast asleep, and listened in amazement. All I knew as a child about wife abuse I learned from those late night conversations. She lived just a few blocks behind our house on Virgin Lane. In 1991 the name was changed to Professional Street. It was Matt Cheney who taught me my first word, "Doggone."

From time to time, the servants were joined by some young daughter of a friend of Lula's, who was given her midday meal and priceless cooking lessons in return for helping wash pots and pans and assisting the cook in any way she could. That was an arrangement strictly between Lula and the girl's mother. Thus traditional cooking skills were passed from one generation to the next. Unfortunately, there were fewer and fewer such opportunities as life in the South became more urban, less rural. Every week or two, Lula's best friend Emma was her dinner guest, usually on Thursday so they could later attend church together.

In late spring and early autumn, the servants ate their dinner on the back porch which was cooler than the kitchen.

All glass and china from the main dining room were washed by Brother Ray in a huge ironstone sink in the butler's pantry, which is where he also polished the silver.

Most of the food was cooked in a huge cast-iron, wood-burning stove with double ovens. It was Richard Ross's duty to keep Lula supplied with wood, which he chopped in the yard and stored on the back porch. There was also a gas stove in the kitchen, for baking cakes. Lula never washed a dish; she hardly had time, cooking three meals, on most days, for an army of twelve to fourteen people. On Thursdays, she took her afternoon off and retired to her house in our yard, a brick building with two large rooms, each with fireplace, and a bath between the rooms. There was a large veranda with a hanging swing which I loved. Lula slept in one room and entertained her friends in the other. All of them envied Lula. Daddy built the house originally for Nancy, Emily's nurse. When Mother complained that Lula kept a messy kitchen, Auntie said, "Ethel, you can have a good cook or a neat kitchen, but you can't have both."

In addition to her culinary skill, Lula possessed a real green thumb. Her veranda was always filled with pot plants of many luxuriant varieties. Except for a beautiful oleander and a trumpet vine, that was the only colorful spot in our large backyard. From time to time Mother had rows of daffodils planted, but they seldom lasted more than a season. The efforts of Mrs. Tom Stewart and other garden club members had not yet transformed the yards of Macon.

All of our servants were far better paid than others in Macon, a well-known fact in the black community, and they were treated with dignity and respect. Let me add at this point that I never knew of any other households in Macon where the black servants were well treated, except in the Burden, Domingos, and Stewart homes. None, despite what one hears to the contrary from persons who remember the past through a rosy haze of forgetfulness. I have a cousin who intends to write a book about how well the blacks were treated "in the good old days." That is sheer rubbish; they were treated like dirt. One can just imagine how black farmhands and factory workers were treated. I could name many a prominent Macon family that treated their servants badly. In my childhood, black people kept records, among themselves, grading the white employers according to working conditions. There weren't many with high marks. One of the richest families was so notorious, primarily for their inordinate demands, that they found it difficult to find help. I think most white families justified their conduct by telling themselves that they were kinder and more considerate than their neighbors and friends. Social conditions are best understood in the context of their time, but that is no moral justification.

After Marylu and her husband and step-son moved to the country, on the outskirts of town, she rarely got to work before ten o'clock, although breakfast was at eight. She certainly made up for it by working late. The lady across the street once remarked to my mother, "Mrs. Massee, I have to keep the shades down on my front windows so that my maid won't notice what time your maid comes to work."

There was a locked pantry opening on to the hall between the kitchen and the butler's pantry. My mother kept the key, but in later years it was seldom locked. Sugar, flour, canned goods, and sugar-cured hams were kept there. In the early years when the pantry was kept locked, my mother would open the door every morning for Lula to get out what she needed. I think it was the inconvenience of that arrangement that led to leaving the door unlocked. Outside, in the hallway was a huge hotel-size icebox—to this day I always call the electric refrigerator the icebox—for which huge hundred-pound blocks of ice were delivered by horse and wagon every day except Sunday. Years later, when we lived in the little house across the street, we had a small icebox on the back porch for "real ice," since my mother didn't like the taste of Fridgidaire ice. At the old house we had a metal box about eight inches long and three inches wide, with a sharp blade on the under side, for scraping the big blocks of ice to make shaved ice, which was delicious for cold drinks. Mother always had Coca-Cola, poured over a tall glass of shaved ice, with her dinner, "for the digestion." That was before it had been decided that Coca-Cola was good for children, even babies. If Martha and I were well-behaved, we were each allowed a shot glass full of the otherwise forbidden beverage at the end of the meal, great care being exercised to see that one shot glass did not contain a drop more than the other.

Lula, on the other hand, favored iced tea with her dinner, which she drank from an old Royal Baking Powder tin can, I suppose because the metal retained the cold longer. Baking Powder cans were much larger then and the whole top came off, not just a small lid in the center.

After Emily and Martha grew up, neither liked carbonated water, so they bought Coca-Cola syrup by the gallon and mixed it with tap water. Each generation had its own eccentricities. At the old house, the chauffeur was sent every Saturday morning to pick up a case of Coca-Colas.

Fresh vegetables were brought to the back yard in a horse-drawn wagon, where Mother and Lula would carefully pick out the best.

Another terribly smelly wagon arrived once a week to pick up slop for pigs. Dozens of live chickens—turkeys at Thanksgiving and Christmas and other special occasions—were kept in a large chicken coop in the back yard. The coop was about twenty feet square. The chickens laid a few eggs, but not nearly enough for our household. We drove to Bolingbroke once a week to fetch several dozen more, always brown eggs from Rhode Island Reds. My father said that Mother had to be personally acquainted with the hens. Brother Ray, then later "Dick" Ross, would ring the chickens' necks and then they would flip-flop around on the ground until dead, which I found disgusting, but not so disgusting as seeing him chop off the head of a big turkey, which was then strung up by its legs from the limb of a tree for all the blood to drain out. The modern way is a distinct improvement.

Inside the wire chicken coop was a covered henhouse where the chickens slept on perches, and where they retired during heavy rains.

There were no supermarkets then and the rest of the food supplies were obtained from Mr. Howard's grocery store, later from Bradley's store on Cotton Avenue. Mother did all her own marketing, with the help of her chauffeur. Martha and I enjoyed going with her to Mr. Bradley's, which smelled of freshly roasted coffee beans. He always had a small goody or two for us. Our real fascination, however, was with one of Mr. Bradley's clerks, who was an amateur ventriloquist. He would "throw his voice," without moving his lips, into the flour bin, to our great delight.

Long before I was born, Nancy would telephone Mr. Howard and without any introduction say, "Baby says send us a twenty-pound sack of flour right away," and hang up the phone. Fortunately, Mr. Howard recognized the voice and knew who Baby was.

After dinner on Sunday, at the old house, the servants took the rest of the day off as soon as the dishes were washed, to go to church. Some of them were more pious than others, but to all of them Sunday afternoon church was the great social event of the week. They dressed in their best clothes, especially Lula, who was a member of the Methodist Church. Brother Ray was also well-dressed, in Daddy's hand-me-down clothes. He always stayed very nearly Daddy's size.

Mother never had a cup of coffee in her life; she didn't even like the smell of it. Demitasse was served only after formal dinner parties. Daddy and Lula had one cup each with breakfast, which was so bad no one else would have drunk it even if given the opportunity. They both favored old-fashioned boiled coffee, not unlike Turkish coffee without the grinds or sugar.

By the time we moved into the little house, I drank coffee regularly but prepared it myself. Jim Brown, Emily's husband, agreed that Lula's coffee wasn't fit to drink. One day, after I had moved to New York, Lula was ill and unable to come in to prepare Daddy's breakfast.

Mother had never cooked a meal in her entire life, nor had Bertha, the fluttery little maid. Between the two of them they managed to boil an egg and toast two slices of bread, but, totally incapable of preparing a cup of coffee, had to give Daddy hot tea, which he had never liked. Emily and Jim lived on Arlington Place, less than a block away, so Emily told Mother, "Next time, just send Daddy through the alley to my house and he can have waffles and bacon and coffee with Jim," but the occasion never rose again. Jim was justly famous for the quality of his coffee, which he made himself. Emily, like her mother, had never tasted coffee in her life. Whenever Jim had coffee at someone else's house, like Mae and Martina Burke's or Sue Myrick's, which he considered superior to his own, he immediately inquired as to the blend and the method of brewing, which in turn led to new equipment in the Brown's kitchen.

Perhaps Lula's coffee never improved because she knew Mother wasn't going to drink it in any case, and she and Daddy liked it boiled. Only one other person did, Judith Wylie.

I am told that Grandpa loved coffee with his breakfast and drank it black and boiling hot. His coffee was prepared with G. Washington powdered coffee, which came in a small tin can and was very expensive. Most people think that instant coffee is a recent innovation.

My father's favorite dessert was sweet potato pie, highly spiced and fortified with rye whiskey. It was one of Old Cook Lula's masterpieces. When we sat down to dinner, the heavy midday meal, Daddy always held up his dessert fork or spoon and asked my mother, "Old Dear, what's the flag?," in order to know how much room to reserve. Now sweet potato pie holds its heat longer than any other food I can think of, long after making its way from the kitchen, through the back hall, and through the butler's pantry to the dining room, where Brother Ray, our butler, cut wedges of appropriate sizes for each member of the family.

Although Daddy must have known how infernally hot the pie would be, he could never wait until everyone else was served before tasting it. Invariably, he scorched his tongue, but being unwilling to wash away the flavor with a sip of water, pounded his feet on the floor, alternately, in rapid succession. When the pie had cooled to an acceptable temperature, he consumed the remainder of his serving with great satisfaction, but slowly, since he never rushed his meals. After a second helping, he pushed the plate away from him, which we children never did, being fully aware that certain privileges were only accorded our father.

Having finished his most favorite dessert, Daddy never failed saying to Mother, "Old Dear, you are a wonder!" And she would reply, "I've always been so considered."

NEW CAR TROUBLE

Automobiles were no longer a novelty in 1920, but they were to Fisher Craft, a young man who worked at the Fourth National Bank. He took driving lessons and then bought his first car from Felton Fincher at the Steve Soloman agency. Soon afterwards he drove to Lizella, about fifteen miles from Macon. When his car stopped, he went to a nearby country store and telephoned his dealer.

"Felton," he said, "This is Fisher. I'm in Lizella and I'm out of gas. Will it hurt the engine if I drive back to Macon?"

"Hell no!," Fincher told him, "Come on in."

FRÄULEIN ALWINA EICHLER

"O lost, and by the wind grieved, ghost, come back again."
Look Homeward Angel, Thomas Wolfe

A book of memoirs such as this must ultimately be judged by its success in capturing, however fleetingly, something of the spirit of its leading characters. That was no problem with my father, who re-creates himself, both through his humorous stories and through his actions; but it would take another Balzac to capture the essence of my mother or Fräulein Alwina Eichler. It is always difficult to portray goodness convincingly, either in fiction or in biography. Most people are a combination of good and bad; pure good is as rare as unalloyed evil, and far less interesting, unless accompanied by heroic actions. There was nothing heroic about my mother or my governess. They lived lives of quiet dignity, each in her own way, as different as two women can be, with nothing in common except love for me. Mother's goodness was one aspect of a perfection that must have been as difficult to achieve as it was difficult to maintain; whereas Alwina's goodness consisted of the practice of disinterested virtues, to the extent that virtue is ever wholly disinterested. Throughout this book I have avoided analysis since motives are always conjectural. I have no idea why the people I knew had become what they were, and for me it is enough to examine their character as objectively as possible, and to record the effect they had on others, although objectivity is especially difficult in the cases of the two women who were most instrumental in forming my own character, and who were dearest to me.

To all appearances Alwina Eichler was a very simple person, while in fact she was extraordinarily complicated. It would be nearer the truth to say that she was consistent. There were contradictions in my mother's character; in Alwina's, none.

Alwina Treuber Eichler was born on December the fifth, 1871, in Weimar, the chief town in Thuringen, less than twelve months after King William of Prussia was proclaimed Emperor of Germany, thereby uniting the four kingdoms of Prussia, Bavaria, Saxony, and Württenberg, along with numerous duchies and free cities. She grew up hating everything Prussian, especially militarism and authoritarian government. Most important, she grew up in the hometown of Goethe, Schiller, Liszt, and Nietzsche, who spent the last years of his life there hopelessly insane, until his death in 1900. Even Bach resided in Weimar early in the eighteenth century as Hofkonzertmeister to the Duke of Weimar.

In Alwina's childhood the ghosts of Bach, Goethe, and Schiller haunted the streets of that small Saxon town, and Liszt and Nietzsche were living presences.

Although Lizst never played publicly, Alwina heard him conduct. As far back as she could remember, music was her greatest passion in life. Well-to-do friends of the family regularly sent opera tickets to Alwina and her younger sister, who took turns attending unless the opera was *Tristan,* which Alwina heard ten times before she was twenty. It was an everyday occurrence to see Franz Lizst walking down the street, or one of his pupils, Emil von Sauer, Mortitz Rosenthal, Eugene d'Albert, Felix Wingartner, Alexander Siloti, Arthur Friedham, Amy Fay, and others. That small town, out of which came so much that is best in German culture, attracted musicians from all over the world. When Lizst resigned as conductor of the opera, where he had given world premiers of Lohengrin and Samson et Delila, he was succeeded by Eduard Lassen, under whose leadership Wagner's *Tristan und Isolde* was produced in 1874, at a time when no other theatre but Munich dared to do so.

The theater in Weimar, built under Goethe's superintendence in 1825, was the scene of the golden age of German drama. Here the greatest plays of Goethe and Schiller were first produced, under the patronage of Charles Augustus, Archduke of Saxe-Weimar.

In 1890, Richard Strauss was appointed assistant conductor of the Weimar opera. As a teenager, Alwina heard Strauss conduct the first performance of Don Juan, and five years later the premiere of his opera Guntram, with Pauline de Ahna singing the leading soprano role. After a stormy courtship, Strauss married de Ahna, who continued to introduce his songs. The opera's coloratura soprano was a close friend of Alwina's younger sister and kept her informed of the latest intrigue in the Strauss household. On one occasion, Strauss was so angry with his wife that he strangled her pet canary, no doubt a symbolic gesture. The leading tenor when Alwina was a girl was Max Alvary, who subsequently became a matinee idol at New York's Metropolitan Opera. "How can he have sung Siegfried with that small voice?," she asked me, although she did not share the German passion for loud tenors. Wagner was undoubtedly Alwina's first love, but she adored the operas of Mozart and Verdi, and, of course, Fidelio.

To understand how a small town like Weimar, with a population of only 21,565 in 1885, could have been the cultural center of Germany, one must keep in mind the towering figure of Goethe and the benevolent presence of Lizst, the father of modern music. It was not a festival town like Bayreuth or, later, Salzburg, but even during the reign of the East German communist government, after World War II, scholars came from all over the world to visit the Goethe and Nietzsche archives. Alwina grew up in a peaceful atmosphere, between the Franco-Prussian War and the First World War, with only a few dark clouds gathering in the shape of the Emperor Wilhelm II.

Alwina Trueber Eichler was the daughter of an officer in the Saxon army. In addition to the two daughters, I think there was a son who died in childhood. The younger daughter studied dramatic art and became an actress, first in Weimar, and later as a life-member of a company in Düsseldorf. Alwina studied to be a teacher and was extraordinarily well-educated. They were brought up in the Lutheran church. Around the age of twenty, Alwina married a young lieutenant, but the marriage was not of long duration, and ended in divorce. After her father's death, she continued to live with her mother and sister. Around 1897, the Kaiser came to Weimar. Everyone turned out for the parade in his honor. After Alwina refused to stand at attention and salute the emperor as he passed, her mother said, "Alwina, I think it is time for you to leave Germany. Why don't you accept the offer you had through your school for a job as governess for an American family going to China?" And so it was that she left Germany and her mother, whom she would not see again until 1926. It must have been a hard decision. She and her mother were unusually close. The chance to earn money to send home was probably the deciding factor. At the age of twenty-five she took a boat bound for China, where she joined Mr. and Mrs. Charles Denby, Jr. and their growing family. She had been recommended for the post of governess by the Weimar board of education. It was her first trip outside of Saxony. At the time of her arrival in Tientsin, there were already two small boys in the Denby family. Edwin, the third child, was not born until 1903. He became the most influential dance critic of this century, as well as a poet of some distinction. When his dance writings were collected and published in book form in 1987, William Mackay wrote in his biographical notes:

Edwin Denby, 1903-1983

Edwin Orr Denby was, indeed, born in Tientsin, China, on February 4, 1903.

On the northeast coast, sixty miles from Peking, Tientsin was at the time a city of seven hundred thousand Chinese dominated by a few thousand Europeans and Americans. It offered its foreigners lush Victoria Park, ambitious Western architecture, golf courses, cricket clubs, concert halls, and several English-language newspapers. Its opera house featured Verdi, Elgar, and Gilbert & Sullivan. Decades later, Edwin still delighted in his mother's recollections of a Tientsin production of *The Mikado:* "So many Chinese playing so many Japanese! Imagine all those extras!"

Much of the foreign enclave considered the Chinese little more than walk-ons anyway. Life in China was simple, Edwin told me. Americans pretended they were in Europe, and the Chinese made believe they were invisible. Edwin's version of the 1900 Boxer Rebellion, which snapped this charade, was wryly Jamesian. "To many of my parents' friends it was a great crisis," he said. "They were never again able to trust their servants."

Few were better positioned than the Denbys to enjoy the fruits of such unapologetic imperialism. Edwin's grandfather, Charles Denby, Sr., arrived in Peking in 1885 as President Cleveland's appointee as minister to China. He served in that post an almost unparalleled thirteen years. A vigorous advocate of the Open Door Policy, he was so respected that China rejected several possible replacements and Japan entrusted him with its interests in China during the 1895 hostilities.

In many ways, Charles Denby, Sr. (who died when grandson Edwin was one), was less remarkable than his namesake son. Charles Denby, Jr., only twenty-three, accompanied his father to China as second secretary of legation. (Actually, the Denby family contribution to world diplomacy was almost washed overboard the S.S. Rio de Janeiro by a typhoon in mid-Pacific.) Not content to be a nepotist, the younger Denby tutored himself until he became "one of the best American scholars of his day in the Chinese language, literature, history and philosophy.... In the Chinese official and written language he attained unusual proficiency, and many important negotiations between the legation and the Chinese government were conducted by him entirely in that tongue." Indeed, as first secretary of legation, Charles Denby, Jr., was the chief draftsman of the treaty ending the Chinese-Japanese War.

By the time of the treaty signing, Edwin's father was already a married man. The match seemed made in heaven—or, more precisely, in Evansville, Indiana. Martha Dalzell Orr had been born and raised in that small town only a few blocks from the Denbys. But it took an around-the-world trip with her family and outgoing Secretary of State John W. Foster (also from Evansville) to pair her with Charles Denby, Jr. They met in Peking in 1894 and exchanged vows in their hometown the following year.

Martha Orr Denby was, by every account, a fearless, intelligent woman. A college graduate, she had waded through crowds of beggars to see burning ghats on the Ganges, wandered teeming Beirut streets, visited a wolf-child in India, celebrated Thanksgiving on the Nile. During the Boxer siege of Tientsin, she hid with her infant son James in basements, while above, the bad situation worsened, people eating household pets and planning "preventive" group suicide.

The Denbys left Asia for the last time when Edwin was seven. Consequently, he had few Chinese memories and doubted the authenticity of most of them. His best recollections, he liked to say, were of the Boxer Rebellion, which occurred several years before his birth.

I assume that Alwina Eichler left the Denbys shortly after their return to the United States. She told me that Mrs. Denby was instrumental in getting her a position with the Kunz family, about whom I know nothing. She continued to correspond with all her boys until the mid-twenties, but unfortunately all their letters and postcards to her were lost some years after I moved to New York. I met Edwin Denby shortly before his death and asked him if he remembered his German governess in Tientsin. Unfortunately, he remembered nothing about his life there, which is surprising considering the fact that he was seven years old when his family left China. He suggested I write his older brother who would surely remember, but the brother was already ninety so I didn't bother him.

FOUR SUMMERS AT GROVE PARK INN

Among the other regular guests at Grove Park Inn were Mr. Seymour and his two daughters, Mary and Anne. Presumably, Mrs. Seymour was dead. Horatio Wilson Seymour was editor of The World, an important New York newspaper, which Joseph Pulitzer had developed into one of the most fearless, dynamic campaign sheets in the United States. Although Mr. Seymour was an ardent Democrat, he and my very Republican father enjoyed many hours discussing politics. He told Daddy that the most difficult decision he ever had to make was when he discovered that one of the presidential candidates had Negro blood, not much but enough to defeat anyone in those days. His sense of fair play overcame his ethics as a journalist, and he suppressed the information. The oldest daughter, Mary Seymour Jones, became one of my mother's dearest friends, one of the few to visit us in Macon. During our first summer at Grove Park Inn, Mary completed two blue and white quilts which she had begun the year before. She embroidered each quilt with her initials and the year, 1914, and gave them to Mother who kept them wrapped in dark blue tissue paper in one of her numerous cedar chests. When Mother and Daddy moved to Martha's house, she gave them to me since I was born in 1914.

Anne Seymour married Curtis Grove, a music student much

younger than herself. They lived in a huge apartment in The Dakota, which had been the Seymour home. Curtis continued his voice lessons but finally gave up singing in favor of banking, at which he was more successful. In the late thirties, Anne and Curtis gave up their Monday evening subscription seats to the Metropolitan Opera because "the standard of singing had declined so deplorably." I assume they didn't care for Wagner. Anne was a rather dowdy woman at the time of her marriage and was often mistaken for Curtis's mother, but when I knew them in the early forties they looked the same age. Curtis had become painfully dignified and Anne had become almost giddy.

In 1935 my sister Emily took her ten-year-old daughter to New York, the child's first visit to the big city. When they called on the Groves, Anne asked Little Emily if she liked New York. The response was emphatic, "No. Yankees have no manners." No doubt to change the subject, Anne asked, "Do you have many beaux?," a sensible question from a woman who had had only one. When Little Emily said she had none, her mother protested, "You shouldn't say that; what about Curtis Rand?" The answer this time ended the conversation: "I wouldn't marry him, he's younger than I am."

When I took up permanent residence in New York, I dutifully called on Anne and Curtis Grove. Anne set a date for a formal party to introduce me to New York society, presumably Murray Hill society since the Seymours did not associate with the nouveau riche. Unfortunately, I forgot the engagement and failed to show up. When I realized what I had done I was so distraught I thought of jumping out the window of my twelfth-floor apartment on Riverside Drive. On further consideration I telephoned my mother for advice. She instructed me to write Anne a note telling her the truth. I wrote apologizing for my lapse of memory and had it delivered with a dozen American Beauty roses. The same day Anne called, gracious as ever, telling me that sooner or later it happens to everyone. We remained good friends, but I had to wait many years before Alice Astor introduced me to "the right people."

The Von Rook House

Like my father, I had a happy childhood, which I attribute mostly to environmental factors. I was brought up in a household with almost no religion and without any personal rancor. In fifty-nine years of married life my parents quarreled only once. It was during the summer of 1924, at the Von Rook House in Asheville, North Carolina. When my father announced he was going into town to get a hair cut, Mother said, "Take Boots with you, he needs a hair cut. But don't let the barber use the clippers around his ears, only scissors." On our return it was obvious that the barber had clipped all my hair except on the top of my head. Mother shrieked, "What have you done to my baby?" Daddy, trying to calm her, said, "Ethel, don't get excited. Let me tell you what happened. When we got to the barber shop, Boots threw his coat on the floor, and while I was picking it up the barber took off a little too much hair on the sides." Mother replied, "That Boots threw his coat on the floor I can believe, but that you picked it up, I know that's not true." Without further discussion she took me upstairs to her bedroom where she wept, then tried to repair the damage with her fingernail scissors.

Daddy drove back to Macon where he stayed until he felt he had been forgiven – all of a week. Emily, Hazel Sparks, and their two beaux decided to record the hair cut for posterity. When they told Anna Lockhardt they wanted to take our picture we suspected nothing and were delighted to pose. Hoping also to capture Anna's figure on film they lured us up in profile and took our picture. Everyone was pleased with the result. That entire summer at the Von Rook house Anna and I were both blissfully happy.

OUR MUSICAL HERITAGE

Music was not my father's long suit. I doubt he ever attended a concert or an opera until after his marriage. He couldn't play a jew's-harp, and certainly couldn't carry a tune. Emily says he was tone deaf, like herself, but I doubt there is such a thing. Individuals differ widely in their ability to distinguish pitches and to remember any sequence of notes, but both skills can be improved markedly with practice, especially with children.

Daddy frequently took Mother to the opera, which she loved; he even came to enjoy the glamour and theatrical extravagance, as well as the social occasion. From the first, they owned the finest Victrola that money could buy and collected single-faced Victor Red Seal records. All the best artists were available on the Victor label, with a few exceptions, most notably Lillian Nordica.

I think my mother's love of music can be traced to her older sister, Mattiebrian Brown Benton, who, after her marriage, spent her few extra dollars on recordings by Marcella Sembrich and Louise Homer. Mother's own collection consisted mostly of vocal music, with a sampling of popular violin favorites by Kreisler, Elman, and Zimbalist. Daddy told me of taking Mother to the Hippodrome, then the world's largest theatre, to hear Alma Gluck and Efrem Zimbalist, who was married to the popular singer, in a joint recital. "So many tickets were sold they had to put chairs on the stage. I thought they threw in the fiddler for good measure, but, by God, he got a bigger hand than she did!" There were no piano recordings in the collections. It was not until Alfred Cortot's "Rigoletto Paraphrase," in the mid-twenties that Mother became convinced that the piano could be faithfully reproduced.

My father never learned to play the phonograph, and I doubt that Mother would have trusted him with her precious records. The 1908 "Sextette" from Lucia, featuring Caruso, Sembrich, Severina, Daddi, Scotti, and Journet, cost seven dollars, a lot of money in those days. At first John McCormack was their favorite singer, but soon Caruso took over. They bought every new recording by the incomparable Italian tenor as soon as issued. I never heard Caruso, alas. No one suspected the 1920 performances would be his last in Atlanta, and Mother felt that I was still too young. Emily heard him often when she was at finishing school in New York, most memorably in 1919 at a gala in honor of the Prince of Wales, but she remembered best the handsome young prince in the royal box.

In the teens and early twenties, Mother bought lots of sheet music, although she couldn't play a note. There was always some friend, like Jonnie Sparks, my godmother, who would oblige. Jonnie could also play "by ear," an accomplishment which I always envied.

During the summers at Pine Retreat in Asheville, young McDowell Preston would play for the family. He introduced me to the "Ave Maria" which Gounod imposed in Bach's "Prelude in C Major" and Schubert's Unfinished Symphony, via "Blossom Time." He persuaded me to buy a recording of Beethoven's Kreutzer Sonata.

Mother and Daddy also owned an Edison phonograph, with lots of cylinders of band music and other low-brow stuff. When I was four or five, the Edison was relegated to the nursery, along with a table model Victrola, for the amusement of the two small children. The cylinders were played with a permanent diamond needle, which should have taught our parents something but didn't. I was very fond of "The Parade of the Wooden Soldiers" and "The Japanese Sandman," "Cohen on the Telephone," and "I Can Dance with Anyone but my Wife." The discs included all the popular entertainers of the day: Nora Bayes, Irene Bordoni, and Blanche Ring, everybody's favorite. There were numerous records by Harry Lauder, although I'm sure Daddy couldn't understand his Scottish brogue. He had trouble enough with Fräulein's German accent. One day he overheard us conversing and asked Mother, "Is that German or American?" At a slightly later day, the Two Black Crows were favorites with everyone, especially the black servants, in that age of innocence. However, the servants regretted we had no records of the Black Patti, Sissieretta Jones. I don't think she made any.

Also in the nursery was an upright player piano on which we practiced before being allowed to use the baby grand in the music room. I was particularly fascinated with the tuner's explanation of how he distributed the notes between the octave.

One day, Rietta Etheridge Calloway brought her daughter

Henrietta to call. The exquisitely beautiful Rietta, a life-long friend of Mother's, then lived in New York. I knew her but had never met Henrietta, who was exactly my age. Our mothers made us play for each other. It was painful for us but they were obviously proud of their gifted children. What a terrible beginning to what would become the most abiding friendship of my life!

Mother and Emily took turns playing Daddy's own favorite selections, in the living room, on the big red mahogany Victrola, with its gold-plated metal trim. These included five operatic excerpts, all Caruso: "Home to our mountains" from Trovatore (with Homer), the "Quartet" from *Rigoletto* (the version with Sembrich, Severina, and Scotti), "Swear in this hour" from *La Forza del Destino* (with Scotti), "The Sob Song" from *Pagliacci,* and "Ah! So Pure" from *Martha.* Both Mother and Daddy liked to see if guests could tell whether Caruso or Scotti sang first in the duet, invoking the printed matter on the back side of the record to settle disputes. Among the semi-classics—what a delicious phrase—Daddy favored all the Gluck-Homer duets, Janet Spencer's "Whispering Hope," and assorted solos by Homer, McCormack, Schumann-Heink, and Evan Williams, especially his "Beautiful Isle of Somewhere." I give the names of the operatic selections in English because that is how my parents knew them. "Ave Maria" was the extent of their linguistic ability, except for food. Much to the amusement of my more learned friends, I still refer to the first Norma-Adalgisa duet as "Impart a sister kiss," since that is the title given, in German, on the Lilli Lehman-Hedwig Helbig recording. Although sung in Italian ("Ah! si, fa core e abbracciami"), it seems perfectly logical to me since I can translate German into English, but not back into the original Italian.

My mother's favorite of all records was "In the Depths of the Temple" from *Pescatori di Perle,* sung by the ubiquitous Caruso and Mario Ancona. "The most beautiful record ever made," she insisted. Apart from Caruso and McCormack, her favorite male singers were Pasquale Amato and Pol Plançon. Among women, she preferred Melba above all others, but she also loved Sembrich, Eames, Homer, Schumann-Heink, Farrar, Tetrazzini, Galli-Curci, and, somewhat later, Rosa Ponselle. Whenever Auntie visited us, she wanted to hear something by Marcella Sembrich. As soon as the record was over, Mother would ask for the same selection by Nellie Melba, to demonstrate, at least to her own satisfaction, the superiority of the Australian prima donna. Confident of my taste, I would insist on hearing the same aria by Luisa Tetrazzini. They both admitted "the little fat one" could sing higher, but Mother complained that very high notes made her nervous. With Tetrazzini she had nothing to fear.

Neither Daddy nor Paul Bigelow shared Mother's enthusiasm for Melba. Around 1939, they were sitting on the front porch of the little house on College Street, while I was listening to Melba sing a fragment of the Queen's aria from *Les Huguenots,* which is, I think, the earliest recording from an actual operatic performance (1901). Finally, Daddy could stand it no more and said to Paul, "To think that noise is coming out of my own house!" He slowly folded his paper and went upstairs to bed. Paul always called Melba the Australian marsh hen.

I myself remember first listening—really listening—to McCormack's captivating rendition of "It's a Long Way to Tipperary," and to Caruso's rousing "Over There," the George M. Cohan patriotic song from the Great War. When Isaac took over as butler after Brother Ray moved to Detroit, he asked Emily if he could hear something by Caruso, the only singer known to everyone, black or white. Before playing "The Sob Song," as "Vesti la giubba" was best known, she explained that the clown was dying of a broken heart after discovering that his wife was unfaithful. When the record was over, Isaac wept copiously, thinking he had heard a recording of Caruso dying.

When the great singer died in August 1921, we were in Asheville. I cried so much Mother took me to ride along the French Broad River, just the two of us and the chauffeur. We passed Dr. Grove, and I wondered if he, too, was upset over Caruso's death. After calming down, I asked Mother, "Who is the greatest singer in the world now?," and she replied, "Probably John McCormack or Galli-Curci." That was the seed from which grew my life-long love affair with Amelita Galli-Curci, but I didn't know that until later when I first heard that incomparable voice in person.

For that event, Mother and Daddy took Martha and me to Atlanta. We stayed at the Biltmore Hotel, which adjoined the Biltmore Apartments, where Mother's dear friend Isabelle Johnston lived. Soon after we unpacked, Isabelle phoned our suite and told Mother to send me over to her apartment as quickly as possible. If she told her why the haste, Mother didn't tell me. Following her instructions, I arrived at her apartment in no time flat. Isabelle led me to a door separating her living room from the adjoining apartment. Through the door I could hear the golden voice practicing for the evening concert. I lay on the floor with my ear close to the crack under the door. I have no idea how long I listened to those scales like strings of perfectly matched oriental pearls, over and over, each time a semi-tone higher. It was the first time in my life that I was aware of being sublimely happy. I don't know how I found my way back to our rooms, and dressed in a small tuxedo with the first long pants I had ever worn.

At last, the great singer strode on the stage with the assurance that comes from knowing that nothing can go wrong. She wore a white and gold gown, of no particular period, with a high Spanish comb in her abundant black hair to make her look taller. It was not until I met her backstage after the concert in Macon that I realized how small she was.

I recall best the miraculous high notes and the ease with which she sang. At that period in her career she was still the complete mistress of the art of bel canto. As Geraldine Farrar described her, "She is as perfect as it is humanly possible to be."

Years later, when Galli-Curci made one of her infrequent radio broadcasts, Terry Murray almost killed his parents and me driving back from Columbus, Georgia, at a dangerous speed in order to reach Macon in time for the program. We made it, and it was worth the risk. Mr. Murray said she wasn't what she used to be, and in comparison with the Galli-Curci of the teens or early twenties he was right, but by any other standard she was magnificent, particularly in the "Un bel di." Better a battered Greek statue than a pristine Roman copy. Every Spring, during the twenties, Mother's oldest and dearest friend, Martha Hunt Cornell, would beg her to bring me to Birmingham for the annual visit of the Chicago Company. Invariably, Mother replied, "I am not going all the way to Birmingham to hear Mary Garden when we can hear Galli-Curci, Bori, and Ponselle with the Metropolitan in Atlanta." Thus I was deprived not only of hearing—and seeing—Mary Garden, but Rosa Raisa and Claudia Muzio as well. Mother had a deep-seated prejudice against Garden, whom she regarded as some sort of notorious strip-tease artist, if indeed she regarded her as an artist at all. I was not to experience the impact of "the twentieth century's symbol of sex and sophistication" until she returned to this country in 1941, when she was no longer singing, and gave a lecture at Town Hall in New York. She was sixty-seven and still weighed one hundred twelve pounds, or less. The old-timers in the audience, except for Carl Van Vechten and Virgil Thomson, were shocked, not by her age but because they had never before seen her as herself, rather than as Mélisande, Louise, Thaïs, Grisélidis, Salome, or *Jean in Jongleur de Notre Dame.* Mary Garden the opera singer had as many faces as she had voices, and as many personalities. In his introduction, Thomson remarked, "I have heard many critics disparage Miss Garden's voice, but never a composer." In 1941 the magic was as potent as ever.

Occasionally, Mother and Daddy took Martha and me to dinner at the home of Mr. W. T. Anderson and his wife, "Cousin Lizzie." The Andersons had a handyman who lived over their garage. One of his duties was to play the phonograph during meals. It was there that I first heard the hauntingly beautiful voice of Mary Garden, singing Cadman's "At Dawning." Since she had gained respectability by switching from Columbia to Victor, I hastened to buy her new recording of "Depuis le jour," from Louise. It immediately became my mother's favorite record, and Garden replaced Melba in her affections. I must have played that record for her more than a hundred times, and she would frequently remark, "If only I had known." I wish Melba had known.

Several years before the Ben Smiths acquired their first radio, an elaborate contraption with numerous dials, which had to be synchronized, and a large curved horn, Daddy bought a combination phonograph-radio, with separate tone arms for acoustic and electric records. Johnny Selden, who was my godfather, owned the finest radio equipment in central Georgia, requiring not only an aerial towering above the roof of his house, but an underground antenna as well. He called our new machine "a nice piece of furniture." Fräulein and I were enamored with the new phonograph but disdained the radio. We seldom left the nursery, by now the family room, listening to everything from Bach to Stravinsky. I learned to sing along with all my favorite sopranos but soon discovered that any note above high C was beyond my range. Unfortunately, we had no mezzo-sopranos singing "Una rosa poca fa," my best aria. Supervía, Tourel, Berganza, and the glorious Marilyn Horne, were way off in the future. I also taught myself to cry real tears whenever I heard "Danny Deever," although I didn't think much of the music. I was proud to add Nordica, Lilli Lehmann, and the incomparable Adelina Patti to our collection.

The price of records was drastically reduced in the late twenties—and they were all two-sided by then—but I could not always afford the latest Ponselle or Chaliapin recording on my two-dollar-a-week allowance. I had few other expenses and for a dime could still see a movie, my other addiction, by pretending to be under twelve. Fräulein would secretly help me out, especially when Mr. Robert Williams had a half-price sale of outmoded acoustic records. I remember her buying the fabulous Caruso-Ruffo duet from *Otello,* coupled with Ruffo's blood curdling rendition of Iago's "Credo," on condition that I not play it when she was around, which meant she had to leave the room, since she was always around when I played music, on the machine or on the piano. It was the Shakespeare plot that upset her, intensified by Verdi's music. She was less interested when I played the ukulele, but that lasted only a few months until I discovered that not even Segovia could play Bach on the ukulele. Martha's banjo lessons didn't last much longer.

The huge new radio-phonograph was kept busy day and night. When I wasn't playing classical music, Martha was playing dance music, erroneously called jazz. She and her friends would gather to dance. On one of those occasions, I met young P. L. Hay, Jr. I told Martha that if she could catch him, she would eventually inherit the Johnston-Hay House, but unfortunately they both had different ideas. Often it was just Martha and Martha Ellis practicing the newest dance steps. Marylu called her "Wild West." I was commandeered to partner the girls. They insisted on leading, which I didn't mind since I could lead or follow equally well. During those sessions, Martha and I mastered the Charleston and the Ann Pennington Black Bottom, even the Gilda Gray Shimmy. Mother was so proud of her gifted children she had us dance for her sister, who was visiting. I thought that very unwise since her sister was rather straight-laced, but Auntie thought our routines were real cute.

Unfortunately, the radio was not a great success. The reception in Macon left much to be desired, except for station KDKA which sounded like a present-day teenager's boom box. Macon's own WMAZ sounded better on my little crystal set, which I assembled from a kit. Once a week Frances Alda broadcast on the Atwater Kent Hour, but it might as well have been Ma Rainey.

Even before we acquired the big machine, I was allowed to play Mother's records, although at first I had to stand on a chair to reach the turntable. I was taught not to wind the motor too tight, and never to wind while a record was playing. I handled the records with great care—no fingerprints allowed—and used only triangular bamboo needles, which could be used only once. The sound was soft and muted, but they were not good for the records. Nevertheless, seventy years later, collectors, who are a race apart, marveled at the pristine condition of my records, probably because I switched in the early thirties to a light pick-up and shadowgraphed steel needles, using a new needle for each record. The compact disc collectors today don't know what we went through, nor do they know any of the joy of collecting rare records.

The year was almost certainly 1931 when Emily and I saw our first television. The set belonged to a friend of Jim Brown, Elliot Beard, who lived in Cherokee Heights, a suburb of Macon. Mr. Beard also had a huge, all-black dog named Snow. We viewed the television picture through a pin-point hole in a black box. I have never been able to determine the source of that early telecast, but it had to be local. In any case, the contraption was extremely primitive. It didn't work well, but like Dr. Johnson's dog that could walk on its hindlegs, it was remarkable that it worked at all. Fortunately, further developments were far off in the future.

Few people have heard an early Caruso recording in perfect condition played at correct speed—not easy to determine—on modern equipment. Good sound is more readily available now than previously, and the fidelity of the latest recordings is something not even dreamed of in the not-so-distant past. Dear Aristotle Panagako maintained that old records in "shockingly mint" condition sound best on an antique machine with a wooden horn and a perfectly calibrated tone arm, sans electricity. His demonstrations were impressive, but I'll stick with Ward Marston and his fantastic equipment, which has more buttons than a Wurlitzer organ. Most of the so-called 78 r.p.m. records in Ward's vast collection are in mint condition—the imperfections that plague the rest of us are usually the result of records in poor condition—and when he produces his transfers to compact discs, he uses the best edition of the previous recording, often in special vinyl pressings from the masters, seldom available to the most avid collector. For example, his peerless transfer of the complete Caruso recorded legacy (all 237 selections on 12 compact discs) includes items so rare only a few wealthy collectors own them. Above all, the original sound is not "enhanced" with artificial reverberation or too much noise suppression.

DIE KÖNIGSKINDER
Geraldine Farrar and the Geese

The annual Spring visit of the Metropolitan Opera Company to Atlanta in 1911 was a social as well as a musical event. That was the golden age of opera, dominated by such singers as Caruso, Chaliapin, Scotti, Fremstad, Destinn, Farrar, Hempel, Homer, and Matzenauer. Opera singers were the most glamorous stars in the firmament in that pre-Hollywood era, and of them all only Caruso was more popular than the American soprano, Geraldine Farrar, "the most gorgeous of all the white peacocks of song." Her remarkable beauty and acting ability almost overshadowed her considerable musical gifts. All the singers loved coming to Atlanta where they were wined and dined and treated like visiting royalty.

Mother and Daddy took a box at the old auditorium and stayed in Atlanta for all four operas, inviting different friends from Macon to join them for individual performances. The highlight of their first season was Humperdinck's new opera, *Die Königskinder,* which had received its world premiere in New York just four months earlier, providing Miss Farrar with her most congenial role.

For Königskinder they were hosts to Uncle Jack and Aunt Gene. A room was reserved for them next to their own. The principal singers had rooms on the same floor of the hotel, and the halls were crowded with trunks containing costumes. The stars wore their own costumes, with which they were identified around the world.

Daddy, as usual, got ready much too soon, making my mother very nervous. Finally, in exasperation, she said, "Jordan, go talk to Jack so I can finish dressing." He went next door and knocked on the Jack Massee's door. Uncle Jack stuck his head out and said, "You can't come in, Gene's not dressed yet." So Daddy paced up and down the hall until he spied a little bellboy who had just delivered a pitcher of ice water to a nearby room. "What are you doing?" he asked him. "Nothing, Boss," the boy replied. "Here's two dollars. Sit on one of those trunks and listen to me talk." The arrangement was most satisfactory to both parties.

Finally, the house lights lowered and the opera began—in German. Before long, Uncle Jack fell asleep. At one point in the opera, Miss Farrar, as a goosegirl, came on stage herding a flock of local geese, unaccustomed to the bright footlights. They promptly set off quite a racket, drowning out Farrar and the orchestra with their "Quack, quack, quack, quack!" Uncle Jack woke up with a start and in a loud voice said, "Thank God! That's the first damned thing I've understood all night."

Jordan Massee Sr. and Jr. with Dusolina Giannini.

DADDY MEETS DUSOLINA GIANNINI

"I don't know anything about music, really. But I know what I like."
—Max Beerbohm (Zuleika Dobson)

In December of 1960, Daddy visited me in New York. He was eighty-seven at the time. My old friend, Maurice Fuggette, gave a beautiful party in honor of my father and Dusolina Giannini, the great Italo-American soprano. I drilled Daddy thoroughly on the correct pronunciation of her name. "You say she's one of the best?" he asked. I assured him, "She is the best," although by then she had almost retired. The meeting was a huge success. When they were introduced, he said, "Mme. Giannini, I've hated opera all my life, but I've always had a weakness for beautiful opera singers." Nothing he could have said would have pleased her more.

Later in the evening, he told her all about Geraldine Farrar as the goosegirl, and Mme. Giannini laughed until she cried. The next time I saw her, she told me how much she had enjoyed meeting my father. "He reminds me so much of my own father, the same warmth and exuberance, and those wonderful stories."

Daddy's fondness for beautiful opera singers probably started with Lillian Nordica and continued with Geraldine Farrar, Frances Alda, Frieda Hempel, and Lucrezia Bori. Daddy was asked to drive Alda to the country club after a concert she gave in Macon, since he owned a closed limousine and the singer refused to expose her throat to the elements in an open car. Mother wouldn't accompany them, which caused considerable talk in our small town. Years after Hempel sang in Macon, everyone still remembered the beautiful yellow dress she wore.

They were beautiful women as well as fine singers, and they were viewed by the general public with the same awe and reverence later accorded movie stars, and now reserved for rock stars, since Hollywood has lost its glamour. Since Farrar and Galli-Curci, only Maria Callas and Luciano Pavarotti command the attention of a Michael Jackson. The singers have changed, as well as the public. I once asked Rosa Ponselle why certain performers in her day were so much more famous than others who sang just as well. She replied, "It's star quality. You have to be born with it." I'm sure that's true, but working at it never hurt. Patti and Sarah Berndhardt were born with star quality, as well as superior talent, but they worked tirelessly to make sure the public never forgot. "The Divine Sarah" became one word, like "Damned Yankee."

CARSON MCCULLERS LIKE IVORY SOAP

Carson McCullers—always referred to by my mother as "your father's cousin"—told the story of Farrar and the geese in her last novel *Clock Without Hands.* She changed the story to suit her own purposes, which didn't please Daddy one bit. Furthermore, he didn't approve of certain scenes in the novel which he considered unladylike, although until then he had been deeply devoted to Carson and very proud of her literary accomplishments. He said to me, "Now I'll never be able to tell that story again: people will think I took it from her book." I even promised to get a letter from Carson acknowledging him as the only begetter of the story, but to no avail.

His initial devotion to Carson extended to her doctor, Mary Mercer, whom he spoke of as "the beautiful lady doctor." Like Carson, Dr. Mercer lived in Nyack, New York, in a beautiful modern house overlooking the Hudson River at the Tappan Zee bridge. Daddy was so upset with Carson he announced he would refuse to visit her even if invited. I convinced him that Carson would be deeply offended if he didn't visit her, so he reluctantly agreed. Dear Mary drove down in her Bentley to fetch us. I was not sure how the meeting would go, Daddy was so put out over the book, but Carson was unaware of all this. After the first amenities, he turned to Carson and said, "Honey, your book is like Ivory Soap: ninety-nine and forty-four hundredths percent pure." Everyone was satisfied.

FAUST AT THE PARIS OPERA

During the summer of 1926, Mother, Daddy, Fräulein, Martha, and I spent several weeks in Paris, where I heard my first opera, the inevitable *Faust.* Although planned days in advance, Mother at the last minute refused to accompany us. She had just had her hair cut for the first time and didn't like the results, nor did Daddy. She couldn't wear a hat to the opera, so she remained at the hotel with Fräulein while Daddy escorted Martha and me on the great adventure. It had not occurred to Daddy to inquire who was singing; after all, this was not the Metropolitan. My first glimpse of the grand stair took my breath away, although familiar from the 1925 Lon Chaney film of *The Phantom of the Opera.* The usher insisted on being paid for our three programs, which annoyed Daddy no end. When I discovered that Marcel Journet was to sing Mephistopheles, I almost fell out of the seat. I wouldn't have been more surprised had it been Faure. To me, Journet belonged to the age of Sembrich and the young Caruso. He had not sung at the Met in many years, so I assumed he was dead, like Plançon. I already knew much of the *Faust* music from the legendary series of records by Caruso, Farrar, Homer/Gilibert, Scotti/Amato, and Journet. If anyone thinks I exaggerate the greatness of the venerable basso's performance, let him listen to the complete recording of *Faust* he made a year or two later. I shall never forget that satanic figure, all in red, even though he wore a floor-length robe instead of the traditional tights. The title rôle was sung by Georges Thill, a name unfamiliar to me then, and I was surprised that a tenor that good was not in New York. The opera was given nearly complete, including the long ballet, which featured a ballerina covered with gold paint. Real live angels descended at the end of the final act to carry Marguerite to heaven, her sins forgiven. Of the soprano, I remember only that she was slender and didn't sing the "Jewel Song" as well as Melba. Goethe would not have been pleased, but I though the opera was the greatest thing ever written.

After we got back to the Crillon, and Martha and Daddy had retired, I kept Fräulein up most of the night with a scene-by-scene description of the performance. I was disappointed that she was not allowed to accompany us since we had a vacant seat, but Daddy wouldn't hear of leaving Mother alone at the hotel.

Faust with Marcel Journet: not a bad beginning! I subsequently heard Pinza, Siepi, and others in the rôle, but no one approached Journet as Mephistopheles. To this day, whenever I listen to the Farrar-Journet recording of "Elle ouvre sa fenêtre," his diabolical laugh at the end sends shivers down my spine. It is the most evil thing I have ever heard.

EUROPE 1925-1926

In 1925 Daddy and Aunt Gene (Mrs. Jack Massee) took my sister Martha and Sims Massee to Europe. The next summer he took Mother, Martha, my governess, and me. With our first meal at the Crillion in Paris Daddy ordered champagne for himself; Mother drank only eggnog at Christmas. When the waiter, who looked exactly like Lon Chaney, brought the bottle of vintage champagne in a bucket of ice, Martha said, "I'll have some." Mother objected on the grounds that she was much too young, but Martha persisted, "I had a glass of champagne last summer and I've felt better ever since." I need hardly add Daddy interceded in her behalf.

THE CRASH

In November, 1929, the stock market crashed and the country entered the Great Depression. As Daddy recalled, "When the Fourth National Bank closed, Joe Neel, Leon Dure, and that whole group got out on a technicality. Only one man in that syndicate came up and paid his assessment, Jim Porter. Your Uncle Jack paid his assessment in full, but he was not a part of the syndicate. I was not assessed. I owed the bank $110,000, the 10 percent limit to one person, which I paid."

"The big mistake Jack and I made was having the Massee Apartments, the two farms, everything in one, with the Bibb Brick Company. We were badly advised by our lawyers, but the final decision was our own."

"The Cherokeee Brick Co. (Bill Dunwody and Sam Coleman) and the Bibb Brick Company (Jack and I) consolidated as the Standard Brick and Tile Company. It was a sales organization only, for the two separate manufacturing plants. Ordinarily, we shipped about one hundred cars a week. Got down to where the two plants together shipped only thirteen cars a week during the worst of the depression."

"In 1929, William Murphy, the brains of the C & S Bank, representing a syndicate, offered me $750,000 for the Bibb alone, along with a lot of common stock in the combine. Neither Jack nor I was wanted in the new organization. Bill Dunwody was to be the president. I turned him down."

"____and____ set out deliberately to steal the Bibb Brick Company, and they did. I saw it sold at the Court House for $75,000, or 10 cents on the dollar; and those two crooked sons-of-bitches are sitting tonight in Hell, just as sure as you're sitting in that chair."

"We had a net equity of about $250,000 in the Massee Apartments, and more than $300,000 in the farms. We had just refused $750,000 for the brick company. All these properties were in the name of the Bibb. If we had left the Massee and the farms as separate corporations, we could have saved the Bibb and lost only the other two. We didn't owe much over 10 percent. I ought to have killed them both the day they closed it. I often wish I had. Sam Coleman did not go out to steal my money—he wouldn't do a thing like that—but he shared the profit."

"Jack and I had two years at the Bibb Brick Company—1921 and 1924, I think—when we made $250,000 net clear each year, and 60 percent of that was mine."

"We owed about $200,000. I had $1,500,000 in properties. I ought to have shot them before I let them take it. Wish now I had. I wouldn't have regretted it anymore than if it had been a couple of rattlesnakes."

(I have retained the repetition, just as he told it.)

"After the failure of the Fourth National Bank, I went down to the plant the next Sunday morning, just to walk around and collect my thoughts. There was an old Darkie who'd been there for many years as watchman. He saw me, and he said, 'What's the matter, Boss, you looks worried?'"

"'God damn it, man, don't you know the bottom's dropped out of everything? In New York, millionaires are jumping out of windows.'"

"He replied, laconically, 'Well, Boss, I wouldn't stump my toe for one of them sons-of-bitches.'; and I realized he was right."

Leaving the Big House on College Street

We left the big house on College Street in 1932. Mother and Daddy had lived there for twenty-two years. It was the end of a glorious period in their lives, and for me it was the loss of the only home I had ever known. Emily and Martha were already married, with homes of their own, but both had spent most of their lives in that house. I knew that Daddy would take the move in his stride, but I also knew that Mother would be devastated. She put up a brave front, as everyone knew she would. Only once was there any outward sign of how she really felt, a moment I shall never forget.

Odille Taylor Preston ("Dilse") and Aunt Gene knew that Mother and Daddy planned to move to the Massee Apartments, which Daddy and Uncle Jack still owned, and had, I suppose, come to offer moral support. Dilse and my mother were born in the same year; they were cousins and very close as girls. She was maid of honor when my mother married. Aunt Gene and Mother became close friends after they became sisters-in-law. They moved in the same social circle. They were temperamentally very different, but I think they were devoted to each other for a long time. Aunt Gene and Uncle Jack had sold their home on Vineville Avenue and moved into the Massee Apartments in 1925. A special apartment had been designed for them on the top floor, complete with a wood-burning fireplace in the extra large living room. They moved there by choice and enjoyed living at the Massee. Aunt Gene was not insensitive to the difference, being fully aware that Mother and Daddy had no other choice.

They came separately to see Mother, but almost at the same time. The four of us sat in the nursery, which had become a sort of back sitting room. Dilse was rather quiet, Aunt Gene doing most of the talking. She told Mother how much she and Uncle Jack liked living at the Massee, and how she felt sure Mother would like it, once she had grown accustomed to the change. She spoke with great tact and genuine feeling. Mother said nothing but slowly the tears began to flow down her cheeks. I am sure that not one of us had ever before seen my mother cry, and no one was to see her cry again until the burial of her sister that same year. Dilse and I sat there frozen, unable to make any gesture or speak a word of consolation. It was Aunt Gene who rose and put her arm around my mother's shoulders, from behind, and held her until the tears ceased.

There are worse things in life than losing one's home, no matter how wonderful that home may be. My mother had survived the death of her own mother, when she was only nine years old; the death of her only brother in 1912; and the death of her beloved father in 1914. Those were terrible losses, losses which she bore with characteristic fortitude and dignity. She did not expect to understand death.

This was more than the loss of a home; it was the loss of a way of life which she had created. She tried to understand, but could not. She didn't blame my father, but said to the children, "I don't know how it happened. Papa would have saved his money." To the outside world she expressed no regret, and set about the business of creating a new world for those she loved. Henceforth, she knew no other life; her own life had ceased to exist. To many people she seemed nobler, warmer than ever; but I knew, as did Emily and Martha, what it cost her to maintain that illusion; and Daddy knew.

He went on living for her, as he always had, sustained by his belief in himself. What he had done once, he could do again. His subsequent success, though partial, was nothing short of heroic.

In 1948, Daddy told me what he remembered of the day he and Mother left the Big House on College Street:

I drove home from the office that day to pick your mother up. She and the servants had cleaned the house from top to bottom. Brother Ray and Lula and Marylu. I think Dick Ross was still with us then. Fräulein helped her, and Emily. But your mother worked harder than anyone. The house was empty except for some barrels of china and things that were to be stored at the plant. Everything we could use had been moved to the Massee Apartments. Some things had been given to friends, some to the servants and their friends. That damned woman who bought the house had been pushing us to get us out, but Ethel had to wash every plate before it was packed. You were in high school then, and Martha was already married.

Mother couldn't understand what all the hurry was about. There wasn't an architect in Macon who would touch the house. They said it couldn't be turned into apartments. Some of them said it out of respect for me, although most of them needed any job they could get their hands on at that time. Mrs. Ullman finally got that woman architect to do the remodeling. What was her name? She used to work for little Snippy.[8] Ellamae League. That was her name, I remember it now. Smart woman, too. You couldn't blame her. But that was later. There wasn't any need for the big rush. Just cussedness, that's all. Mean as the devil. You know, she was related to Douglas Fairbanks, the movie star. Well, she hadn't lost her money, and she wanted that house. It wasn't even finished when we bought it from Wallace McCaw. I should have burned it to the ground.

Do you remember the night of the big fire, when John Moore's house burned? I was in the middle of a big poker game at the Progress Club when Ethel called and said, "Jordan, you'd better come home. The Moore's house is on fire and the fire chief says we must get out of the house, it may catch on fire." I told her to get the children out and lock the door, and if the house caught on fire before I got there, to let it burn.

We left our chips right there on the table, put our cards in our pockets, and drove home. Leon Dure, Max Lazarus, Mose Newman, Dutch Fried, Morris Michael, and the rest of us. I knew that if Ethel called me at the club, it was serious. Don't you remember that? It was a big fire.

Anyhow, the day I came to fetch Ethel, Brother Ray let me in when I got there and said to me, "Madam's ready, Mr. Massee, just waiting for you."

I walked into the front hall, all alone. Those hardwood floors looked like they'd been waxed for one of the big dances. And while I was standing there, your mother came down those front steps, looking just like Mary Queen of Scots. I'll never forget the way she looked as she came down the stairs for the last time.

She said, "Jordan, do we have any money at all?"

I reached in my pocket and took out three hundred dollars bills, which was all we had in the world.

8 We never knew why Daddy called Elliot Dunwody "Little Snippy." Certainly he was a particular favorite of Daddy's, as well as Mother's, as a boy and as a young man visiting us every summer at Pine Retreat. It must have started after Elliot became a prominent architect, and occasionally specified handmade brick from Virginia instead of brick from the Standard Brick and Tile Company. Daddy really blamed the senior Dunwody. "Why doesn't he tell that boy what to do?" Anyhow, he was deeply touched when Elliot refused to alter the Big House on College Street.

"We've got three hundred dollar bills. You want them?"

And she said, "I want two of them."

"My dear, you can have all of them. All I have is yours." And she took two of the three bills and put them in her purse.

I asked her, "My dear, I don't give a damn what you do with the money. It's yours. You can chuck it out of the window if you like. I'm just curious. What are you going to do with the money?"

And she said, "I want to hire a crew of professional cleaners to come in and give the house a final, thorough cleaning."

I said, I remember, "My dear, if that's what you want, that's what you must do."

And that's what she did.

I sat in silence when he told me all this. I didn't doubt that he knew about Mary Queen of Scots and her tragic fate, yet the comparison seemed so unlike him. I remembered, however, that he and Mother had seen Modjeska, probably on their wedding trip. Mother once told me that Modjeska was the greatest actress she had ever seen, greater even than Ellen Terry. They may well have seen her as Mary, Queen of Scotland, which was one of her most famous roles. It's only a guess, but with these small keys we sometimes unlock the secret compartments of the heart. I knew that the comparison was more than visual, and that, however obliquely, he had revealed the depth of his love for my mother, and something of its nature as well.

The Massee Apartments

GEORGE ELIJAH ROSSER AND HIS SAINTED WIFE

The Early Years

George Elijah Rosser was a widely recognized biblical scholar who taught at Wesleyan College, the oldest chartered college for females in the world. Although not as old as the college, Dr. Rosser seemed to me, in the mid-thirties, to have attained a biblical age, not because I was young, but because he was born old. He was an authority on Hebrew, Aramaic, Sanskrit, and Ancient Greek; and his translations were published in learned journals. He also wrote a slender volume describing his pilgrimage to the Holy Land.

Dr. and Mrs. Rosser lived at 507 Georgia Avenue in a house facing the college campus. Unfortunately, the house was only two doors from the Mary Baker Eddy headquarters. The doctor always referred to Mrs. Rosser as his sainted wife, and she may well have been, since she informed generation after generation of girls that she and her husband were both virgins, which sounds to me more like Saint Augustine than the good John Wesley. He was a familiar sight to all Maconites; walking, always walking, in his rumpled linen suit, straw hat, and umbrella. He is said to have walked as far as Gray, occasionally.

The Rossers lived in a large frame house and rented rooms to individuals with proper credentials. One couple, alas, slipped from grace. They ordered a bottle of whiskey from a Vineville Branch liquor store. Dr. Rosser happened to be sitting on the porch when the delivery arrived. With a nose for sin, he asked the boy what he wanted, and the hapless lad naively told him. He snatched the package and smashed the bottle on the concrete walk, shouting imprecations that could be heard long after the youngster had disappeared. There were no impartial witnesses to what happened inside the house, but within minutes the couple had joined the broken bottle on the sidewalk. A neighbor half a block away reported that she had heard him shouting, "Out! Out! You have defiled the home of my sainted wife!"

Dr. Rosser was ahead of his time in some respects, but only a few. He regularly jogged around the mile track at Central City Park, usually reserved for speed demons and Alfred Willingham, Jr. Remember, this was roughly sixty years before Marguerite Matthews, Albert Reichert, Jr., and the half-naked Mercer boys graced the streets of Macon. But Dr. Rosser jogged with a difference: he had developed a technique whereby he could jog and read the Gospels simultaneously. God knows how he did it, but there were many things known only to God and Dr. Rosser, as you will discover.

Dr. Rosser arrived one day to find young Willingham dismounting in something of a temper after a turn or two around the track. He approached Mr. Willingham, whom he knew only by sight, and said, in the voice of the prophet Elijah, "Sir! May I be permitted to ask why you address the noblest of God's four-legged creatures as the son of a female dog?" I hate to reveal that a Willingham ever cussed, but this was in the depraved thirties when family values were at an all-time low. Alfred Willingham's response was not recorded, but like any good historian, I shall tell you anyhow: he recognized the voice of divine authority when he heard it, even from a Methodist.

When I Was Seventeen

"Comedy is more serious than tragedy"—W. B. Yeats

I had heard of Dr. Rosser all my life but hadn't the opportunity to meet him until a few days after my first, and last, appearance as a public speaker. A charitable group of women at Christ Church decided to present a well-known musician—that was me—lecturing on his favorite subject, "Classical Music and the Phonograph." For me there wasn't any other kind of music, and phonograph and Victrola were synonymous. My mother informed the committee that I would be delighted. She had more faith in me than I had in myself. After all, wasn't I forever lecturing on one subject or another? I should explain that in 1942 I was an early drop-out. After three years at Mercer University, during which I studied English literature and any subject taught by Otis Dewey Knight, I had announced that I refused to go back to school. Mother knew, in her heart, that with Dr. Knight on sabbatical at the University of Chicago, there was no one left at Mercer who was likely to teach me anything; but that was beside the point. A diploma was a recognized badge of merit which could open any door should I ever choose to open any. In order to restore peace and save the family from disgrace, I agreed to enroll at Wesleyan Conservatory of Music, which was less than a block from the Massee Apartments, where we lived. Not even my mother supposed that I would become a concert pianist; I lacked both talent and patience, but it seemed to her a good way to keep me out of mischief until I returned to my senses. How touching is the regard for schooling among those who have little.

The eminent pedagogue-pianist, Joseph Maerz, accepted me as a pupil since I had already studied with Margaret Adams for eight years. It was understood that the lessons would continue until I absorbed what Professor Maerz had to offer before returning to academia. I knew that could take years, so everybody was happy with the negotiated peace. My father had been happy all along because he knew that no one except doctors, engineers and plumbers ever learned anything useful at school and their techniques could be acquired in apprenticeship. His faith, or lack of it, would have remained the same even if he had heard of actuarial science, archaeology, and computer processing.

Mr. and Mrs. Pliny Hall lent their home for the great event. The house was built on top of Mr. William B. Johnston's artesian well, which still supplies the Y.M.C.A. with fresh, frigid water. A large sum of money was raised for Christ Church, money which my father insisted should not go to China. In his opinion, the heathens were doing well enough without any help from Episcopalians. I did not convey his wishes to the committee.

In addition to my two teachers, who were honored guests, my mother's friends attended en masse, with their husbands, if any. The crowd was so large, husbands had to sit in a back room where they couldn't hear me or the sopranos selected to illustrate my lecture. After a learned introduction by Professor Maerz, I rose to speak, purposely lowering my somewhat limited volume to make absolutely certain that no one in the back room could hear me. Professor Maerz wisely chose to focus attention on his pupil's prodigious knowledge of recorded music, especially vocal music, rather than on his keyboard accomplishments. Suddenly, all my fears vanished—almost all. I knew I could charm a bunch of women with my good looks and genteel manners, but I was nervous over the open piano, although I knew that in an emergency I could call on my teacher to illustrate the more arcane points with a few selections of his own choice. The dear man would bail me out. Everyone knew that I was an authority on singing, recorded or otherwise, past and present; all they needed were a few details. The ladies sat on the edge of their funeral parlor chairs; they couldn't have heard me otherwise. But charm them I did. I regaled them with examples ranging from the divine Patti to Galli-Curci and Ponselle, with whom the art of singing once again died forever. The applause was thunderous, loud enough to be heard in the back room. I still recall a few heartfelt compliments and lots of kissing. In those days, one kissed only close relations, children, and boys of seventeen.

Three people silently applauded my every pronouncement: Professor Maerz, Mrs. Adams, and my mother. They grinned from ear to ear, showing their eye teeth. For a few hours Mother forgot all about Mercer. After delicious refreshments, the crowd reluctantly dispersed, no one more reluctant than I. It was my greatest triumph since I was four and crowds of women gathered on street corners to hear the infant prodigy recite the entire twenty-third psalm from memory.

Next day the happening at Hall House elicited the highest praise for any cultural event since Adelina Patti sang at Ralston Hall in 1854. The review must have been written by Professor Maerz. The editors of both papers—The Telegraph and The News were separate then—knew they could rely on Professor Maerz for an unbiased account; anyhow, neither Susan Myrick nor Blythe McKay could have followed the intricacies of young Massee's thoughts on singing.

A few days after the rave review, I received a telephone call from a man who identified himself as Dr. Rosser of Wesleyan College,

Biblical Studies Division. He had read the article in the paper with great interest and wondered if, during the holidays, he might bring his sainted wife to hear a few of the golden treasures in my collection. Not knowing which holidays he meant, I suggested the next day, only too happy to have found another fan, particularly a male fan. I sincerely believe young people are more vain than old people, and with far less reason. But first I had to assure Dr. Rosser that it was truly convenient.

At the appointed hour, the doorbell rang and I welcomed the couple. Formal introductions were exchanged, very formal, which pleased me because I had always been Master Jordan, Mister Jordan, or plain Jordan, even to clerks in stores, depending on their degree of familiarity with my mother. We three retired to the music room, conveniently located near the front door. Due to my extreme youth, guests would not expect to meet their hostess until they were leaving. I had spent hours trying to decide what to play. Dr. Rosser had not given me so much as a hint on the telephone. I chose to open the program with Handel's "Largo," which when sung in Latin by the great Caruso, sounds religious. I didn't have any Methodist hymns, and I wasn't going to risk playing Luther's "A Mighty Fortress is Our Lord," or "Ave Maria," Schubert or Gounod. That is as far as my plan had progressed.

The "Largo" was met with polite murmurs of approval and wonderment that so much sound could come from one throat. Was it not likely that the volume had been mechanically increased? I assured them that electrical amplification was not invented until several years after Caruso's death. "And why should it have been," he asked rhetorically, "there was no need for it then." Pretty smart, I thought, and Mrs. Rosser silently agreed. On the spur of the moment, through no process of ratiocination, it occurred to me to play Chopin's "Funeral March" as the second selection. How much more religious can you get than at a burial? Then came Elman's recording of the "Air for the G String," regarded as religious music by everyone except Bach. Having exhausted instrumental music and preempted the march for the dead, I drifted back to singing.

Finally, I got down to Galli-Curci's exquisite rendering of "The Last Rose of Summer." Not all the words were easy to follow, even on the latest equipment, but Dr. Rosser was a linguist, so why worry? I could sense we were getting closer but had not yet hit the mark. Mrs. Rosser began to stir in her rocking chair, not rocking, just stirring, suggesting they may have overstayed their welcome. The little gentleman would never tell them, but it was high time her dear husband took the hint. Sensing her feelings, I begged them to stay, they were giving me so much pleasure. After much persuasion they agreed to linger a while. "Ashamed as I am, Mr. Massee, to impose still further on your great generosity, may I ask if by any chance, I mean is it possible that you might have in your evermore surprising vault a lovely tune I heard as a boy, I think it was called, 'An Italian Street Song,' although time and premature senility may have robbed me of the more precise title of that sublime melody?"

I thought, "Oh! My God, can he mean the song from Victor Herbert's *Naughty Marietta?* Surely, even as a boy, Dr. Rosser cannot have had such carnal tendencies." Recovering as best I could, I picked out the infamous melody on the piano, with one finger. "Is that it?" I asked, fearing that it might be. "My dear boy! That is indeed the very song itself." I quickly located my mother's single-side, purple label Victor record, sung by that sterling artist, Lucy Isabelle Marsh. As the final notes faded into infinity, I glanced at Dr. Rosser; his eyes were closed but there was an expression of pure ecstasy on his face, an expression that expanded until it filled the entire room. The Massee rooms were small, so I assume his ecstasy extended through the closed door, down the hall to where my mother and governess were waiting.

Dr. Rosser slowly opened his eyes and after a short pause, whispered, "My dear, dear, dear boy, that is the most beautiful thing I have ever heard, outside my church." I dared not speak, nor Mrs. Rosser. Finally, he continued, with a slight chuckle, "And now a final request—I almost said 'small favor'—may we hear that inspired performance again?" We heard it again three times before my guests felt compelled to make preparations for their stately departure. I fetched their wraps from the closet, and while they were getting wrapped, the doctor said to me, in a true pianissimo, "Kind Sir, every night, before going to bed, on your knees in prayer, I want you to thank the Lord God Almighty, in the name of His Only Begotten Son, for giving you this glorious recording; nay, I say without fear of blasphemy, you should thank Almighty God three times each night for his Divine Grace, and during the day, whenever you find yourself in silent prayer." Thrice, once, once again; already in my mind the numbers were multiplying. The name of the Almighty must have alerted Mother and Fräulein, who met us at the front door. Mother spoke first, "I know this must be Dr. and Mrs. Rosser, and I want to thank you both for giving up so much of your time to my little boy."

"Oh! No! Mrs. Massee, for I know you to be young Mr. Massee's blesséd mother, it is we who must express our gratitude to you, etc., etc." When she could get a word in edgewise, Mother introduced Fräulein as the child's only mentor and guide. Now there was another voice praising the marvelous boy, and the round might have continued into the night had not Mrs. Rosser decided enough was enough, and moved into the lobby outside our apartment. There, Dr. Rosser turned, again addressing my mother, "Gracious Lady, I beg you to grant me a last favor: won't you and Miss Eichler join us for one final musical offering?" They assured him the pleasure would be theirs, and joined us, along with Lucy Isabelle Marsh, in a room already overcrowded with my piano and Victrola, to hear that trite song transformed. When we returned to the lobby, Dr. and Mrs. Rosser each pressed Mother's hand, Fräulein's hand, then mine. Just before the elevator arrived, the Doctor looked at me but spoke quietly to himself, "When the pearly gates open to my sainted wife and me, I hope the heavenly choir will be singing 'The Italian Street Song' in unison."

The afternoon began comedic, reached transcendence, then settled back into serenity, all through the absolute purity of one man's fantasy.

A GUEST IN THE HOUSE

In 1938, Paul Bigelow moved to Macon, after spending several weekends here visiting friends he had met in Atlanta. He immediately fell in love with Macon, particularly the climate, which endeared him to the natives who could do nothing about it. Although born in Maine, Paul had spent several years in Guatemala and Mexico, so he felt at home in the Macon heat.

Paul stayed at the Y.M.C.A. several months before accompanying me to New York City, where we took rooms at King's College to be near Roy Domingos and Terry Murray. On returning to Macon, Paul was a guest in my parents' home until he located suitable quarters at Dr. Rosser's, consisting of a single room in the attic. There was no window, but the door opened into a wide hall with a dormer window overlooking Georgia Avenue. It was conveniently located near the Washington Memorial Library and my mother's dining room. He shared a bath with the doctor, on the floor below. With the room came fresh linen once a week and a small electric fan, a luxury which the doctor would not allow himself. The rent was two dollars a week, which I thought rather steep, considering the accommodations. I shouldn't have been critical, since Paul was delighted with both the room and Dr. Rosser. Mrs. Rosser had passed over by then, waiting somewhere in limbo for her beloved husband so they could enter heaven together, as planned. Paul had no trouble being accepted into the sacred precinct, armed as he was with a note of recommendation from Mrs. Massee. I suppose Cousin Roy alerted Paul to the availability of a room in a respectable Methodist home. Roy never forgot his humble origins after he became an Episcopalian.

It was not long before Dr. Rosser became enchanted, if that is not too pagan a word, with Paul's exquisite manners and cultivated speech. Furthermore, Paul was able to listen intelligently while Dr. Rosser expounded on the relative merits of Hebrew and Greek, although not overly familiar with either. Thus began a friendship that would have pleased Carson McCullers, as indeed it did when she learned of it later.

The bathroom had two doors: one opened into Dr. Rosser's bedroom and the other into his sainted wife's bedroom, now preserved as a shrine where he meditated. I must point out to my young readers that this was true meditation, no Oriental heresy. At first, Paul had to enter the bath through Dr. Rosser's room, which was cause for no embarrassment since the doctor bathed and dressed before sunrise and retired long after Paul had gone to sleep. When Paul won his host's trust, he was told that he might enter through the other room, a privilege which Paul fully appreciated. One day, after his bath, Paul inadvertently locked both doors on leaving. I don't know how the locks worked, but the next time the venerable doctor used the bath, he found himself locked in. After a lengthy wait, he saw through the window a woman walking around in the backyard of the house next door. Finally, the woman realized that a voice was addressing her, "My good woman! My good woman! You are in a position to do me the greatest of favors!" Fortunately, she knew something of her neighbor's sterling character through hearsay and immediately came to his rescue. I have known many people who supposed that Paul's numerous stories about Dr. Rosser were colored by his vivid imagination, but I assure you, they were toned down for the sake of credibility.

In January 1942, Dr. Rosser was so pleased with his tenant in the attic, he decided to open the space across the hall to provide another room to rent. Space was left at the rear of the new room for a bath if needed at some future date. Around April or May, Paul asked if he might invite a friend from New York to spend the summer with him. Ordinarily, the mention of New York would have aroused suspicion in Dr. Rosser's mind, but any friend of Bigelow's was a friend of his. The bathroom was hastily completed in time for the arrival of the guest, none other than Tennessee Williams, whom Paul and I had gotten to know in New York.

Dr. Rosser Entertains Tennessee Williams

Shortly after Tennessee's arrival in June 1942, he and Paul encountered Dr. Rosser returning home accompanied by a boy carrying a wicker basket half full of small pebbles. The doctor, though almost breathless, greeted his guests, "My good friends, I must apologize for the horrendous noise that must have disturbed your slumbers last night, as it did mine. Everyone is complaining of a pack of stray dogs that roam the streets at night. This is a respectable neighborhood and I will not tolerate it. I covered the area for several hours and each time I spotted one of those miscreants, I ordered my boy to stone the beast." Whereupon the child, with all his might, threw a pebble at each culprit, one by one, until peace had been restored. It goes without saying that the doctor had not forgotten that we are all God's creatures, great and small, but even children and dogs must be punished, albeit gently. Anyhow, it was long before Edwina Barnes came to protect our animals. Ours is a more enlightened society now, in which every civilized American knows that dogs as a species are just as good as people, if not better. A truly good person is infinitely better than any dog can possibly be, but the worst dog cannot begin to approach the wickedness of a truly bad person. Therefore, the median goodness among dogs is considerably higher than among humans. If Germaine Greer wishes to make use of the same argument to demonstrate the superiority of women to men, I hope she will feel free to do so. Not even Bertrand Russell could have refuted my logic.

Tennessee and Paul frequently ran into Dr. Rosser in the hallway or on the front steps of the house on Georgia Avenue. On one of these occasions, they encountered the distinguished scholar as they were leaving for Recreation Park, a favorite Williams haunt. Dr. Rosser greeted the gifted young playwright with these words, "Good morning, Mr. Williams, I can recommend most highly the reading of the Psalms in the original Aramaic, both for moral value and for literary style." I can set down Dr. Rosser's exact words, but unfortunately I am unable to reproduce the sound of his remarkable delivery. Suffice to say he spoke from the pulpit, regardless of place or subject. Alas, when Ann Maria and I are dead and gone, who will remember that astounding combination of Barbara Jordan and the prophet Jeremiah.

On still another occasion, as Tennessee and Paul were leaving the house, Dr. Rosser stepped out of a taxi, armed with pail and mop. The two young men stopped in their tracks, hoping for an explanation of this unprecedented occurrence. It was forthcoming; and with no introduction, Dr. Rosser explained, "My good friends, late yesterday afternoon as I was homeward bound from my daily constitutional, I passed the Bibb Mills, where I noticed that small urchins had written certain obscenities in chalk on the sidewalk. Dusk was descending, but I decided then and there that it was my duty, both to God and to Society, to remove those offensive words as soon as possible. Therefore, before sunrise this morning I returned to the scene, before God-fearing employees of the mill were likely to be up, and scrubbed the sidewalk thoroughly. The gatekeeper most generously provided me with all the water necessary for the task." Without further ado, he swept into his own house leaving his two friends to wonder whether he had required a taxi both ways or only for the return trip. I am left wondering why the creator of Amanda Wingfield, Stanley and Blanche, Miss Alma, and Big Daddy never used his rare and incalculable gifts to immortalize George Elijah Rosser. Like Wittgenstein, Dr. Rosser would consider my question inappropriate.

The story of Dr. Rosser and the stray dogs was utilized by Truman Capote in "Children on their Birthdays," one of his most charming stories. The characters have been changed, but the incident of a child stoning the beasts remains the same. The Capote short story bears the dedication "This story is for Andrew Lyndon." The delightful and irrepressible young Lyndon was a frequent companion of Tennessee Williams and Paul Bigelow when they went swimming at Recreation Park during the hot summer days of 1942.

A luncheon party at Carson McCullers' home on February 5, 1959. Left to right: Marilyn Monroe, Arthur Miller, Isak Dinesen, Felicia Geffen, Jordan Massee, and Clara Svendsen. Carson's back is to the camera.

AN INDEPENDENT LIFE

New York, 1950-1979

[Because Jordan never wrote this chapter, these two entries are transcribed directly from a videotaping done shortly before his death by Dan Griffin. We are extremely grateful to him for his generosity in allowing us to include them here. They suffer only from Jordan's lack of opportunity to edit and re-write, something he did constantly. RJH]

My roommate, Paul Bigelow, was working as assistant manager at the Franklin Arms Hotel in Brooklyn Heights. While he was there, Mrs. Wolfe, Thomas Wolfe's mother, came to stay at the hotel. She got the flu, or at least she said it was the flu. It was actually just a bad cold from malnutrition because she was too stingy to eat in the dining room downstairs. She would go out and buy little messes and put them on the window sill because it was winter and they would stay fresh. Finally, they sent for her daughter, Mabel Wheaton, who is, of course, Helen in *Look Homeward Angel.* Mabel is a large raw-boned wonderful woman, very frank, and she came up from Washington where she runs a boarding house similar to the one her Mama ran in Asheville.

While she was there, as soon as she reassured herself that Mrs. Wolfe was not really ill, she went down to the nearest drug store. In typical fashion, she sat on a stool and said to the soda jerk, "I'm Tom Wolfe's sister." After he had gotten pretty bored with her, because all members of that family have total recall, he said "You see that woman over there? She's a famous writer, too. Her name is Carson McCullers." "Oh, I've heard of her," she said. So she went over and said, "Carson McCullers?" And Carson said, "Yes." She said, "I'm Tom Wolfe's sister." Carson, not to be outdone, said, "Well, Tom Wolfe's sister, have a seat." So she sat down. After they discussed various and sundry things, Mabel said, "You know, my mother never read a book until the publication of *Look Homeward Angel.* But since then she's read all contemporary fiction to be sure for herself that her son is the best. And I know she would love to meet you. Would you come up to the hotel to see her?" So when they arrived at the hotel Mabel introduced Carson to Paul Bigelow and Paul said, "Carson, I room with Jordan Massee, a cousin of yours." "Oh, my goodness," she said, "he's a legend in the family. I must meet him!" Well, of course, it was my father she was thinking of, not me. Carson was always vague about things like that. So eventually I went over to meet Carson and that's how it all started...

Carson phoned me at the office and she said, "Boots, I want you to come to lunch next Friday. And I said, "Well, darling, I don't think I can because it takes 45 minutes to get there on the bus and 45 minutes to get back and I don't have but an hour for lunch. I can stretch my lunch to an hour and a half but that's it!" And she said, "But you must come, because it's in honor of Isak Dinesen." And I said, "Oh, my God, why didn't you tell me that in the first place? I'll take the day off." I said, "Who else is coming?" And she said, "Well, Arthur Miller and Marilyn Monroe." So when I went in and told my boss I wanted the day off because I was going to have lunch with Isak Dinesen, Carson McCullers, and Marilyn Monroe, he said, "Marilyn Monroe?" And I said, "Yes." And he said, "Well, you can take the week off if you want to – just remember everything she says." And that was one memorable luncheon.

Isak Dinesen came with Marilyn and Miller and they were about 35 minutes late and you could see that the Baroness [Dinesen was the Baroness von Blixen] was not pleased about that because punctuality meant a great deal to her. As we were to find out later, Marilyn Monroe was compulsively late everywhere she went. I thought it was because she had to be sewn into that black dress. I used to say that jokingly until I read a book recently that she was sewn into that black dress. There was no support. No eye hooks, I could tell that. They could have gotten it on her and sewed it up. Well, she looked like a million dollars. I won't say that she was beautiful but one of the prettiest women I ever saw. She and Lollobrigida had the two most extraordinary figures I ever saw. I never saw Sophia Loren.

She had a friend who was a cinematographer named Sam Shaw. He did the cinematography for the movie *Alexander the Great* with Richard Burton. He knew all these people. He came to me one day and he said, "I understand from Paul Bigelow that you have a great collection of photographs of Eleanora Duse." And I said, "Yes indeed, some very rare ones that I bought in Italy." He said, "Will you lend them to me to copy for Marilyn Monroe?" Well I took a double take because the idea of Marilyn Monroe even knowing who Eleanora Duse was was too much for me. Well she knew all about her. She did collect pictures of her.

When we all sat down to lunch, she was sitting next to me. I said, "Miss Monroe, I'm the person who lent Sam Shaw my pictures of Duse to copy for you." Well, that broke the ice. From then on she was most charming and very animated and most appreciative. She was absolutely delightful. Of course, everyone had to take a second fiddle to Isak Dinesen who talked non-stop.

At lunch, Isak Dinesen told a story that was later to become one of her most famous stories but at this time it had not been published. It was about the first lion she ever killed in Kenya and sent the lion skin to the King of Denmark and he wrote her a letter. That letter was believed by the natives to have magic properties. Every time there was a woman who was having a difficult birth, they would run and get that letter and she would hold it and her pain would disappear. One time a wagon turned over on a man and crushed his leg, and while they were getting the mules to pull the wagon off the man they let him hold the letter and he felt no pain at all. It's a metaphor for the magical properties of writing, and I think it's the best of her *Out of Africa*-type tales. I asked her why she didn't include it in *Out of Africa* and she said, "I meant to but I forgot it." So it came out later in a book called *Shadows on the Grass.*

But she told that story – and it's a very long story – it must have taken 45 minutes to tell it, and we all had never heard or seen anything like it. We were just dumfounded by it. Later I went to the YMAG to hear her speak and she told the same story from memory. There was not one syllable difference – she had memorized it. I thought that was astounding. I'm sure she recorded it for the Library of Congress but I never heard those records.

Then she talked a great deal about going to see Albert Schweitzer who was one of my gods, and one of Carson's. She told Schweitzer that she wanted to open a hospital in her part of Kenya the way he had. He said, "You stay a week and we'll talk about it." So she stayed there a week. After it was over, he said to her, "You see now, don't you, that you're not physically able to do this?" She said, "People talk so much about his saintliness but they don't tell you that he was a bear physically – he was so strong – he was like a strong man in a circus. She said, "I realized I was too weak to open a hospital like his." ...

But my favorite story of hers concerned Aldous Huxley. She said, "You know, I'm very proud of the fact that I introduced to my publisher in Denmark Aldous Huxley and Ernest Hemingway." Hemingway was writing *The Sun Also Rises* and Huxley's was either *Barren Leaves* or *Chrome Yellow.* She said, "It's awfully interesting now in retrospect to realize that neither one of them was ever to write a book that good again." But that's true.

She said she got a charming letter from Huxley about a month before this luncheon party. When she arrived in London at the Savoy there was a note there for her from Huxley asking if he could come by the Savoy and see her. So she wrote him and made an appointment and he came. Well, he was 45 minutes late getting there. As I've told you before, she didn't cotton to that. Well, when he came he said, "Don't be angry with me for being so late, let me explain what happened." He said, "On the way I had to stop and see Lady Somebody," (I don't remember the name. Let's call her Lady Blossom.) "You know Lady Blossom is a medium. When I got there she took me in the dining room and before my eyes in broad daylight she materialized a whole dining room table top of white roses." He said, "I brought you one," and handed this rose to Isak Dinesen. In telling us this story, Dinesen said, "You know, it wasn't even a very good specimen." That summed it up.

Appendix

Macon has produced two very distinguished writers: Sidney Lanier, the lyric poet, and Harry Stillwell Edwards, novelist and short story writer. Mr. Edwards was deeply devoted to my father and always called him "Nephew." My father, in turn, called Mr. Edwards "Uncle Harry," although they were not related by blood.

Mr. Edwards' most famous story, *Eneas Africanus,* the story of a Georgia slave who is entrusted with the safekeeping of his master's family silver during the Civil War, has fallen into neglect in recent years, though not from lack of merit.

Letter from Harry Stillwell Edwards to William Jordan Massee. Mr. Edwards was collecting information for an article which appeared in The Macon Telegraph, Sunday, 8 June 1919, entitled:

Dreamers
Hon. W. Jordan Massee
Harry Stillwell Edwards
Hon. W. J. Massee Macon

My dear Nephew:

Kindly give me the data on your marvelous work at Jackson—date of start; capitalization; length of time consumed, with details as to height, length of dam, backwater, power etc. etc. In fact everything you can think of in connection with the enterprise. You are about to be immortalized by

Sincerely yours,
Harry Stillwell Edwards

William Jordan Massee
August 1, 1873-October 19, 1961

It cannot have happened often that a son wrote his father's obituary, nor was it my intention at the time. During Daddy's last visit with me in New York—June 4 through August 19, 1961—I took copious notes for a biographical sketch, which I completed shortly after his return to Macon. I had known the basic facts for a long time but was not sure of dates nor of the sequence of events.

When Emily called me on October 10, 1961, to tell me that Daddy was critically ill, I left for Macon at once. He was operated on for cancer of the stomach shortly after I arrived. Emily, Martha, and I were all opposed to the operation because of his advanced age—he was eighty-eight—but the doctors felt that with his strong constitution there was a good chance he would survive. Under the circumstances, they left us no choice. He lived only a week, regaining a degree of consciousness intermittently.

During that week, our old friend Susan Myrick, who wrote for the local papers, asked for information regarding my father's career, in case of death, which seemed imminent. I gave her the biographical sketch I had written the month before and brought with me in order to make copies for Emily and Martha. After Daddy's death on October 19, the editor of the paper, to my surprise, decided to use my sketch, just as written, with only the addition of names of the survivors, which I myself added. At the time I didn't want it known that I had written it, but now I'm glad that I did. Both my father and my mother would be pleased with its accuracy. When Grandpa Brown died in 1914, The Macon Telegraph published a lengthy obituary referring to the wrong Lawson sister as his wife.

When I returned to New York and showed Daddy's obituary to Alan Kelly, he said, with no disrespect, "I didn't think that old man would ever die," a deeply felt sentiment shared by many.

(Reprinted with permission from *Macon Magazine,* March 1998; written by Jenny Noller):

Coming Home To Roost:
Native son Jordan Massee reminisces about life in Macon in simpler times

"My fame is based upon reflected glory," says Jordan Massee. This native Maconite has crossed paths with some of the most famous people of our time, from Bette Davis to Tennessee Williams to Carson McCullers, so his words have the ring of truth. Some people he only saw from a distance, some he just exchanged a few words with, and some were close personal friends. All impacted his life; he has many stories to tell.

Jordan had been away from Macon for a large portion of his life, but returned seven years ago to the place of his family and his heart. When he talks about Macon, he gets a glimmer in his eyes that can't be mistaken for anything but Southern pride. When he and his close friend, Andrew Lyndon, would argue about Macon having more nuts per capita than another city in the country, Lyndon would always retort that Jordan just knew more about Maconites' skeletons. Those skeletons may soon be revealed; Jordan is working on a biography complete with stories of some of Macon's most eccentric characters. He will call it *Accepted Fables,* a name that struck him when he read a statement of Napoleon's: 'History is accepted fables.' Jordan's philosophy is that history just keeps repeating itself; every time we rewrite it we get closer to the truth, but that takes a long time.

Hanging vertically above the fireplace is an abstract painting – a gusty puff of minty greens explode through two brown circular forms. "I call it 'A Cave of the Winds,'" Jordan Massee says. Then he explains when he bought the painting it hung horizontally, but he likes it better this way. He cocks his head upward; his eyes linger for a moment, and he exhales a trail of blue smoke. He found "A Cave of the Winds" at the same place he bought his other favorite pieces of art. He rises from the orange chair that almost swallows his body and beckons me to the hall. Here are some of his prizes: three etchings of watercolors from 1744, copies of Pompeii wall murals, and even more unique, replicas of Greek art – columns jutting out into the starless, black night, goddesses cloaked and garland-crowned. "Can you believe they were hidden in the attic?" he asks.

Out of the corner of my eye I watch Jordan's eyes on the paintings; it reminds me of a woman touching her moth-balled wedding gown or of a hunter cleaning his great-grandfather's musket. He stands for a moment, sunlight falls onto his face and I notice his prominent cheek bones as he sucks in on a cigarette. He squints his eyes. Yes, Jordan is an art lover. It is at this moment that I realize there is a difference between art enjoyer and art lover. The enjoyer looks but the lover savors. The thing about art lovers is that the savoring becomes contagious, my eyes, too, stop to linger on the painting and notice a shadow on a face or the brush-stroke on a cloud I would have missed the first time.

We return to the sitting room; as he sits by the fireside. I now notice a white bust behind him. "Isadora Duncan," he says, and then with a smile, "She is my obsession." Isadora Duncan was the founder of all modern dance and Jordan spent years amassing a collection of art work depicting her. Sixty-three newspaper clippings he collected from sources like the Hearst scandal sheet will be displayed as part of the Isadora Duncan exhibition in the Georgia Museum of Arts in Athens. Jordan liked her wild streak; the fact that she opposed marriage and flaunted her escapades intrigued him as a boy. But, in 1922, the racy dancer died when her scarf tangled in the wheels of her roadster and strangled her to death.

He carefully crosses his legs and blows another stream of smoke toward the ceiling. The smoke hangs in the air like a still ribbon above his head. He has just finished telling me of his passion for art and how many of his collections have now been given away to various museums and such to be shared with the public.

Jordan grew up in Macon as one of three children, who lived for a time in the grand brick house on College Street with a slate roof, 18 columns and 22 rooms. The entire third floor was a ballroom for his sisters' entertaining. Jordan says Martha and Emily never used the ballroom, but the parties the family had downstairs were a sight to be seen, complete with five-course meals at midnight and orchestras that played the Cakewalk. The biggest party of the year called "Crème of the Crop" was a costume party, but Jordan says his father, who was the character model for Tennessee Williams' Big Daddy, refused to ever dress up. Jordan only went to one party, and the Museum of Arts and Sciences has the little black velvet suit he wore. Even though it was during prohibition, the drinks flowed; the Massees bought beer trucks in Louisiana and drove them up for the parties.

From the time Jordan was six years old he attended Gresham Grammar School. His parents, however, didn't like to listen to his lessons, so they hired teachers such as Otis Knight (former Dean of the College of Liberal Arts of Mercer University) to tutor him. Jordan dubs Knight as "the best educated man I ever met." The children's German governess tried to teach him her language, but he was too interested in picking her brain for the details of European history. Later, he went to Lanier High School, a chapter in his up-coming autobiography he calls "Five Years in Hell." It was a time when segregation was rampant, not just black and white, but male and female, as well as the farm boys and the city boys. Jordan remembers it being difficult and teachers not making it any easier for him to blend in; one in particular announced to the whole class that the first book Jordan ever read was "The Hunchback of Notre Dame." She was wrong though. He tells me that it was the third book he read, "Seven Champions of Christendom" and "The Count of Monte Cristo" were the first two. But even then, the teacher's pet was a black sheep.

"You can get a pretty good education now," he says. But as he told his sister Emily (who refused to go to school until she was 14), "There is no relationship between education and schooling. You can be highly educated, but unschooled."

The Massee household was, like many others, extremely active, but at dinner time everyday all five members would sit down together. Emily would come back from wandering on her own; Martha and Mother would return from errands, Jordan would come in from roaming in Pleasant Hill; and Father would come back from a day at the brick yard. Jordan's father loved to eat. Occasionally they would have his father's favorite, sweet potato pie, and he would burn his mouth in his eagerness to consume it; and the family would laugh. At some point each evening, Jordan says, his father would look at his mother and say, "Old dear, you are a wonder." And she would reply, "I have always been so considered."

After Jordan graduated from Lanier High School, he attended Mercer University. He left Mercer to travel in Europe and spent most of his time in Germany; he regretted not learning the language from his governess. In March of 1938 the war forced him home; the American embassy had asked everyone to leave. Before he left he did actually see Hitler. The streets of Berlin were packed with hordes of people because of a mandatory welcoming for Mussolini. "The only other person who was that riveting was Pope Pius XI. And that, of course, is on the opposite end of the spectrum," he says wryly.

The German servants whispered about his odd undergarments, colored silk shorts, made by three ladies who lived in Bolingbroke. So, Jordan Massee could be said to have been on the cutting edge of fashion. All the Massees were used to high fashion, though. One time, he says his sister Emily was stopped on the street by a stranger to ask where she got her beautiful clothes and she proudly answered,

"Paris, New York and Bolingbroke." Jordan chuckles and lights another cigarette. "And that was the truth," he assures me.

Jordan returned home in 1938 after traveling in Europe for two and a half years. His father would joke that he only came home to get clean linen. Jordan wasn't home too long before he decided to move to New York City to appease his yearning for excitement. He found an apartment on 57th Street and began working in an art gallery. He loved his work, but most of all, he loved meeting the artists and the people who happened to wander in to look at the art. Not long after he started working the manager left him to tend shop with a sole instruction: do not accept any checks. An hour or so later, the manager returned and asked Jordan if he had sold anything. He had, but the purchase had been paid for by check; before the manager could speak Jordan handed him the check and watched as the manager recognized the signature – Mrs. Theodore Roosevelt.

After two years in New York, his sisters convinced him to return home and help his father with the new family business. Coleman and Dunwody bought out the Massees' Cherokee Brick Yard, one of the largest in the world. Mr. Massee continued to have a hand in the company until a conflict of interests arose, at which point he took out a $70,000 loan to open a concrete block business. Jordan kept the company's books for a time, but Macon still didn't hold his interest and he longed to be back in the big city.

The summer of 1942 was spent with Tennessee Williams and friend, Paul Bigelow, at Sea Island. This is where Mr. Massee inspired the bawdy character in "Cat On a Hot Tin Roof." "The character had Big Daddy's zest for life," Jordan says. People are always asking about what Tennessee Williams was like, Jordan says, and he finds it amusing that people never realize Tennessee was "a walking anachronism." It wasn't normal to wear a 1900s Panama-style hat in the 1940s. "Maniacal" laughter was a trademark of Williams'; Jordan thinks that the excessive laughter was a shield for emotion. One afternoon, a group of guests at Sea Island sat together and, at Tennessee's insistence, took turns reading from Chekov's "The Seagull." At one seemingly inopportune time, Tennessee burst into his "maniacal" laughter and when Jordan asked why, Tennessee replied, "The trouble with people is they don't laugh enough." When the pope spoke out against Tennessee Williams' play, "Baby Doll," Tennessee laughed and told Jordan he wished people would worry more about the things that matter.

Jordan finally returned to New York and landed a job with Welch's Grape Juice, Inc. where he stayed for 26 years. But when Congress lost control of the Postal Service and was trying to revamp its procedures, Jordan was hired by Bristol-Myers to conduct marketing research on postal operations.

When he was 61, Jordan retired and began projects such as

annotating Virginia Spencer Carr's biography of Carson McCullers, the famous Southern author. Carson was Jordan's cousin and one of his dearest friends. He donated a collection of her letters which she had given him for safekeeping to Duke University. Carson had realized that people were stealing things from the trunks in her basement and entrusted Jordan with her correspondence. Tennessee Williams gave Jordan Massee some of his letter for protection as well.

Seven years ago he and a friend, Bismarck Reine, left the North and moved back to Macon. "I love it. I wouldn't live anywhere else in the world," Jordan says. "Macon is just right – a little too big, but the historic district hasn't changed. In fact, it's gotten better now – more trees and flowers." Jordan explains that yards and landscaping were not a priority back in the early part of the century; people weren't interested in flag lily-lined walks and shrubbery, just what was inside of a house mattered.

He leans back in his orange chair without reaching for another cigarette. I can't help but wonder about his favorite books and plays, his forgotten dinner conversations, or what those eyes of his have seen of Macon and the world. "You know," he says, "my father always told me I was a walking encyclopedia of useless information." I think but do not say, "Useless is a relative term."

Eulogy delivered at Jordan Massee's funeral at Rose Hill Cemetery in Macon, Georgia, on March 23, 2002, by Richard Jay Hutto:

Jordan's close friend Tennessee Williams wrote in the last line of his own autobiography, "high station in life is earned by the gallantry with which appalling experiences are survived with grace." If that is the case, then no one achieved a higher station than Jordan. Born to great wealth and privilege, he had it taken from him when his father's fortunes were reversed. Yet throughout that period and, eventually, his last few years umbilically linked to an oxygen tank, and, finally, during three weeks in intensive care, he never surrendered his dignity.

In one of my recorded conversations with him, he told the true story of a mean-spirited man who contrived a reason to visit the Massees after they had lost their home. He and his beloved sister, Emily, were sitting on the floor packing away the family possessions when this man said to him (and here I directly quote Jordan), "'You children were born with gold spoons in your mouth, and now you can't even afford to hire some blacks to pack up your china.' Well, it pushed me one step too far, and I said, 'What we were born with we cannot lose and you cannot buy.' My mother later said, 'Well, that's true, but it was wrong for you to say that.'"

Anyone else would have ended that story before his mother's remonstrance, but not Jordan. Although he was never deliberately cruel, he never varnished the truth. He combined sharp wit with an unparalleled mind and they were both his defense and his weapon.

Although I did not have the honor of knowing him when he was young, evidently he was just as iconoclastic in his youth. One of the earliest mentions of him in the local newspaper was just after he had returned from a six-month trip though central Europe. While visiting a Moslem home in Albania he saw his host's harem all veiled as required. The newspaper then quotes Jordan as saying, "Judging from the harem-women's figures, I was not anxious to see beyond the veils."

But throughout his life, that is just what Jordan did – he saw beyond the veils of hypocrisy, prejudice, and distrust. Perhaps that is why he engendered such fierce loyalty among friends both famous and obscure – he always gave far more than he took. He did not apologize for the way he lived and in staying true to that course there became no reason for him to apologize for his life. He was accepted and eventually embraced by those who would have disapproved of someone else in similar circumstances.

On the afternoon he went into intensive care, he began to hallucinate because of the lack of oxygen to his brain. Anyone else would have seen pink rabbits or figures from their childhood. But Jordan told me, through his oxygen mask, that the ceiling tiles above his bed were painted by a German Bauhaus designer from the thirties and it troubled him that he could not come up with the name. I have no doubt that, by the time the breathing tubes had been forced down his throat, he had remembered the designer's name and the salient facts of his life. Indeed, Jordan had probably had dinner with him.

Those who did not see him in the past few weeks should be assured that he received excellent care. Dr. James Upshaw led a team of devoted and compassionate caregivers at Middle Georgia Hospital. Early on I told one of the nurses that Jordan would hate being seen unshaven even though he was unconscious. From that moment on, he was shaved every night. After he regained consciousness he spent his last week communicating only with his expressive eyes. One of his doctors said that she had never seen anyone with the ability to insult someone, albeit good naturedly, while having a breathing tube down his throat.

In the past few years, it would have been impossible for him to live at home without the love and care of Bismarck Reine whose life will be incalculably poorer for his loss. Bismarck had the privilege of sharing forty years with Jordan and only regrets that he will not have forty more. Jordan's great-nephew, who was "little Bob" all the way to the end, reminded him constantly of his family's love and unconditional acceptance. When the end did come, it was quick and merciful as Jordan deserved.

In looking through Jordan's meticulous notebooks, I was particularly struck by one of his own thoughts. I had always wondered how he mastered such an encyclopedic memory and how easily he called forth facts from it. There, written in 1995, were these words of his: "A thought must be personalized before it becomes useful, and must be filed and cross indexed in the memory. Only universal thoughts require no transformation." He had not only conquered that vast knowledge, but had come to terms with understanding it as well.

He also kept a notebook of his favorite quotes, naturally alphabetized by author, and his choices offer us a glimpse into a man who was insightful in both spellings of the word. Here are only a few:

"One is rich not through one's possessions, but through that which one can, with dignity, do without."

Epicurus

"Experience is not what happens to you; it is what you do with what happens to you."

Aldous Huxley

"The higher we soar, the smaller do we appear to those who cannot fly."

Nietzsche

"We gain freedom when we have paid the full price for our right to live."

R. Tagore

And, perhaps somewhat surprising for a man who once said, "The person who proclaims himself to be a good Christian is probably neither," the last quotation in Jordan's book, and the only one not in alphabetical order, is from the Biblical Agrapha. Although we know that Jordan was not a religious man, it would be a mistake to assume that he was not a spiritual one. The Bible verse is, "Jesus saith, Let not him who seeks ... cease until he finds and when he finds he shall be astonished; astonished he shall reach the kingdom and having reached the kingdom he shall rest."

Today we offer thanksgiving for the life of this extraordinary man we all loved so well. Each of us thought that Jordan loved us best, and each of us was correct. I would like to end with a poem by W. H. Auden whom, of course, Jordan knew:

"Stop all the clocks, cut off the telephone,
Prevent the dog from barking with a juicy bone.
Silence the pianos with a muffled drum,
Bring out the coffin, let the mourners come.

Let the aeroplanes circle moaning overhead
Scribbling on the sky the message, 'He is Dead.'
Put crepe bows round the white necks of the public doves,
Let the traffic policemen wear black cotton gloves.

He was my North, my South, my East and West,
My working week and my Sunday rest,
My noon, my midnight, my talk, my song;
I thought that love would last forever: I was wrong.

The stars are not wanted now: put out every one;
Pack up the moon and dismantle the sun;
Pour away the ocean and sweep up the wood,
For nothing now can ever come to any good."